A Heritage of Faith

Juanita Nobles

authorHOUSE®

AuthorHouse™
1663 Liberty Drive
Bloomington, IN 47403
www.authorhouse.com
Phone: 1-800-839-8640

First published by AuthorHouse 2/25/2010

ISBN: 978-1-4490-7685-6 (e)
ISBN: 978-1-4490-7683-2 (sc)
ISBN: 978-1-4490-7684-9 (hc)

Library of Congress Control Number: 2010901392

Printed in the United States of America
Bloomington, Indiana

This book is printed on acid-free paper.

FOREWORD

--by Dr. David Tolliver, Executive Director,
Missouri Baptist Convention

Jesus was a storyteller. With precision and understanding, Jesus told stories, known to us as parables, designed to make a point. The Reverend Marvin "Charlie" Nobles is also a storyteller, also telling stories with great purpose.

It is proper, at this point, that I pause long enough to acknowledge that I had not heard the name "Charlie" in reference to Reverend Nobles prior to reading the stories found in this book. For more than twenty years I have known Reverend Nobles as Marvin Nobles. From now on, I affectionately know him as "Charlie." Marvin's "many names" is a story of its own that begins in the first chapter, but runs throughout this book.

Charlie Nobles is a storyteller, to be sure. Everyone who has heard him preach would say that he is a storyteller in the way of our Savior. For more than 70 years, Charlie has been telling the stories of Jesus by the way he lived his life. As a Baptist pastor and Director of Missions, Charlie retold those stories as he applied Biblical truth to everyday living. The story of Charlie Nobles is a wonderful mix of history, family story-telling, and theological truth. Now that I have read this story, and the particular stories that Mrs. Nobles has included, I have every confidence that some of these stories will find their way to my own preaching. I will be sure to give proper credit.

In God's time, the lives of Juanita Wier-Nobles and Marvin "Charlie" Nobles intersect and merge to form a genuine and lasting Heritage of Faith. I recommend that you read their heritage carefully and prayerfully. It will enable you to lay the groundwork for your own "Heritage of Faith".

CONTENTS

DEDICATION

This book is dedicated to our grandchildren:

Debbie's children:
Andrew Jeffrey DeGroot
Austin Noble DeGroot
Jensen Anne DeGroot
Coleman Gray DeGroot

David's children:
Daniel O'Dell Nobles
Sarah LaVell Nobles

Cindy's children:
Marissa Nicolette Scanio
Charles Glenn Scanio

Remember God loves you and so do we.
Look to God often. Let Him be the Lord of your life as you travel
through this world.

ACKNOWLEDGMENTS

Thanks to all the staff at Author House who were so helpful as we went through the writing and publishing process.

Thank you for buying my book. I hope you enjoy reading about our family and experiences, people we have met, and places we have been in service to our Lord and Savior, Jesus Christ.

> *"You are a chosen race, a royal priesthood, a holy nation,*
> *a people for God's own possession, that you may proclaim*
> *the excellencies of Him who called you out of darkness*
> *into His marvelous light."*

--I Peter 2:9(NAS)

INTRODUCTION

Marvin Nobles has served as pastor or staff member in twelve Southern Baptist churches in Texas, Missouri, and Florida, since 1955. In 1983 he became a Director of Missions in Jefferson Baptist Association, Missouri for the last eleven years of his ministry, retiring in 1994.

In this book I have told about the churches we served and the places we have been. Most of the churches we served had just had a traumatic experience prior to our going there, and all of them profited from a pastor with his loving, caring personality. The calming spirit and peacemaking manner that God gifted Marvin Nobles with caused him to be able to lead the people to love and grow again as we served together; sometimes for only a short time, sometimes for a few years.

Many of these stories were sermon illustrations—situations that impressed him as he grew up; events that led him back to the Lord and caused him to give his life totally to God. I also recounted some things that happened to me as a child and led me to give my life to Jesus. Stories about our children are included; sometimes they were told during Marvin's sermons and sometimes they were shared because they were so funny.

Through the years as I listened to my husband preach, I kept thinking, "Somebody ought to preserve these stories that he tells." They had great meaning, and I didn't think they should be lost when we are no longer on this earth. So I began thinking about them, writing them down, making a legacy for our children and grandchildren to help them as they live this life.

I wanted our grandchildren to know about their parents when they were children, and about us and how we came to be the persons we are. I want our grandchildren to live for the Lord, to give Him their lives and to look to Him always, and with these stories to remind them, I hoped they might be encouraged to do just that.

As I wrote these stories, of course my husband and I discussed them together. He would read the stories I had written and he usually would say, "Now, it didn't happen *exactly* like that. I remember . . . " and he would tell me what he remembered regarding the incident that I had written about. So I would revise and embellish the stories I had written, and then write another one or two. But sometimes my memories prevailed over his. He didn't get the last word on every story!

As I shared these stories with friends and acquaintances, I was encouraged to compile them and to make a book that others could read and enjoy. The book was published in 1999 with the title It Wasn't Always Easy, but it Sure was Fun.

All the books were sold, and people are still asking if I have any more books, so I decided to do it again, but this time I have changed it somewhat. I have added some stories and left others out. I have told a little about some of the things that broke our hearts, as well as the incidents that made us happy. I have also told a lot about the churches we served, and how Charlie did things in them to turn them around to begin to love again. The format of the book has been changed and some chapters were added that were not included in the first book. If you bought the first book, you will see some familiar stories, but you will see many others.

We have had quite an interesting life. Those twelve churches and one Association in three states have provided us with a wealth of memories. We have met hundreds of people through the years. Many people impacted our lives and some of them are mentioned in this book.

This was our life as we lived through these years. This is
A HERITAGE OF FAITH.

Marvin T. Nobles, Director of Missions, JBA, 1991

1
GROWING UP IN THE COUNTRY

In the Kimbell Bend of Texas, early in the twentieth century, a few sharecropper farmers lived in poor shacks working the land along the Brazos River. The owner of the land hired people to live in those shacks and farm an amount of land he could manage with a plow and a team. They worked the land, picked the cotton, and made their way in the world, giving "the man" most of their earnings. Among these sharecroppers were two families—Walter and Lilly Nobles and their six children: Jack, John, Clint, Bill, Carl, and Ethel; and William and Mattie Lou Hendrix with their four children: Roy, Minnie, Marvin, and Thula Jane.

Because of the close proximity of these families, three children in each family intermarried. Roy Hendrix married Ethel Nobles, Carl Nobles married Minnie Hendrix and Bill Nobles married Thula Jane Hendrix. The children of these couples were called "double cousins." They saw each other often, stayed in each other's homes, and grew close until time and the pressures of life took them in different directions.

This used to be the way people lived. They stayed in their own communities and married people they knew and had associated with all their lives. Because travel was more difficult then, people didn't go very far from home. Later in time, big companies began moving people around and travel became more commonplace, so people began to find mates in other places, strangers, as it were. But in those days, community ruled and this was the way it was.

Times were hard in the nineteen-twenties and thirties. This was the time of the Great Depression and people everywhere were scrounging for money to just get by. But in the Kimbell Bend, life went on as it had for a long time—still farming, sharecropping, and living as their parents had.

When Bill and Thula married in 1923, they set up housekeeping on a farm a few miles from the small town of Kopperl, Texas. William Edward was born in 1927, Marvin Thuriel was born in 1929, and George Glynn came along in 1933, while they lived in the Kimbell Bend, rich farmland along the "bend" of the Brazos River. The brothers were about two years apart, little tow-headed boys in stair-step order, having the time of their lives and not knowing they were poor.

The family had a garden and raised the vegetables they ate, they raised their own beef and pork, and Bill sometimes shot squirrels, rabbits, and other small animals for food. Thula washed on a rub board, she fashioned clothes for the family with her needle; Bill had an old shoe last and he would put the boys' shoes on it and rebuild the soles so that each boy could wear the passed down shoes as they grew.

Two other boys were born later—Walter Raymond was born in 1937 and Charles Melvin was born in 1942, after Bill found a job in Lake Worth, Texas, a suburb of Fort Worth, as foreman on a ranch on Silver Creek. They lived in a larger house on the ranch, and as the boys grew, they had lots of woods and creeks to explore. It was a wonderful place for the boys to grow up, even though moving on to another place was something almost unheard of in those days, but something that would come to be commonplace as society grew and the times changed.

The Nobles' house was two and a half miles from the one-room schoolhouse where the boys learned their basics. They would start out walking to school, and as they passed by the houses of neighbors, other children would join them, until by the time they got to school they usually had gathered up a crowd of twelve or more kids, all walking together and having a great time. These kids would grow to adulthood in this new community and become life-long friends.

This book is about Bill and Thula's middle boy—Marvin Thuriel. When he was born, his mother named him "Marvin" after one of her brothers, and "Thuriel"—a name she must have made up. Thula called him "Thuriel", but Bill had a hard time remembering that name, so he called him "Man" from the time he was born.

When he was about six years old, one of Bill's friends who lived in Dallas gave all three of the older boys their nicknames. Ed was "Gump", George was "Hotshot" and Thuriel became known as "Charlie McCarthy"—like the dummy used by Edgar Bergen, a ventriloquist famous in those days. Everybody called him that, until they thought it was too long and it became shortened to just "Charlie". His mother continued to call him "Thuriel", his dad called him "Man", his friends and brothers called him "Charlie", and when he had to sign anything official he wrote his name as "Marvin". Anybody else would have had an identity crisis because of all these names, but easy-going Charlie went right along and remembered who called him what.

When I met him in college, he was introduced to me as "Charlie Nobles", so that has been the name I used. I could never call him anything else. His brothers, sisters-in-law, and many of our church members through the years have called him "Charlie", but some still call him Marvin.

This has been a confusing thing all through our life together. Every time we went to a new church, he was Pastor Marvin Nobles, but I called him Charlie. Some people thought Charles was his legal name. We have received mail addressed to "Marvin Charlie Nobles", "Charles Nobles", and any other imaginable combination of names.

"Marvin's Many Names" became something we would always have to explain when we started out in a new place. After we became engaged and I wrote my parents about Charlie Nobles, they told people in their church where my dad was pastor that I was marrying Charlie Nobles. Then the invitations went out with the name Marvin Nobles, and people thought I had changed my mind and was marrying Charlie's brother!

But I think the worst problem was when Charles Massegee preached a revival in our church in Texarkana, Texas. He had gone to Hardin-Simmons University in Abilene during the years we were there, and my husband was known as Marvin Nobles in college. When Beverly, Charles' wife, heard me talking about Charlie, she whispered to her husband, "I think that preacher's wife is having an affair! She's always talking about someone named "Charlie" but her husband's name is "Marvin."

Even in our last pastorate in DeSoto, Missouri, I managed to have a problem with "Marvin's Many Names." I was at the church with a group of senior ladies, working on a quilt to be donated to the Baptist Children's Home, and during the conversation, of course I said something about "Charlie".

After several references to Charlie, the senior quilter, Reba, a sweet lady about 86 years old at the time, looked at me. She took off her thimble, stuck her needle into the quilt, folded her arms, and said, "I just want to know who this "Charlie" is.

"Why, he's my husband," I told her.

"No," she said, "Your husband is Marvin Nobles and he is our pastor. Who is this Charlie?" (I think she thought she had me there— just about to give some fodder to the rumor mill.)

So I proceeded to tell her the story of Marvin's Many Names. She thought for a minute, then picked up her needle, put her thimble back on, and resumed quilting as she said, "Well, that's all right then. I just didn't want you to have *TWO* men when I don't have *ANY*!"

Even after we retired, "Marvin's Many Names" continued. We began working as volunteers with Campers on Mission and were at Salem Baptist Church in 1998 with a group of builders. As they organized the devotionals for the week a sheet of yellow paper was sent around. The leader said, "If you are willing to give a devotional this week, sign your name on this paper."

Charlie was talking with a group of men, so as the paper came around he hurriedly wrote down "Marvin" and passed it on.

Later in the week a lady came around asking, "Is there anybody here named Maxine?" No one answered, and I paid no attention and went on with what I was doing.

She continued with the yellow sheet of paper, going from group to group, asking, "Do you know anybody named Maxine?" She is supposed to give the devotional tomorrow and I can't find her."

I knew my husband planned to do the next day's devotional, so I said, "Let me see that paper."

I looked at it and said, "That's my husband's name. That says 'Marvin'."

The lady looked again and said, "Marvin? Who's Marvin? I thought your husband's name was Charlie."

Some of the men in our church picked up on that pretty fast and said, "Maxine? Another name for Marvin! Oh, I'd hate for anybody in our church to hear about this!"

After we returned home, quite often we heard one of our fellow volunteers telling this story and introducing people to "Maxine".

When Charlie was about three or four years old, he did something he never forgot! One of the "double-cousins", a girl about ten or twelve years old, was caring for the younger children while the grown-ups picked cotton.

Charlie's mother and her sister, Minnie, both dipped snuff, as did some of the other women in the family, and he had seen them do it many times. He knew where the snuff was kept so he decided to try it. He climbed up to the shelf where he had seen his mother put the snuff, took out a pinch of it, pulled out his lower lip as he had seen her do, and inserted the snuff. He got so sick he thought he might not live to see his parents return from picking cotton! He learned that snuff was something he would never try again! He did try some other things later, but he never dipped snuff!

When the family lived in Kimbell Bend, the house they lived in was a very poor shack. There were holes in the walls and floors and sometimes the doors and window screens fell off. Charlie vividly remembers the family returning home one day and finding goats and chickens in the house! There was a goat on the table and furniture had been overturned. His mother began yelling and chasing the animals out. Because she was normally calm and easy-going, this experience made a big impression on him. After getting all the animals out of the house they set about putting things in order again.

One Christmas some people from the church came and brought food and toys to the Nobles family. Along with the items was a little car that a small child could ride in! Ed was too big for it and George was too little, so it was Charlie's. He still remembers that little car and how much fun he had with it when he was about three or four years old.

While Charlie, Ed, and George were little, their mom came up with a plan for teaching them how to share. If there was only one of something and more than one boy wanted it, she chose one of the boys to cut it or divide it, and the other two got first choice of the part they would take. After getting the smallest piece a few times, the boys learned to divide things as equally as possible

Whenever one of the boys did something wrong, their mom would go out and get a "switch" to spank them with. Modern children today don't know what a "switch" is, but these boys did! When that young, limber branch from a tree swats a young boy's or girl's tender legs, it can teach them pretty fast that whatever they did that was wrong was not worth doing again! Charlie says his mother killed two peach trees and three lilac bushes breaking off "switches" to use to spank them. I, too, remember being spanked with a switch, and it was not a pleasant experience!

Correct your son, and he will give you comfort; he will
delight your soul.
Proverbs 29:17(NAS)

When Charlie was a little boy, he had to change his clothes all the time. He would get up in the morning and put on his old clothes to do chores around the ranch. Then after breakfast he would put on his school clothes, and after school, he had to change back into his old clothes for playing or working. He said he and his brothers only had two suits of clothes—the good school clothes and the old work clothes, so he could not work or play in his "good" clothes. That's why he **hates** to change clothes now. He just does whatever he needs to do in whatever he happens to be wearing. If he buys clothes at the store, he picks them out and doesn't try them on until he's home and ready to wear them. If they don't fit, guess who takes him back and exchanges them for a different size? If he gets grease on his sleeves because he's doing a dirty job, guess who get the grease out? It isn't Charlie. Whenever I would ask him why he didn't change clothes before doing a dirty job, I would always hear the story about how often he had to change clothes when he was a child.

Since the Nobles family lived on a ranch far from town and they didn't have a car, they did not get to go places very often. They had to walk wherever they needed to go, and with several small children, that was a difficult task. If something was needed from town, Bill would walk into Fort Worth—a distance of about 16 miles—to buy what was needed and then walk back home, unless someone he knew gave him a ride. In later years, they got a car, and the whole family would go into town once in a while.

On one of those trips when the whole family went into town, Bill decided to buy the boys an ice cream cone. Of course, they had never had one before and didn't really know what to do with it. As the boys hesitatingly reached for their cones, their dad said, "Just eat it, boys." Charlie can remember eating it very carefully, making especially sure that he didn't break the cone, and then handing the cone back because he thought it was just a holder for the ice cream and it had to be returned!

One day when he was about eight or nine, Charlie found himself far away from the house out in an open field, with a pocket full of matches. He doesn't remember how he got there or how he got the matches, but he remembers the incident very well.

He struck one match, threw it down and stomped the fire out. That was pretty fun, so he struck another match and let it burn a little longer before stomping it out.

After a few experiences with the matches, he thought, "I wonder how big a fire I could make and still stomp it out?" So he struck two or three matches and threw them all down. He danced around, stomping out the little fires, until he realized that the fire was bigger than he could handle. He began to panic! He was trying so hard to put out the fires, but they were growing and getting farther and farther apart.

He was jumping around from one spot to another, trying to stomp out the fires when he heard something. He looked up and saw his dad driving the old Ford truck, stirring up dust, coming up the road to help him out. He didn't know whether to feel glad or worried. But he didn't have time to think about it. Bill quickly set to work with tow sacks and pails of water, slapping the sacks on the fires before it took out the whole countryside. Then Bill made another fire—on Charlie's backside!

He often told this story as he preached, saying, "This is what happens when we begin to dabble with sin in our lives. The little fires are easy to put out. But then a big fire comes up and we can't put it out by ourselves. We have to call on our Heavenly Father, and after He puts out the fire, He gives us correction, just as my dad did."

He who turns a sinner from the error of his way will save
his soul from death, and will cover a multitude of sins.
James 5:20(NAS)

Charlie, his brothers, and his cousins all liked to wear cowboy hats. They were all playing outside together one day and they got their hats wet in the rain. They knew there was no way to get some more, and the floppy wet brims were falling down in their eyes, so they began trying to figure out a way to fix them. One of the boys suggested that they try to iron them.

So they put some wood in the stove, put their mom's heavy irons on it, and began to heat them up. After ironing the brims, the hats looked pretty good, except for the round part that went over their heads. Then Thurman, one of the double cousins, said, "I know!" Holding up his knee, he said, "Put the hat here!"

Charlie put the hat on Thurman's bony, skinny knee and began to iron. Of course, Thurman quickly jerked his knee out of that hat! It was a long time before the burns on Thurman's knee healed.

Charlie loved to read Buck Rogers comic books about space exploration. The pictures of spaceships, laser guns, and far outer space thrilled him. But when his mother would catch him reading them, she would grab the books and say, "I don't want you reading about those things! That's something that will never happen and you don't need to fill your mind with that!" She would get rid of the books, so her boys would not be influenced by such "far-fetched" ideas.

But anytime they were at their friends' houses, if they found Buck Rogers comic books, they read them with pleasure, absorbing the ideas and dreaming about the possibilities of travel in space.

As time went on, those ideas were not so "far-fetched." Charlie read those books before they had electricity in his part of the world, before airplanes became commonplace, when space travel was only a dream.

So much has happened in only eighty years in America and in the world. Those "far-fetched" ideas became reality. The dreams of many have come to pass, even though some looked at those things as impossibilities.

During the summer Charlie, his brothers Ed and George, and their friends spent a lot of time swimming in the creek. They would shuck off all their clothes and just jump in. Their friend, Kyle O'Donald was usually with them. Kyle and his dad lived in an old shack up on the mountain, and Kyle spent a lot of time at the Nobles' house. They were best friends and remained so throughout their lives.

There was about two years' difference between each of the boys, Ed being the oldest and George the youngest. Ed and Charlie had learned to swim, but George was still pretty little and had not yet mastered that skill. However, George wanted to be with his big brothers and Kyle, and do what they did, so they rigged up a little raft for him. They had a wooden sled that they used for hauling wood to the house for cooking, but they also used it for George to play with in the water. He would put his body over it and as he kicked his legs, it would float. So he was able to play in the water and be with his big brothers and have a good time, just as they did.

Once while they were swimming with several boys, one of them accidentally came up under the raft and knocked George off into the deep water. He went down, and by the time the boys realized what had happened and got to him, George had swallowed so much water that he was unconscious.

The older boys dragged him up onto the bank and turned him over on his stomach. None of them had ever heard of CPR or how to revive someone who had drowned, but they knew they had to get him breathing again, so they began to beat on his back and pump his arms up and down. They kept on until George began to cough and sputter, and then he opened his eyes! You can bet those boys were happy to see George looking up at them again!

They didn't tell their mother about this incident until many years later, when all the boys were grown. They said, "If Mom had known about it, we knew we would not be allowed to swim and play in the creek. George was all right, so we just kept it to ourselves."

In the one-room schoolhouse where Charlie and his brothers and friends went to school, the teacher taught all the grades at the same time. She would get one grade going on a lesson, then start with another group, and so on until all the kids were busy. At recess time, all the children played outside together at the same time.

Electricity was coming to that part of the country during that time in the mid to late 1930's, but people knew nothing about electricity and many of them were afraid of it because they feared the unknown "new things" that were coming. An electric pole had been put up in front of the school and workers had begun to string wires on it to provide electricity to people in the community.

The janitor at the school, an old man who was called "Old Jess" by the children, feared that if people had electric wires in their homes, the wires might blow up and kill them. He watched warily as the poles were being installed because he felt a strong responsibility to protect the school children, as well as to take care of the building and grounds.

One day while the children were playing outside in front of the school, a grass fire started on the playground near the electric pole. The pole had been coated with creosote, a preservative that would catch fire easily. Old Jess looked at that electric pole and the wires on it and thought, "If that grass fire spreads to that pole, it will catch fire. The fire will go up the pole and the electric wires will explode and kill all these kids." In his mind, he had to do something to save the lives of all those kids.

As the fire neared the pole, Old Jess ran up to it and put his big, old hands around the pole as high as he could reach. Holding tight to the pole, he brought his hands down to the flame, stripping the creosote off the pole and taking the fire away from the wires. He put the fire out with his bare hands!

But the creosote was hot and his hands were burned unmercifully. The pole had splinters in it and many of them were imbedded in his hands along with the blisters from the burns. Because of the injury to his hands, they had to be bandaged and he was unable to use them for many weeks. But in his mind, all the pain he endured was worth it because he felt he had saved the lives of all those kids playing on the school playground.

This is a sermon illustration Charlie used to tell. He said that Old Jess was willing to do anything to save those kids, and that we ought to try to do anything we can to tell people about Jesus and then help them learn to love Him and live for Him. Our son David said that he could remember this story clearly from his dad's preaching. In David's mind, as he read this story, he saw the church, the place where he was sitting, and even the kids in the youth group who were sitting on either side of him. Old Jess made an indelible impression on him, too, when he was a young teenager.

In that one-room school, the children did their math problems on the chalkboard. One class would line up at the board and the teacher would give them a problem to do. Since Charlie was not very good at math, he would wait until the person next to him put down the answer and then he would look at it and write down the same answer.

Of course, the teacher quickly caught on! She got a little slate and put it on her desk. Charlie had to stand with his back to the rest of the kids who were at the board, and do his math problems. But he finally learned his math facts!

Since money was hard to get, Charlie and his brothers came up with a plan for making some extra Christmas money. They caught small animals like raccoons, possums, and skunks, skinned them, and sold their hides for a small amount of cash. One day they found a skunk in their trap, so they skinned it and sold the hide. But they soon discovered there was no way to get the smell of skunk off them and off their clothes. They bathed, they bathed again, they scrubbed, but the smell of skunk lingered on and on. Their dad made them sleep in the barn. Their mom made them eat outside. She washed their clothes again and again, trying to get rid of the skunk smell. They were not allowed to come into the house because the strong scent of skunk followed them everywhere!

Monday morning came and it was time to go back to school. Upon arriving at the school, they were cold, so they went up to the old wood stove and stood close, trying to get warm. But the skunk smell was so bad that the teacher sent them home and told them not to come back until the stink was gone. So they found that skinning a skunk had its good side—it got them out of school for a few days!

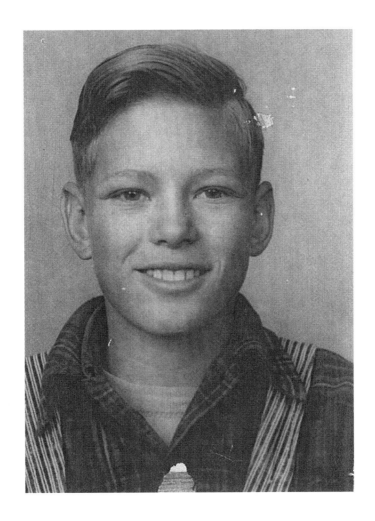

Marvin T. (Charlie) Nobles, age 11 or 12

2
A MAN'S GOTTA DO WHAT A MAN'S GOTTA DO

When Charlie was about thirteen years old and in the eighth or ninth grade, he decided that he'd had enough of school. So one day when report cards were given out, he took his and kept it; he didn't return it to the teacher at school. About a week later, he came home, tossed his card on the table, and said, "I quit school today."

His parents sat at the table, looking at him and trying to decide what to make of this development! Charlie's brother Ed had quit school before graduation, and at that time, he was living with a family who had a dairy, helping with chores. So it looked like the pattern had already been set. Apparently their second son also thought he did not have to finish high school.

After awhile, his dad said, "Well, what are you going to do now?"

"Get a job, I guess," Charlie shrugged and said.

Bill Nobles shook his head, dejectedly, and said, "Well, if you're not going to go to school, you can help me for awhile."

So the next day he went to work on the ranch. He worked with his dad, doing chores around the ranch until he heard of a job at the Silver Creek Ranch, not many miles from where the Nobles family lived.

Silver Creek Ranch was a huge cattle operation that raised and sold Hereford cattle, sometimes selling to a ranch in another state, far away

15

from Fort Worth, Texas. Lots of men were needed to do the work on the ranch. By the time Charlie was fourteen years old, he was living in a bunkhouse with grown men and doing the work of a grown man. This was during the beginning of World War II, when every available man was needed to work. Many men had gone to war, and the only people left to do the work were men too young or too old to be in the Army. A teen-aged ranch hand was better than no ranch hand at all, and Charlie was a good worker. Later his younger brother, George, quit school and went to work with him, also living in the bunkhouse.

As Charlie lived on the ranch and worked with the cattle and horses, he began to dream of one day having a ranch of his own. Even though he had no money and no possible way of getting enough to someday buy a ranch, he learned how to do all the things that have to be done by a rancher. He would get up early in the morning and feed several hundred head of cattle before breakfast. He rode the range, rounding up cattle and caring for them. He loved to sit on his horse and look over the softly rolling hills in that flat part of Texas and dream of the day when he would have his own ranch, and he would be the boss. He got a driver's license before he was sixteen, and drove the truck to deliver cattle that had been sold to other ranches.

He was always smiling and whistling as he went about his work, so he earned the nickname "The Happy Cowboy" there on the Silver Creek Ranch.

Charlie and another guy not much older than he were given the task of driving from Fort Worth to Roswell, New Mexico, to deliver a bull that had been sold to a ranch there. They were in an old truck without a heater and it was winter, so they got pretty cold. The two fifteen or sixteen year old boys were shivering and shaking as they drove many miles across the countryside, hauling a trailer with the large animal inside.

After they made the delivery and were headed back home, Charlie's co-worker was shaking so bad that he couldn't stop. Charlie wanted to help him get warm, and he knew they had some hay in the truck, so he stopped and built a fire in a field. They stood around the fire, trying to warm up as much as they could in the cold winter weather. When the hay had burned up and they were a little warmer, they started out again. But the other boy was so sick, and was shaking so uncontrollably that they decided to stop and spend the night at a motel. Charlie hoped that after some rest and warmth, his friend would feel better and he could help him drive the many miles back to Silver Creek Ranch in Fort Worth.

The next morning, much to their surprise, Charlie's friend was covered with measles! They were two young kids, doing the work of men, and getting a children's disease along the way!

They got in the truck and headed out, but Charlie had to drive all the way, because the other guy was just too sick to help him drive.

About ten miles from Silver Creek Ranch there was an old shack where one of the workers lived. He was an old man with Parkinson's disease, which caused his hands to tremble all the time. The boys working on the ranch laughed at him and called him "Old Shaky." They were young and knew nothing about age and disease.

Old Shaky had a Model-T-Ford that he was always working on when he was not busy doing something for the upkeep of the ranch. When the young cowboys rode by his place, they would sit on their horses and watch him as he worked and listen to him tell stories about his younger days and how strong he had been then. He would say, "When I was young like you, I could just pick up this engine and take it out of the car and set it on the ground to work on it. Then, when I had it fixed, I would pick it up and put it back into the car." While he was talking to the boys, he would always get around to telling them how much God loved them, and that one day he would be young and strong again in Heaven.

Years later, God reminded Charlie of "Old Shaky" and the things that he had told him and the other cowboys about God's love. Charlie often said, "When we tell somebody about God, we never know how long they will remember it, or how it might change their lives when they do remember it." He was not living for God when he knew "Old Shaky", but God used that witness many years later to help bring him back to Him, and His plan for Charlie's life.

While he worked at the ranch, Charlie always took his dirty clothes back home for his mom to wash for him. One day, he rode his horse over to his folks' house to deliver the laundry and thought he would stop on the way back to visit his girlfriend who lived along the way.

While riding back to the ranch, he saw an old cow, trapped in a swollen stream. She was bawling, trying to get out.

He thought, "I'd better help that cow," so he rode his horse into the stream.

While sitting on the horse and trying to get hold of the cow, he realized that he would have to slip out of the saddle in order to catch her. He slipped out, but didn't manage to get hold of the saddle horn, and the horse got away. Meanwhile, the cow moved further upstream and just walked out on the other side. The horse managed to get out, too, but there he was, still in the rushing water, and it was carrying him to the opposite side of the stream.

He managed to get out, but was on the other side from where the horse and cow were and where he needed to be. There was no way he was getting back in that rushing water to swim across, so he had to walk about a mile upstream to a bridge, cross over, then walk the mile back downstream to get his horse. And he was soaking wet!

He went on back to the ranch to get some dry clothes, and didn't visit his girlfriend that day!

When Charlie was old enough to get a driver's license, he wanted to buy a car. He found an old 1929 Model-A Ford that he could buy for $200.00, but he didn't have any money and he knew his parents didn't, either. Charlie Rothlis, a man in the community who owned a service station and grocery store, was about the richest man he knew around those parts. Charlie had worked for him a few times, so he decided to ask him to loan him the money to buy the car. He went to Mr. Rothlis and asked if he would loan him $200.00 to buy the car he wanted.

Charlie Rothlis knew the Nobles family well. He said, "Bring your dad by and we'll see about it."

So Bill and Charlie went to see Mr. Rothlis. After some discussion, he said, "Bill, do you think it would be all right for this boy to have that car?"

Bill said, "Yes, I guess it would."

"Then that's good enough for me," Mr. Rothlis said, and he handed Charlie the money.

Charlie said, "Don't you want me to sign something, saying I'll pay the money back?"

Charlie Rothlis replied, "If Bill Nobles says it's all right, I know it will be all right. I don't need anything else."

Charlie Nobles learned that the good name of his dad was all it took to borrow the money. His dad had such a good reputation in the community that people knew he would do what he said. He knew that if anything happened and the younger Nobles could not pay back the loan, his dad would. Back in those days, a good name was the best thing you could have.

And something did happen. Before the car was paid for, Charlie was working on it and the car fell on his hand, breaking his thumb. He had to have his hand in a cast with a long pin sticking through the thumb to make it grow straight, and because of the injury he could not work for awhile. So his dad made the payments until he could work again, just like Charlie Rothlis knew he would.

A good name is more desirable than great riches.
Proverbs 22:1(NAS)

Charlie had a few other jobs along the way after he quit working at the ranch. For awhile he and his friend Kyle O'Donald worked for the city of Forth Worth in the tree service department, climbing trees and pruning limbs. Then he worked for the Pittsburgh Plate Glass Company, installing windows and mirrors in buildings. Sometimes he worked in offices or bank buildings and sometimes he installed mirrors in people's homes. He said that once he put mirrors on the whole ceiling of a bathroom!

Early in his career at the glass company, he and another man were working to remove a broken plate glass window in a store. The older, more experienced man told him, "This is very dangerous. Don't let go of the glass, no matter what happens, or somebody can get hurt." As they were handling the big and bulky piece of glass, suddenly it started to topple over. Because he was so new at working with glass and so unsure of what he was doing, Charlie dropped his end. The huge piece of glass fell on the older man and cut his arms badly.

Of course, Charlie felt very sorry that he had let his fellow worker down and that he had been hurt, but the older man didn't blame him. He said, "That's all right. You are new at this. But next time, hold on to the glass and don't let go."

Years later, as he recalled this incident, Charlie likened the man's reaction to the mercy, love, and forgiveness that we find in God. Sometimes He tells us to do something and we get scared and don't remember what He said. We let go or we do something stupid, and sometimes disasters happen in our lives. But He always forgives and gives us another chance! God's mercy is everlasting and His forgiveness is unending.

I will give thanks to the Lord with all my heart; I will tell of all thy wonders.
MPsalm 9:1(NAS)

During World War II the United States government had a program called "the draft." Every young man was required to register with the government on his eighteenth birthday, and when they called his number, he had to go into Military Service. If he didn't want to go into the Army, he could serve in the Navy, Air Force, or Marines, but every young man was required by law to train in the military so he would know how to fight and protect our country. Of course there were deferments, which allowed a man to opt out of the draft, but strict rules applied to this. Everyone knew that when a young man was drafted, he had to go. No matter what a person had planned, this took precedence over everything.

Charlie registered for the draft on his eighteenth birthday, and a couple of years had passed since then. He was working for Pittsburgh Plate Glass Company, and every day when he came in to work, people would say, "Did you get your draft notice yet?" or they would ask some other question related to the military situation.

Charlie got tired of answering their questions, and tired of waiting, so one day he went to the draft board and said, "Can I volunteer to be drafted?" He didn't want to wait for his name to come up in the draft; he wanted to get this part of his life over, so they allowed him to volunteer. In a short time, he was sent to Fort Hood, Texas, for his basic training. Then his unit was sent to Germany, where there was no fighting, only military occupation.

The men continued their military training in Meinz, Germany, just as if there had been a war, so they could be ready for whatever job they were called to do. Charlie's job was in communications as Chief of Fire Direction for a 105 Howitzer. He was to listen for the orders and then pass them along, telling the men when to fire their guns on the big tanks. The men marched and drilled, but there was no enemy gunfire and no danger there.

He found out later that the unit he would have been in, if he had waited to be drafted, was sent to Korea, where a war was going on. Many of the men who went to Korea did not come back. So he was blessed by his impatience. Volunteering kept him away from a very dangerous confrontation.

When he had time off, he and his friends rode the train and visited many parts of the beautiful countryside in Germany. They would go to the train station, buy the cheapest tickets they could get, and then they would get on the first-class car and sit in the plush overstuffed seats. They leaned back and enjoyed the refreshments. That is, they enjoyed them until the conductor came along and asked for their tickets. He would look at the tickets and tell them that they were in the wrong section of the train; that their tickets were for a cheap seat in another car, where there were no nice seats or pleasant surroundings, only old wooden benches.

Charlie and his friends would pretend they did not understand, saying that they were Americans and could not understand the German language. So the conductor would motion for them to get up and follow him, and he would lead them all the way back to another car with no frills—just a bare train car with wooden benches. Then, as soon as the conductor was gone, they would get up and go back to the soft seats in the first-class section of the train.

Later in life, as Charlie preached about living a victorious Christian life, he would tell this story. He said, "We bought cheap seats and sat in the first-class section of the train, but God has bought and paid for first-class seats for us, and too often we sit in the cheap section of life. We don't take advantage of the first-class life that God wants us to live."

God has made every provision for us. He has given us the best place in His kingdom, the privilege to learn from Him, to come into His presence and to know His will for our lives. Too often we find ourselves on the old, hard benches, not even listening to Him or reading His Word, not taking advantage of the wonderful blessings afforded to us through His Son, Jesus.

Bill Nobles was a Baptist deacon and he taught a men's Sunday School class. Every week as he studied, he would write out his entire lesson and mail it to Charlie while he was serving as a soldier in Germany. After Charlie became a preacher, he often wished that he had kept those letters from his dad, but he didn't. Those letters would have been a wonderful treasure, but as a young person we don't always know what great things are until we have lost them.

Charlie's mother, Thula, sent him pineapple-upside-cakes while he was in the service. He said that sometimes by the time the cakes arrived the pineapple would be so old that he and his friends would peel it off, scrape the mold away from the cake, and eat what was left. It was her way of reminding him of her love for him while he was away from home in a foreign country, and he always remembered it with fondness.

When Bill Nobles was a young man, God called him to preach. But he was living through the Great Depression and he was a grown man. Since he did not feel that he could go to school and learn to be a preacher, he made a bargain with God. He said, "God, if you will release me from this calling and give me a son, I will try to live before him a life that will cause him to want to be a preacher, and I will give him to you."

God gave Bill and Thula five sons, and one of them did become a preacher. Charlie was saved when he was a little boy, about ten or eleven years old. He doesn't remember how old he was, but he does remember vividly how it happened.

The church in the community where they lived had been closed for a long time when a group of students from Southwestern Baptist Seminary in Fort Worth came to hold a two-week revival meeting. Charlie and his family attended several nights, then both he and his brother, George, felt the need to give their hearts and lives to God. They talked with their mother about how to be saved and decided that they would go forward during the revival meeting to make their public decision to accept Jesus as their Savior.

But on the night they were planning to go forward, a lady who belonged to a church of a different denomination stood up and began arguing with the preacher right in the middle of the sermon! The boys were so frightened that they didn't go forward that night, but later in the week they did, telling the congregation that they had accepted Jesus and wanted to be baptized. They were baptized in Silver Creek, out in the open, when the revival meeting was over. Charlie says that when he came up out of the water, he had the cleanest feeling he ever had! He knew for sure that Jesus had saved him.

But the church was still closed, and they did not have opportunity to go to Sunday School and to learn about the Bible and how God loved them. The men from the seminary had only come to do a revival, and there was still nobody to lead the church.

Time went on. Charlie quit school and began working on the ranch and then worked on other jobs. He did not live for Jesus during those years.

Several years passed; then Bill Nobles and some other men in the community decided to try to get the church opened again. After they cleaned the church building, they talked to administrators at the seminary and arranged for them to send out a preacher. A young man named Art Brewer, who worked for Southwestern Bell Telephone Company while getting his seminary education, was called as pastor at the Elm Grove Baptist Church.

One day Charlie was at home visiting with his parents when Art Brewer came by. They talked awhile and Art said, "Why don't you come to church next Sunday?"

Charlie said, "All right, I will." Later he wondered why he had said that, but he had given his word, so he went to church. After that first Sunday, he went back the next week and the next, and soon he was attending regularly.

God began to speak to him and he was called to preach when he was about twenty-two years old. He went into the Army and tried to live a Christian life. He and his friends did not get involved in some of the things the other soldiers did. But he had a hard time breaking the smoking habit. And he really didn't give his life to God to be a preacher until he was out of the Army.

He was trying to come to terms with what to do with his life when one of his friends said, "Why don't you go down to the Army office and take an aptitude test? That might help you decide."

He decided to go. At the Army office he answered page after page of questions about what he liked to do. After he turned it in, one of the testing personnel took it and asked him to wait. Then he took him into a little room, and asked him some questions. One of the questions was, "Did you ever think you might like to be a preacher?" Charlie said, "I lied like a dog when I looked him in the face and said, 'Oh, no, I never thought about anything like that!'"

But that was what made him finally surrender his life to the ministry.

He knew he would have to go back to school and to the Seminary. Since he had not finished high school, he had earned his G.E.D. (General Equivalency Degree) while in the service, so he didn't have that hurdle to get over. He was accepted at Decatur Baptist College in Decatur, Texas, in 1953. He preached his first sermon at Elm Grove Baptist Church on September 20, 1953.

Marvin T. Nobles, Army photo, 1950

3
A CITY GIRL DURING THE DEPRESSION

When my parents, Coy Wier and Allene Phipps, married, they were very young. Mother was 15 and Daddy was 18 when they married in June of 1934, and I was born nine months later. Because my mother was so young, my grandmother, age 35 at the time, just took over the raising of me, treating me as her baby instead of her grandchild. My parents, grandparents, and my mother's younger sister all lived together in Dallas, Texas.

Charles and Mae Phipps had moved from Oklahoma to Dallas when my mother, Allene, and her sister, Jewell Frances, were young children. My grandfather, called "Papa" to me, was busy in the trade of bricklaying. Mama was a "practical nurse" and she took care of sick and older people all her life. Papa was always busy working or reading the paper. He never talked to me much, but I remember my grandmother singing to me as she held me in her lap and rocked me.

She sang an odd song about a little girl whose father was a drunk, and he stumbled around and kicked over the little girl's chair and sometimes even hurt her. Later in life, I wondered why she sang that particular song all the time. I guess maybe she didn't know any others, but to this day I can remember many of the words to the song "Poor Little Innocent Blossom", because she sang it so often, as I sat on her lap, her rocking chair moving rapidly back and forth.

One Christmas when I was five or six, I got a beautiful doll. I carried it around with me, but like all children, I lost interest and dropped it on the floor when I started playing with something else. A little while later, I was looking for my doll, and Mama told me, "You didn't take care of it, so Santa Claus came and got it. He's going to take it to a little girl who won't drop it on the floor and who will take care of it."

I was heartbroken and cried and cried. I was so sorry. A few hours later, I saw the doll lying on the couch. I grabbed it and hugged it to me, asking what had happened. How did I get my doll back?

Mama told me, "Santa Claus brought the doll back because he saw how sad you were and he thought you had learned to take care of it and treat it better."

That made an indelible impression. I never wanted Santa Claus to be mad at me again!

My grandmother was from a very large family. Some of her brothers were active in the Pentecostal Church, but our family didn't go to church at all, except occasionally, when we attended their church for special things.

Papa chewed tobacco and I can remember whenever he smiled, his teeth looked all brown and nasty because of the tobacco juice. He would go and play dominoes in the evenings at the domino parlor, and spit his tobacco juice into a "spittoon" which was a big metal pot that was kept in places where men met during those days in the 1930's, like hotel lobbies, barber shops, and back rooms of the domino parlor. At home he would spit his tobacco juice into a tin can he kept for that purpose. Chewing tobacco was a nasty habit.

Any time I got stung by a bee or wasp, Papa would make a sort of potion out of his old tobacco juice and put it on the place where I had been stung. That's the only useful thing I know about tobacco juice, but it kept the stung place from swelling.

Once we went on a trip from Dallas to visit some of his relatives in St. Joseph, Missouri. We had an old car, and since there was no air-conditioning, we had the windows down to let in air. All of us were crammed into that car, so I sat by the window and put my hands or head out to get cool. Once when my head was sticking out, Papa spit his tobacco juice out and it went in my face! Another time a June bug got caught in my hair and I was frantically yelling and swatting at it until somebody got it out and threw it out the window. I've hated bugs and the smell of tobacco ever since.

When I was little, mother kept my hair cut in a "Dutch boy" style, which was a popular children's haircut in the 1940's. It was straight all around and clipped very short in the back.

As I got older, I wanted a permanent wave like the other girls had, so we went to the beauty shop to get one. In the 1940's the permanent wave machine was a large hood hanging down from the ceiling, connected to electric wires. Inside the hood were rollers on wires. Hair was rolled on the rollers and then the electricity was turned on. It went through the wires into the curlers and the object was to have curly hair when you got done, but my hair was always "fried" and very frizzy.

When "cold waves" were invented, a girl could get curls without being hooked up to electricity. That was a more pleasant experience.

When I went to the beauty shop with Mama, I would watch them color and curl her hair. They used a rinse that was supposed to give silver highlights to gray hair, but her hair was always blue when they got finished. Once I heard her talking about another lady who said she couldn't get a permanent because of her "fine" hair, meaning, of course, that her hair was thin. But I heard Mama say, "Huh! Fine hair! My hair is as fine as hers or anybody else's! She thinks she's better than anyone else because of her 'fine' hair!" Mama mixed up the meanings for the word "fine", but she was as good as anybody else, and nobody better try to tell her anything different!

It was a rare experience to go to a beauty shop. I only remember a few times that I was in one. When I was about fourteen, I was in a piano recital and got to wear a "formal" and get my hair fixed at the beauty shop. The stylist washed my hair, rolled it on rollers and styled it before lacing ribbons through my hair. The ribbons hung down my back, making me feel quite elegant in the long dress that I wore for the recital. I don't remember the song I played, but I sure thought I looked good while doing it!

If I was sick, Mother would make up my bed with clean sheets and tuck me in. I had to stay in bed all day if I was too sick to go to school, so I very carefully weighed the options before declaring any sickness. I still remember the wonderful smell of clean, fresh sheets, and the feeling of being loved by my mother as I crawled into the bed.

If I had a bad cold, Mama would make a mustard plaster and put it on my chest. That feeling is not as pleasant as the other one. She would mix up a paste with dry mustard and a little water and spread it on an old rag with a knife. She then put another rag on top and plastered it to my chest. It was very hot, and of course, I had to stay in bed while the potion did its work. The purpose was to make the congestion in my chest go away. I hated to have to have a mustard plaster.

Home remedies were what she knew best because of her training as a "practical nurse." During my first year of school, I caught whooping cough. Then my baby brother got it, and so did my mother. We might not have lived if it had not been for Mama's watchful care during the long coughing and whooping spells.

Mama made me take vitamins and cod-liver-oil and other awful-tasting medicines regularly through my growing-up years. She said it would make my stomach work better, or keep me regular, or some such thing. One summer she made me take a spoonful of mineral oil with orange juice every night. It almost made me hate oranges!

As a teen-ager, I had serious problems with my periods and many times I would faint because of the severe pain. Whenever that happened Mama or Mother would make me a cup of hot tea and I would drink it and feel better. Mama often put paregoric into it. Paregoric was a pain-killing drug that people used to ease pain and help them sleep.

In those days you could buy this over the counter in a drugstore. When my first child was born in 1957, you could still buy paregoric over the counter. He had colic and mama advised me to put a little of the medicine into his bottle so he would sleep and not cry with his stomach pain. While writing this book, I decided to look up that medication on-line. I was horrified to find out that it is 45% alcohol and is basically made from opium with morphine! This was a common medication when I was a young girl. We were never without it in our house!

When I was about six years old, my grandmother told me my mother was sick and I was sent to play with one of the neighbor children. When I returned home, I had a new baby brother! They told me that the doctor brought him in his bag when he came to see mother because she was sick.

I had no idea that a baby would be joining our family. In those days, that was something that was not discussed, at least not in my hearing. My brother, Coy Allen, was born in 1941, at our home. I thought the doctor could have put a girl in his bag, because I really would rather have had a baby sister! I had to wait several years for a sister. I eventually got two sisters; Becky was born in 1946 when I was eleven, and Julie was born in 1953 when I was eighteen and already out of high school.

Daddy worked for the Checkerboard Feed Store and Hatchery, and delivered feed and baby chicks to farms. I would get to go to the store and pick out the feedsack I liked, then when the feed was sold, mama or mother would make me a new dress from the sack the feed came in. They even made my underwear! Everything was homemade in those days. Well, everything except socks.

Every Friday, my grandmother and I would walk to the inter-urban station and go to downtown Dallas on a big streetcar that was connected to electric wires. The wires determined the route of the car as it wound its way from our neighborhood into the downtown area of Dallas.

We would eat lunch in a cafeteria downtown, do some shopping, and usually go to a movie. In the plush Dallas theaters called "The Palace," "The Grand," or "The Rialto" we watched many of the elaborate old-time musicals with Doris Day, Deanna Durbin, Mickey Rooney, Judy Garland, and Fred Astaire, Esther Williams, and other stars of the

1940's. I loved to sing and I used to dream of being "discovered" like Deanna Durbin or Judy Garland.

After the movie, we would go shopping. When we shopped for socks at Kress's 5 & 10 Cent Store, mama would say, "Juanita, make a fist." She would open the package of socks and put the foot of them around my fist. If the heel and toe met at the joint of my thumb, she said, the socks would fit. There were no stretchy socks in those days, so you had to be sure they would fit, and the size of the sole of your foot is exactly the same size as your doubled-up fist.

Sometimes on Saturday, my brother and I would go to a neighborhood theatre and see a "kid's show." There was no television, but the theatres showed 'serials', stories that were continued each week. Nobody wanted to miss an installment because every week the main character would be left in some precarious situation, and we always had to find out what would happen next!

We lived in several different houses in Dallas and I attended several schools during my early elementary years. Whenever we moved and I started to a new school, I always felt "different" and alone. I was in a wreck when I was seven, and I had to wear ugly glasses. Sometimes I had to wear a patch over my "good" eye because the doctors thought it would make the "bad" eye work better, but it never did. It just made me feel very different from the other kids, as they laughed at me. My name was Juanita Wier, and I can remember the kids chanting, "Juanita Wier Dear Queer", and other rhyming words, as I stood on the playground at a new school, wishing for a friend. Of course, I had no idea what those words meant, I only knew that I was new and alone, wishing for a friend.

Our last move was to an old two-story house on Overton Road in Dallas. It was just a shell of a house. It did have running water, but it did not have a hot water heater, and there was no bathroom. There was an outhouse in the back yard, which was used for a few years, until my dad built a bathroom when he built more rooms onto the house.

We had a round #3 washtub that we used when we took a bath, which was not very often. Every night we would wash our feet so we wouldn't get dirt all over the sheets on our beds, but we took baths about once a week. Taking a bath was a backbreaking job! Bath water had to be heated in large pans on the stove. After the water was heated and poured into the washtub, cold water was added to make the water the right temperature for bathing.

First the kids would bathe, then mother, and then daddy would bathe in the same old dirty water. If the water got just too dirty to use, they would have to take the tub to the back door, pour out the water, then heat more water, pour it into the washtub, and start over.

One day daddy came home with a long tub. He set it on the kitchen floor and I got in it and found that I could stretch out my legs! It was still a washtub and the water still had to be heated, but it was great being able to take a bath without your knees being as high as your shoulders!

Whenever someone was taking a bath in the kitchen right next to the kitchen stove, everybody else had to stay out to provide a little privacy. Once one of my grandpa's sisters came to visit, and I didn't know she was in the kitchen taking a bath. I ran into the room just as she stood up to get out, and I was scared to death! I didn't know she was in there, and I was startled to see a wrinkled, old lady getting out of the tub!

Later daddy built a bathroom and put in a hot water heater and a real tub with running water. Everybody could take a bath in water that had not been previously used by somebody else. And the door could be shut so that a person could be in there alone! Ahhh—we thought we had really arrived! But we were still very frugal. Old habits are hard to break. We couldn't put much water in the tub, because of the feeling that it was wasteful. And with so many people in the house, we couldn't stay in the bathroom very long before somebody was yelling, asking you to hurry up.

A wooden "ice box" in the kitchen was where we kept perishable foods. The iceman would come by the house to deliver large blocks of ice. Everyone put a sign in their front window to let the iceman know how much ice they wanted. He would come in, carrying a 25- or 50-pound block of ice in huge tongs, and put the ice in the top of the icebox in a metal-lined compartment. If we wanted a cool drink, we would have to chip off some ice with the ice pick. That was a dangerous job because you could easily stick it into your hands, so the children were not allowed to get their own ice. As the ice melted, it dripped into a metal pan under the icebox and we had to keep an eye on that pan or we would have water all over the kitchen floor.

People never locked their doors in those days. If it was too hot to sleep in the house, we would take our quilts outside and spread them on the lawn and sleep there. I remember many nights when we looked at the stars and tried to find the big dipper and other star formations before going to sleep, with the cool breezes blowing on us. The next morning the sun would wake us up.

Sometimes an old tramp would come to the back door, asking for a plate of food in exchange for some work. My mother would give him some food and he would sit on the back steps to eat it. When he knocked on the door to return the plate, she would give him a job to do in the yard to pay for his meal. There was never any fear, and most any housewife was willing to give a little food to a hobo. He would go on his way and we never saw him again. But there were others who came. I think they must have known which houses were friendly and would give them something to eat – maybe information was passed along like it was in the days of the Underground Railroad. I think they all knew there was good cooking at our house!

When Daddy worked for the Checkerboard Feed Store, he got a promotion and moved the family to Gonzales, a town way down in South Texas, where he was manager of one of the feed stores. It was a big step upward for him, but a problem for the family, especially for my grandmother, who didn't like for her family members to be very far away from where she was.

That was during World War II, when people had to use ration books to buy many things needed in the home. My brother was very young, about three or four years old. One day he grabbed the ration book and headed to town, which was right around the corner in the small town of Gonzales. He didn't have any money, but he knew he needed that book! My mother caught him before he got too far, and fortunately he had not dropped the precious ration book!

My grandparents came to see us, and I begged to go back home with them. Mother let me go, but mama didn't bring me back. She enrolled me in school in Dallas, and kept me there instead of taking me back to my parents. I was used to going to new schools, since our family moved a lot, but I remember this one vividly.

The school was in a mixed race neighborhood and Mama would get me dressed and give me money for lunch. She would wrap up coins in a man's handkerchief, putting the money in the corner of the handkerchief, then wrapping and knotting the cloth so that the coins would stay enclosed. Then she would put the handkerchief in my hand and with her hand over mine tightly, she would say, "Now don't you let any of them *other* kids get any of your money!"

During that school year, Mother and Daddy moved back to Dallas, and we all moved into one house again. We all lived together most of my life until I left for college.

Another job my dad had was working with Papa, learning to lay brick. One day the foreman came along and asked Papa, "Can I borrow that boy to drive some nails?" So daddy went with him and began to learn about carpentry. He discovered that he really liked carpentry better, and went on to become a master carpenter, building houses with cathedral ceilings, bay windows, and many fine materials. He became a contractor, supervising several jobs at one time, and he made a name for himself in Dallas.

He always put special touches on the houses where he worked. He never had any respect for builders who built homes quickly—homes that would not last and might even have inferior materials in them. He would walk into a building and immediately look at the corners to see if they were square or if the builder had cut corners just to make more money. And he could tell if that had been done! He remodeled homes in exclusive parts of Dallas, working for famous people like Lee Trevino, the golfer, and Mary Kay Crowley, the founder of the Home Interiors decorating company. Some of the remodeling jobs in these homes cost half a million dollars and took a year or more to complete. He learned to read and interpret blueprints without any formal education. He was quite a man! He taught me to be a hard worker and to try to do a good job of whatever I was doing. He said, "Don't ever back up to get your pay. Be proud of what you do."

My dad had a very good work ethic. I see people now who won't work, or who want the government or others to support them, and it makes me sad. Doing a good job is a great accomplishment, and the person who learns to do it is happy and blessed. It gives a person a sense of pride when they know they have done something worthwhile to earn their own way in the world.

If any man will not work, neither let him eat.
2 Thess. 3:18(NAS)

When I was eleven or twelve, my brother met me in the yard one day as I came home from school, saying, "Don't go to the garage! You can't see what is in the garage! It's a surprise!"

Well, as soon as I could, I made a bee-line for the garage. Daddy had bought an old used bicycle. He had taken it apart and was painting and oiling it and fixing it up for me for Christmas. He painted it blue and silver and it was the only bicycle I ever had. I rode it everywhere I could. Daddy kept the chain oiled and the tires pumped up, and I was really proud of that bicycle!

Many of the gifts we got were homemade. There were doll cradles made from an oatmeal box, with a homemade quilt over it, books made from pieces of paper, tied together with string, go-carts made from scrap lumber—all sorts of things we put together to have a little fun. And part of the fun was in making the toys!

I grew up way before the days of Barbie dolls. We had "paper dolls" and I loved to cut them out and play with them and their paper clothes. I liked to keep them neat, so I would put them into big, heavy books, usually a big dictionary or encyclopedia. Daddy loved to read, so he would pick up a book, and out would fall all my paper dolls, all over the floor. I would have to rescue them and smooth them all out and put them back together in groups. I also liked to cut dolls out of the Sears and Roebuck catalog.

One Christmas I had a little extra money, so I bought myself a book of paper dolls and wrapped it up and put on the tag "to Juanita" so I would get an extra present!

When Mama was sewing, I would sit on the floor beside her and organize all the buttons! I would choose the ones that were the same color and make them into families—the big ones were the daddies, the middle sized ones were the mamas, and all the little ones were the kids.

We really did make up our own fun during the beginning of World War II when money was hard to get and commodities were scarce!

I tried this button game once with one of my granddaughters, and she quickly found something else to occupy her time!

My mother has always been an avid reader. I loved to read too, and the summer when I was eleven or twelve years old, mother encouraged me to keep a list of the books I read.

We went to the library regularly to get books that summer, and that was the beginning of my life as a reader, which continues to this day. My brother and sisters also became readers, and we appreciate our mother teaching us to love to read. Even though my mother and dad never finished school, my two sisters and I have completed college and some graduate school. Two of us became teachers ourselves. My sister's daughter and my two daughters also became teachers. Reading opens many doors!

Daddy, too, was an avid reader and learner. At one time he read a whole set of encyclopedias, just to learn about new things! Even though Dad only went to about the seventh grade, he taught himself anything he wanted to know. He was always finding something interesting in the newspaper and reading it aloud to whoever would listen to him. Daddy was a unique individual—a man who wanted to learn more and more, even though his education had been so limited as he grew up.

When I was in second or third grade, the school offered group piano lessons to those children who were interested. Six or eight of us would be taken into a small room and given pieces of cardboard that looked like piano keys. We learned how to position our fingers and how to move them, but there was no sound. We moved our fingers on the cardboard piano, and were taught a little about reading music. The teacher talked to us about how to play the piano, but no instruments were there for us to use.

I took my "cardboard piano" home and put it on an old apple crate and practiced, moving my fingers up and down on the cardboard and singing. The teachers said this would help us to learn how to use our fingers correctly. I would pretend it was a real piano, and make my little brother sit and listen. Once in awhile at school, we did get to play on a real piano, but not very often.

After awhile, my mother could tell I was not learning much, so she found me a teacher. By then, we were going to church, and our pastor's wife, Mrs. Nelson, gave me my first lessons. She observed that I was learning to play "by ear" and was not learning the notes. So she told mother to hold a piece of paper over my hands so I could not see them, and I would begin to rely on the notes. And I did. Mother would stand for half an hour as I practiced, not letting me look at my hands.

Mother and Mama bought a piano, an old upright that was very heavy. Sometimes when they cleaned the house, they would move that big piano across the room, grunting and pushing, and talking a mile a minute as they worked, cleaned the room, and rearranged the furniture. I really loved to play and Mama liked to listen to me. She always wanted me to play and sing "The Tennessee Waltz".

I learned that if I said I had to practice the piano, I could get out of doing dishes. Mama would say, "You go on and practice. I'll do the dishes for you and listen to you play." She enjoyed it, but papa was not so understanding. He would say, "Can't that kid do anything besides bang on that piano? A man comes home tired and wants to read the paper and all he can hear is that kid beating on that piano."

When I came home from school on my sixteenth birthday, I found that the piano was different and it had a huge red ribbon around it. My parents had sent it off and had it somewhat modernized. A little shelf was at the top with a mirror all the way across. I continued to play that piano until the 1970's. After I married, we took it with us, and it was moved several times. My husband can tell you it was really heavy.

When we moved to the house on Overton Road, I started to Lisbon Elementary School in Dallas in the 5th grade. I stood before the class as the teacher introduced me, looking at the children sitting in desks bolted to the floor in straight rows. A girl sitting on the very first row in a "double desk" with no one beside her said, "She can sit with me!" So the teacher assigned me to that desk and Caroline Mizell became my best friend. We were best friends all the way through school.

We spent a lot of time at each other's houses and we got to know each other's family. She had four brothers and they always listened to "The Lone Ranger" on the radio while eating dinner at night. At home, we listened to the radio, too. I remember listening to "Fibber McGee and Molly", "Amos and Andy", and a scary show called "The Shadow Knows" that had an evil laugh track throughout the program. During the day my mother and mama listened to "Stella Dallas", but they always made me go somewhere and read or play while they listened to that show. I think that must have been one of the first "soap operas" in the days of programmed entertainment.

When I was about eleven, our family became owners of a television set. It was a large box on legs with a round black-and-white screen. There were not many programs, but every Saturday night the whole family watched wrestling. Papa played dominoes a lot, but not on Saturday night. He made sure to be there to watch the wrestling matches.

After we moved to the house on Overton Road we began going to church. My mother, brother, and I walked the few blocks to Ramona Avenue Baptist Church and began going regularly. I took part in the Junior department, then in the Youth group. Two dear ladies, our pastor's wife, Mrs. Nelson, and the grandmother of one of the boys in the group, Mrs. Dandridge, were our leaders. I learned Bible verses, the books of the Bible, how to find passages by taking part in Bible drills, and I learned what it means to live as a Christian. I took part in Sunbeams and Girls' Auxiliary, Training Union, and worship services. I was eleven when I sang my first solo on a Sunday night.

Many years later, as I sang, "Thank You for Giving to the Lord," the faces of these two dear ladies came to my mind. I thank God for what they taught me.

At church, I listened and watched as the pastor's daughter, Louise Oliver, played the piano for the services. She added chords, embellishments, and extra notes and I would go home and try to play the hymn just like she did. I practiced, tried to recall the notes she used, and worked until I got it right. I thought that if I could be as good as Louise, I would be set for life!

I was about twelve when Louise asked me to play for the Sunday evening services once in a while. She gave me a chance to learn how to be a church pianist by stepping aside and letting me play. Lots of times I would worry because I knew I had hit some wrong notes, but most people didn't even notice. I have been in a lot of places, and I have never seen another church pianist so willing to let a young person learn as she was. Most church musicians are territorial, very protective of their jobs, but this dear lady was a caring person who stepped aside and let a little girl learn.

Soon after we started attending Ramona Avenue church, I sang a solo in the Christmas program. I was dressed as an angel and I stood in the baptistery and sang, "Help Somebody Today" as a part of the Christmas play. The pastor went to our house and asked my daddy personally to come and hear me sing.

Daddy was not a Christian and he usually would not let a preacher come on the place to talk to him. But that time he went to church, and God began to speak to him. Rev. Harlan Nelson, the pastor, visited my dad regularly every Thursday night. On one of those occasions, when the pastor was talking to dad, my mother saw that he was really listening, so she took my brother and me upstairs.

Dad gave his attention to the pastor's teaching and God saved him. I was nine years old when dad was saved, in September of 1944.

In 1999, as I was doing a book signing for my first book <u>It Wasn't Always Easy, But it Sure Was Fun,</u> I met a man who had been a member of Ramona Avenue Baptist Church when I was a child, and had been my daddy's friend through the years. Craig Freeman was pastor of a little church in Dallas and he wrote in his church newsletter:

> *She was just a little eight year old girl in 1943. Without her parents, she came to Ramona Avenue Baptist Church. Teachers loved her and taught her. She was saved and later so was her father.*
>
> *Her father then surrendered to preach. The girl grew up and married a preacher. Coy Wier, the father, spent many years in Texas as a bivocational pastor. The little girl, Juanita Nobles, and her husband have just retired from 40 fruitful years in the ministry. She has written a book about those glorious experiences.*
>
> *Juanita's sister is a public school teacher and a Sunday School teacher.*
>
> *Complain about just about anything, but you will get little sympathy from me in suggesting cutting back on children's work in our church.*

My dad came from a very large family. His parents, Doyle and Exie Wier, had eleven children, but five them died when they were babies. My dad, Coy, was the oldest. Next came C.V., then Dee, Kenneth, Daniel, and the last one was Edna Fay, the only girl. Grandma had two sets of twins that died at birth, and another boy, Archie, who died at about age two. Daddy said he was always taking care of babies and he had a permanent wet spot on his hip from carrying a baby around on it. Sometimes he had to stay home from school to help his mother with the babies. He wore a ragged old shirt to school because that was all he had, and he was very ashamed of his clothes. He would not take off his jacket because he didn't want the other kids to see his shirt.

Somebody told him one day that if he found a safety pin and picked it up, it meant that he would get a new baby brother or sister. After that, every time he saw a safety pin on the ground, he picked it up and threw it as far away as he could!

Grandpa Wier was a barber. When his eyes became so bad he could not see well to do a good job of cutting hair, he became a migrant worker. He and my grandma, Exie, would pick crops and when the job was done they would move on to another place and pick crops for somebody else. All the kids helped, trying to earn enough money to keep the family going financially. This was during the time of the Great Depression, when jobs were hard to find and money was extremely scarce.

One year when his parents and siblings were ready to begin moving to pick the crops, Daddy stayed in Dallas. He had met my mother, he was 18 years old, and he didn't want to risk losing Allene's affections by going away. While his family went to pick crops, he stayed in Dallas, and often he would go to her house and visit her. They didn't go on dates, because nobody had money to do that. So they played games, made cookies or popcorn, or went for walks, and got acquainted with the whole family.

Once Dad was getting ready to go to see my mother before they were married. He had washed and ironed his clothes, which he had to do himself, and laid them on the bed. While he was taking a bath, his brother C.V. came in and saw the clean clothes and decided to play a trick on him. C.V. put on the clothes and went to my mother's house. When Coy got out of the bath and went to get his clothes, they were gone! He had to put on his old, dirty clothes. He walked to Allene's house and there sat C.V, on the couch next to her, wearing his brother Coy's clean clothes! When my mother told me this story, she said, "I don't know what happened after that, but they walked away together and your dad was really mad!" And Coy became my dad, not C.V.!

Daddy's brother Dee was always running away from home. When my dad was about twelve years old, his grandpa, A.J. Wier, died. Doyle and Exie lived in Cleburne, Texas, at that time. They got enough money together to buy one train ticket and Doyle was to go to the funeral, since they could not afford for all of them to go. Dee wanted to go too, but since he couldn't, he ran away from home.

He was always wanting to go somewhere else and running away to get there. When he was grown, he drove an 18-wheeler and went many places because of his job. Dee died with a heart attack before he was fifty years old.

Daddy's brother C.V. ran away from home a lot, too. When he was about seventeen, the Ringling Brothers-Barnum and Bailey Circus came to town. C.V. went out to where they were camped and hung around, doing anything he could to be a part of the circus. When they left, he went with them, and worked for the circus for four or five years. When World War II started, he joined the Army. He was in the Second Division Texas unit and when he came home, he had a chest full of awards, medals, and ribbons.

Exie Hyatt, my dad's mother, was about five years old when her mother died, leaving her and two brothers, Winston and Houston. Her father remarried, but her new stepmother and she did not get along well. When she was thirteen, her father also died. She and her brothers moved around and lived with different relatives until they were grown and able to be on their own.

Later she wanted to keep in touch with her brothers but they had moved around so much, living with relatives, that she could not find them. She loved children. When anyone in the family had a new baby, or married a new husband or wife with children, they were "her kids." She was always telling people about her grandchildren, and even raised some of them. The telephone was her most prized possession. She loved to talk on the phone to family and friends. If the phone rang and she didn't get to it in time to find out who was calling, she called everybody she knew, asking them, "Did you call me?" until she found out who had wanted to talk to her.

Julia Anne Windsor, my mother's grandmother, lived in Iowa in the 1800's. She was about five years old when she fell at the door of the house and broke her ankle on a big stone. In those days not much was known about setting bones, and she was crippled. When she was a young woman, James Marcus Lafayette Jenkins came to Iowa, working as a cowboy. He met Julia Anne and they were married. Although she walked with crutches the rest of her life, she raised a large family. I never knew my mother's grandmother, but I remember a large picture of her that hung in our home. She was standing with her crutch.

My mother told me she had many wonderful memories of her grandmother, and that she felt very close to her when she was a little girl. She said that when I was born, she proudly took me to see her grandma. Grandma Jenkins laid me on the bed, then picked me up haphazardly and my mother was alarmed. Grandma told her, "She's real pert. She'll do all right."

My grandmother, Mae Jenkins, the youngest of Julia Jenkins' children, was born in 1900. The family moved to Oklahoma from Iowa when Mae was about eight years old, riding in a covered wagon to get to their new home.

My grandmother was a "tomboy". She loved to run around barefoot and play games with the boys. She rode a horse with just a blanket on its back instead of a saddle. Her only sister was thirteen years older than Mae, and she had several older brothers. Grandma Jenkins was past the age of forty when Mae was born.

When Mae was about nine years old, the family happened to be in Galveston, Texas, when a big flood came to the area. One of her older brothers saved her from drowning in the flood. This made her very afraid of water, so she never wanted any of us to be in a boat or to go swimming, or to have anything to do with water. She never did like school, either. The best part of school was riding the horse there and back. She did not like to read or study. When she grew up and had a family, she did not care whether her daughters went to high school or not. She never cared about education—for herself or for anyone in her family. She just wanted family to be near.

She liked hanging around her brothers. When her brothers began smoking cigarettes and sneaking around to do it, she would say, "Ummm, I'm going to tell on you." So, to keep from being told on, her brothers gave her a smoke. They said, "Now, if you tell on us, we'll tell on you." Because of this, she began smoking at a very early age.

She smoked until she was about forty years old. She was told by doctors that she should quit because of her health, so she came home, put her cigarettes up high in a cabinet, and never smoked another one. She said that whenever she really wanted to smoke a cigarette she would take them out of the cabinet, smell them, and put them back

I always hated the smell of cigarette smoke, so it was not hard for me to make the decision at age eleven that I was not going to ever smoke or drink. And I didn't. My real reason for this was that I thought God wanted me to be a preacher's wife, and I wanted to keep my body clean from these habits. I still remember the day I told God that I would never take part in smoking and drinking, and honestly, I was never even tempted to do either one.

The closest I came to smoking was in high school. I had a crush on a good-looking boy who smoked and I started carrying a small book of matches in my purse, just in case he ever needed one! But he never paid much attention to me.

One winter when I was a teen-ager, one of papa's distant relatives came to stay with us, to work with him and learn to be a bricklayer. He was a good looking young man not much older than I, and one night he asked me to go on a date to see the Ice Capades in an arena in Dallas. We started out on a very cold evening, and he lit up a cigarette. I promptly rolled down my window. He said, "It's cold. Roll up the window." I said, "Put out that cigarette and I will." So he put out the cigarette.

My daddy was a smoker when I was little. I remember him telling me after he was saved he knew he had to quit smoking. We were on a streetcar in Dallas and he threw his cigarettes out the window and never did smoke another one.

My husband, Charlie, did not have such an easy time breaking the smoking habit. He had a nice 1952 powder-blue Chevrolet when he went to college. He had determined not to smoke, but he didn't empty the ashtray in the car. Whenever he had an uncontrollable urge to smoke, he would go out and dig out one of the old stubs from the ashtray, take a puff or two, and then put it out. I heard him say, "The Lord didn't give me that nasty habit, and I wasn't going to ask Him to take it away." But he later admitted that he should have asked God for His help in breaking that habit. He did break the habit. I never saw him smoke.

Bill Nobles, Charlie's dad, smoked all his life. He often said he wished he could quit, but he just didn't think he could. After we were married, we heard an advertisement for some filters for cigarettes. The ad said you could just put your cigarette in the filter and smoke it, and keep on with each filter, one after the other, until finally after the filters were used up the desire to smoke would be gone. We decided we wanted to help Grandpa Nobles quit, so we bought him the filters. We proudly took them to him, and told him what the ad had said about how to use them. He looked them over, took out the first filter, and put his cigarette in it.

A person was supposed to use each filter for a week. Bill used them faithfully, each one for a week. When the last filter was gone, he went on smoking his cigarettes—with no filter. Charlie lit a cigarette for him the day he died.

My grandmother, Mae, was a really good cook. I remember her going out and getting a chicken and wringing its neck, then after it flopped all around the back yard until it died, she would pluck out all the feathers, cut it up and fry it. We also raised rabbits for food, and I always cried whenever Papa killed one of the rabbits so we could eat it for supper. I never could eat the rabbits. I could see their big eyes and think of their soft fur, and I'd just eat vegetables and leave the meat alone on those nights.

Because of the good cooking in our house by both my mother and grandmother, we always had lots of company. When people came to visit they always managed to stay for dinner. Mama spent most of the day in the kitchen fixing food and making the guests welcome. The women would sit in the living room visiting with others, and not offer to help very often. A family friend, Mr. Welch, would come, bringing his son, Truett, and his daughter, Thomazine. Of course, there was not room at the table for everybody to eat, so the men would eat first, then the women and children would eat. The children always had to wait until the men had finished. There was a popular song during those years, called "Take an Old, Cold Tater, and Wait." That was really what we did, only sometimes we didn't even get the old, cold potato; we just waited!

One day Papa, Mr. Welch, Truett, and another man were playing dominoes at the kitchen table while Mama prepared dinner. She said to Papa, "Charlie, you need to put them dominoes up so I can get dinner on the table." He said, "All right, as soon as we finish this game."

Pretty soon she would say again, "Charlie, have you finished that game yet?" And he would say, "Oh, we finished that one and dinner was not ready, so we started another one." She had a hard time getting him to stop his domino game long enough to put the food on the table. He was an avid domino player all his life.

Mae was an expert at crocheting. She made beautiful tablecloths, bedspreads, doilies, anything that could be done with a crochet hook and some thread. I don't remember many times when her hands were not cooking or wielding a needle or crochet hook.

We had doilies pinned to the top of all the chairs, and on every surface in the house.

Doilies were beautiful open-work scarves. When they had to be laundered, though, they were a headache. After washing, they had to be heavily starched (and starch was made with boiling water, another long process.) Then they were laid on towels on the table to dry. They had to be checked regularly and pulled so they would dry straight and even. Then they were ironed with a very hot iron and placed back on the table or chair where they had been.

Mama was also a very good seamstress. She taught me to sew when I was fifteen. That year I made skirts and blouses for school, and wore them proudly, and have been making clothes and other things ever since.

She sewed for us and for many of the kinfolk. One of the aunts, Rosie, had several children. Mama would begin in the summer saying, "Rosie, you'd better get me some material so I can make them kids some school clothes." Finally Rosie would bring the material over, along with all six of her children, and stay all day while Mama sewed for them. She would sit at the sewing machine and watch as Mama sewed. She would say, "Why are you cutting it like that?" "What are you doing that for?" and "What do you want to do with that piece of material?" My grandma said she was always glad to see her leave at the end of the day.

But when she came, she brought only material—no buttons, no thread, no lace or trimming. Mama had to come up with everything to make the school clothes look kind of nice. Rosie would sit all day. Mama would get up at noon and fix lunch, then stack the dishes and go back to the sewing machine. Rosie would continue to sit and ask questions.

Finally, when the job was finished, Rosie would say, "Well, Mae, I would stay and help you with them dishes, but I've got to go home and give the baby a dose of medicine."

After that in our family, whenever somebody didn't want to do something, they would say, "Well, I would do it, but I've got to go and give the baby a dose of medicine."

Juanita Wier, age 16

4
LOVE LIFTED ME!

The year was 1942. I was seven years old and in the second grade, and my brother, Coy Allen, was more than a year old, but not quite two. We lived in an old farmhouse out in the country. The place where the farmhouse was located is now covered with houses, shopping centers, and businesses, but then it was an undeveloped piece of ground with an old farmhouse and some outbuildings. My dad worked at the Checkerboard Hatchery and his boss, Mr. Becker, allowed us to live in the house as a little "perk".

In the old farmhouse there were two bedrooms, a kitchen, a large living room with a fireplace, and a little room off that one that was barely big enough for a bed. Mother and Daddy and my brother shared one of the bedrooms, and my grandparents were in the other one, and I had my own room—the little room off the living room. Part of the time while we lived there, my mother's sister and her family lived there, too, when her husband was out of a job and they needed a place to stay, so it was really crowded. We had cows, pigs, chickens—lots of animals for the adults to care for.

I went to school in a little one-room schoolhouse where the teacher taught all the grades. Our house was well back from the highway and I had to walk a long way to the road to catch the school bus, but there were cows in that pasture, and I remember being deathly afraid of them. I would stand at the gate and yell for my mother to come and walk with me when I got home from school.

One morning my brother and I were playing on the porch when my mother called us and said we were going to visit Aunt Effie, Mama's sister, who lived a good distance from where we lived.

Mother, who was only twenty-two years old in 1942, had learned to drive on the busy streets of Dallas. Since my grandmother never drove, mother was determined to be independent, so one day my dad just gave her the wheel and told her to drive—and she learned in the midst of traffic. I'm sure that was a traumatic experience, but by the year 1942 she drove anywhere she wanted to go.

Aunt Effie managed a large apartment house in Dallas, and after visiting her we visited with one of my mother's cousins who had a daughter about my age. I was always asking her mother to let her come and spend the night, and she had never done that, but that day her mother said she could. I grabbed her hand and said, "Come on, Elizabeth, let's wait in the car."

We started running down a hill. The car was facing the opposite way and was parked on the other side of the street at the bottom of the little hill. As we ran, Elizabeth dropped my hand and yelled, "Wait!" because she saw a car coming. I never heard her, but kept on running.

The next thing I remember was later—about a week later—when I woke up in the hospital. My right leg was broken and I was encased in a body cast from my waist to the knee of my left leg and the toes of my right leg. Of course I was immobilized and confined to the bed. I had broken some other bones as well as my leg, and had a fractured skull, and my eyes had been damaged so that I would wear glasses the rest of my life.

Later I learned that I had been in a coma for a week and the doctors had told my parents that they had done all they could, and whether I woke up depended on God. Even though my dad was not a Christian at that time and had no time for God, he cried and prayed, asking God to let his little girl live. He even promised God that if He would spare his daughter's life, he would surrender his life to Him to do whatever God wanted him to do.

God answered my dad's prayer. I woke up and began to get better. The man whose car had hit me came to see me in the hospital. He asked if there was anything I wanted and I told him I wanted some red shoes.

We had money for school shoes, the sturdy tie-up high-top shoes that I wore, but not money for something frivolous like red shoes. I remember waking up one day and there on the bedside table was a pair of shiny red patent leather shoes! But before the cast was off, my feet had grown and I never got to wear those beautiful shoes!

When I was released from the hospital and we went back to the farmhouse, daddy rigged up a little swing over my bed so that I could raise myself up to look out the window. The body cast kept me from getting out of bed, but I could look out the window as he and my brother would catch lightning bugs and put them in a jar. Then they would bring them to me, turn off the lights and let me watch them light up.

That doesn't sound like much fun to kids today who have all kinds of electronic gadgets, games, movies and TV. But in those days, we didn't have that and we made do with simple pleasures, like a jar full of lightning bugs, or homemade toys and stories that were told and retold.

Once I tried to get out of bed and fell with a thud. Mother and Mama came to pick me up and get me back in bed. I'm sure it was hard, being seven years old, and unable to get out of bed.

The accident happened in May, near the end of the school term, so I didn't miss a lot of school. The children in my class made get-well cards and I remember spending hours looking at them.

After I got well, my daddy forgot about his promise to God. We moved away from the farmhouse into the apartments managed by my great-aunt Effie. She was very faithful in her church attendance, and took me with her as often as she could so that I could go to Sunday school. My mother and grandma went to church and made professions of faith, but daddy and papa would not go.

That summer Aunt Effie took me to Vacation Bible School and she encouraged my mother to go and be a helper. Mother went along and helped in the department where I was. She told me years later that she learned a lot she didn't know about the Bible stories, just by being a helper in a children's department.

On Decision Day, the preacher told the story of Moses, the children of Israel, and the plagues of Egypt. That story really scared me! I had never heard of a God who could do things like that! So when the invitation was given, I went forward, more out of fear than anything else. I wanted to be on the good side of a powerful God who could do bad things to me if I didn't do what He wanted. I don't remember being counseled, and everything was foreign to me because I had not grown up in church. A time was set for me to be baptized on a Sunday night. There was a big fuss at home because Daddy could not understand why we had to go to church at night, and by the time we got there, the baptism service was already over.

A year or two after the car accident, we moved to the house on Overton Road. I walked to Ramona Avenue Baptist Church, a distance of a few blocks, and soon my mother and brother began to go, too. One Sunday I went forward at the church and said I was already saved and wanted to be baptized. The preacher, Brother Harlan Nelson, came to our house to ask my parents if I could be baptized.

After I was baptized, Bro. Nelson came to talk to daddy alone. The Holy Spirit began to prepare his heart, and it was not long until he accepted Jesus as his Savior, too. Daddy said later, "I used to curse and be mean to preachers. I wouldn't even let them come on my property to talk to me about Jesus. But something made me listen to this preacher. I went to see Juanita baptized, and the Lord saved me." After that, everything became different.

Daddy began to want to preach. He said, "I always knew that if I ever accepted Jesus, I would have to give Him my whole life." He preached his first sermon when I was eleven years old. I was so proud to be a preacher's daughter. During my teen-aged years, I went with Daddy when he preached at a rescue mission in downtown Dallas. I would sing and he would tell the story about when I was hurt in the wreck and how God used that accident to bring him to a saving faith in Him.

After Daddy's salvation, God began teaching him lots of things. He had never gone to high school; in fact, he had only completed seventh grade before stopping school to help his family. He was only thirty years old, with a family, and he felt he could not go back to school. So he took some night classes through Southwestern Seminary, located in Fort Worth, and began to read and learn all he could about the Bible. He had a natural desire and a hunger for learning so it was not hard for him to educate himself. He was a compassionate preacher. He often cried as he preached, telling people about how God had saved him, and could save them, too.

He told me about an experience he had shortly after his salvation. He was working at the church at night, helping with some building project, while the choir was inside, rehearsing. He heard the choir sing,

I was sinking deep in sin, far from the peaceful shore,
Very deeply stained within, sinking to rise no more,
But the Master of the sea heard my despairing cry,
From the waters lifted me, now Safe am I.
Love lifted me, love lifted me,
When nothing else could help, love lifted me!

That song, "Love Lifted Me", from the old Broadman Hymnal that Baptists used for many years, described my daddy, he said. He told me years later that when he heard those words, he stood in awe and thought, "That's what God did for me! I was so deep in sin I could never get out, but He lifted me and took me out of the muck and mire of sin and set my feet on solid ground! Nothing else but Jesus could have helped me!"

Any time I hear that song, I think of my dad. After his salvation at age 30, he preached or taught the Bible until he was almost 80. He taught Sunday School and attended church on the day he died. I am thankful for the heritage of honesty, love, and faith that he gave me.

In addition to learning about the Bible, my dad continued to learn more about the carpentry trade. He was a "tentmaker" preacher because he worked full time every day as a carpenter, then came home, got a bath and put on a suit, and went out to visit at hospitals or to win somebody to the Lord. He wore striped bib overalls, a hammer hanging from his side during the day. He had nicks, scrapes, and Band-aids on his hands because of the work he did during the day as he went out at night to witness for Jesus.

Church became important in the life of our family. We became active in everything that went on—Sunday School, Training Union, Wednesday services, mission organizations. All of us went to church except Papa. He would not have anything to do with church or God.

We all prayed for Papa, and finally, a few years before he died, he did accept Jesus as his Savior too.

After Daddy began to preach, he bought a small building and remodeled it, and began the South Cliff Baptist Church. He preached there for several years—on fire for the Lord. He would shed tears when he thought about what God had done for him. He would cry unashamedly as he told about the car wreck and how God had saved him and called him into the ministry. I played the piano and taught children's Sunday School classes, but I was not sure about my salvation.

Years later, after I was married to a preacher myself, one of our friends came to our door in Abilene, Texas. It was noon and we were home from work for the lunch hour when Cecil Foster hesitatingly knocked on our door. He walked in and paced the floor for a few minutes, then blurted out, "Juanita, the Lord sent me over here to ask you about your soul. Are you saved?"

I looked at him and burst into tears. For years I had been seeking reassurance of my salvation and just couldn't find it. I had "rededicated" my life many times. I told Cecil about my fears and indecision and he said, "Have you ever *asked* the Lord to save you?"

I admitted that I never had. I had just gone forward in church as a little girl, I was baptized a couple of years later, then I lived the life of a Christian, going to church and doing all the things that I thought a Christian would do. So there in that kitchen, I knelt and asked Jesus to be my Savior. And He saved me.

I was the first person my husband baptized in the little church where he was pastor. Most preachers get to baptize their children, but Charlie got to baptize his wife, his children, and several of his grandchildren!

When we told my dad about my decision to accept Christ in 1954, after I was a preacher's wife, he refused to accept it. He said, "It was because of you that I was saved. You were a Christian since you were a little girl."

I thought, "What does it matter whether I accepted Christ then or now? I have had problems for years, doubting my salvation, and now I am sure." I thank God for that assurance.

Trust in the Lord with all your heart and lean not on
your own understanding; in all your ways acknowledge
Him, and He will make your paths straight.
Proverbs 3:5(NAS)

Juanita and her dad, Coy Wier

5
THE TWO BECOME ONE

After I graduated from high school I wanted to go to college, but family pressure and a lack of money kept me from doing that. I had studied secretarial skills in high school, and my family was of the opinion that a college education for a girl was wasted money, since girls just got married and became wives and mothers.

I found a job and worked for a couple of years in an office. In the back of my mind I wanted a college education, but no one in our family had ever gone to college, and very few had even graduated from high school. So I worked and tried to save money with the goal of eventually going to college.

I was dating a boy I had dated in high school. We had been "going steady", and we had talked about getting married, but had not set a date. He even had given me an engagement ring.

Some of my friends were in college and I was invited to go with them to a Baptist Student Union meeting at East Texas State University in Marshall, Texas, just to see what it was like. I was riding the bus to work, reading my Bible, and I heard an audible voice saying, "Juanita, give James back his ring and go to college. There you will meet the man you are to marry." I actually turned and looked around the bus because I thought someone was talking to me.

Shortly after that, I broke up with James and began to see what colleges were out there that I might be able to afford. I heard about Decatur Baptist College, which was fairly close to Dallas, so I began to make plans to go there, in spite of my family's discouragement. I believed that God wanted me to be a preacher's wife.

I went to Decatur College and began the summer session in 1954. An office job helped with my bills, and I lived in the dormitory on campus.

In the old two-story girls' dormitory, we didn't even have twin beds. The two girls in the room shared a double-sized bed, something that would not even be imagined in today's world. Once I tried to wash the sheets for the bed in the bathtub, which was down the hall. There were no bathrooms in our rooms. There was no laundry area and clothes had to be taken somewhere else to be laundered, so I was trying to do it myself. After wringing and wringing, I just couldn't get all the water out of those sheets, and I never tried that again!

The boys' dorm was directly across the campus, with the administration/classroom building in the middle. It had been built in the early 1900's, a large stone structure with a lot of creaking stairs and old facilities. There was a large courtyard between the two dorms, with lots of room for walking around, playing games, etc.

Charlie had enrolled in Decatur College in March of that same year, after having been out of school for about 12 years, when he decided to totally give his life to the Lord and to study to be a preacher. He went into the office that day in June, on the first day of the summer semester, looked around, and thought, "Hmm, something new has been added to the office." He said, "I saw this girl with big eyes, a new worker in the office. I was eyeing her and she was eyeing me, and that was the start of it all!" He commuted from Fort Worth with Chick Harrell and another preacher, and he told them about seeing me in the office. So the two older preachers dared him to ask me for a date. And that's how our life together began.

When I met Marvin Nobles, one of the girls I knew from the dorm introduced him to me as Charlie Nobles. He had already been there one semester and he was known by most of the students, since it was such a small college. And he was so good-looking! Everybody knew him and most of the girls wanted to date him.

He didn't live on campus but he commuted daily. He would drive up on the weekends and we would go out or just stay on campus and talk. There were not many places to "go out" in Decatur.

We were both members of the Volunteer Service Band, a group of students who did services in Baptist churches in the county. He preached and I played the piano or sang, or we would go along and listen to the others, just so we could be together. Sometimes we just stayed on the big porch of the girls' dorm and talked, or walked around the campus.

I liked to play my ukulele and sing "Beautiful Brown Eyes." I would clown around, singing loudly, until one day Charlie got one of the girls to go into my room and get that ukulele and bring it to him. He hid it in the boys' dorm and thought that would stop me from my silly singing. But I just got one of the boys to get it and bring it back to me. No one of the opposite sex was allowed in either dormitory. If a male walked past the big living room on the main floor of the girls' dorm, someone would yell "Man on the floor!" and girls would scurry to their rooms, making sure they were decent!

We had English class with Mrs. Esther Watkins, a down-to-earth lady who taught us to speak and write correctly. She stressed the importance of prayer while she was teaching English. She once said, "I wouldn't even trade mules without talking to the Lord about it first!" Her classes were always lively and interesting.

Charlie Jones was the music instructor, and of course, I was involved in music. I sang in the chorus and was also part of one of the girls' trios, along with Wanda Womack and Mary Lee Butler.

We sang on "Western Day," wearing fringed skirts, boots, and big hats. We had to borrow boots from the boys, and the ones Wanda wore were so big, she had to stuff newspapers into them and shuffle her feet so they would not fall off!

Charlie and I were in Biology class together, and I would never touch any of the specimens. He would do the dissecting, and I would write about it and turn in my papers without ever touching those gross dead things! Dean Tom Gettys, who taught the class, said I was the first student he had ever had who passed the course without touching anything!

Dr. Otis Strickland, the president of the college, taught the Bible class. I learned about the Old Testament and the Tabernacle, which was a great awakening for me. When I learned about the veil of the tabernacle being torn in two at Jesus' crucifixion, I was mesmerized. To think that Jesus would die for me and make a way for mortal man to approach a holy God in prayer!

Behold, how great a love the Father has bestowed on us,
that we should be called the children of God!
I John 3:1(NAS)

One weekend Charlie drove me home from college, about a two-hour drive from Decatur to Dallas. We left on a Saturday morning, stopped in Fort Worth to meet his parents and brothers, and went on toward Dallas. We stopped at a park and had a leisurely time talking. By the time we got to my house, about eight hours had passed! That evening as we walked into the house, I could see that my parents were visibly upset. They told me they had driven to Decatur that morning to pick me up and were told that I had left with a young preacher, and they had been worried when I didn't get home in a short length of time.

Even though I was 19 and had been out of high school and working, I felt I was under my parents' supervision, and when I realized how upset they were, my mind went blank. I said, "Mother and dad, this is –" I couldn't even remember his name! Charlie stuck his hand out to Dad, and said, "—Charlie Nobles." Dad shook his hand, but mother was still pretty upset!

In August, after we had met in June, Charlie picked me up at the college campus and we drove to Fort Worth to attend a citywide youth revival. That was in the early days of the "Youth for Christ" movement, when young preachers held services around the country to lead young people to the Lord. After the service, before driving back to the campus, we stopped for awhile and that night Charlie asked me to marry him.

We had not known each other very long, but we felt that God planned for us to put our lives together.

By the time we realized what time it was, it was about 1:00 in the morning. When we got back to the campus about an hour later, of course, the doors to the dormitory were locked. The rules were that we "signed out" when we left and "signed in" when we came back, and the doors were locked at about 10:30 p.m. Wondering how in the world I would get back in, I ran around the building, trying to wake up somebody to come and unlock the doors. I finally threw a rock at a window and one of the girls inside heard it and came and unlocked the door.

She was the only one I told that we had become engaged, but by the next morning, everybody in the dormitory knew it, and even some of the boys from the dormitory across the campus had heard it! Later that day, the dorm mother called me in and really gave me a going over about "keeping her awake all night wondering where I was." I wondered where *she* was when I was trying to get into the dorm.

On Monday nights, Charlie and some other young preachers made a habit of going down into the "wino" section of Fort Worth to the Rescue Mission. They would stand on the corner and invite people to come in. If they went in and listened to a preacher for about half an hour, they were given a bean sandwich and a bed for the night. Many of the homeless men and women on the street went into the Rescue Mission for the food and the warmth, and they endured the preaching to get it.

One night Charlie was preaching and he had a little Gideon New Testament in his hand. After the service, one of the men came up to him and said, "I sure wish I had a Bible like that. If I just had something to read, I think it would help me."

Charlie has always been a giver, so he handed the man the New Testament. He noticed that the man left and went across the street, rather than going into the mission for the night. He watched as the man went into a bar. He thought, "I'm going to follow him and see what he does." He went into the bar and the bartender had the little New Testament in his hands. The man had traded it to him for a drink.

Since my mother was only 35 and daddy was 39, they had a hard time accepting the fact that I was going to marry a man aged 25. They said, "We don't want you to marry that *old* man." We had met in early June and were making plans to be married in November. But after our marriage, they soon realized that Charlie was the best one I could have ever married. Eventually, Mother and Dad came to love Charlie and he and my dad became very good friends.

As we talked about getting married, we discussed getting a ring. We couldn't afford an engagement ring, but in my fairy tale mind, I hoped for a miracle and a diamond engagement ring!

As we drove to Charlie's parents' house one day, traveling down a little dirt road, he said, "I got you something." I knew he had been shopping the week before and I was so excited when he leaned over and brought a small velvet box out of the glove compartment and handed it to me.

I could hardly breathe as I thought, "He bought me an engagement ring!" I held the box and carefully opened it.

There, inside the box, was an old, broken man's ring. The gems had all fallen out, the leather band was broken, and even the back of the ring was broken. It was a piece of junk! After a minute I looked at Charlie and he started laughing. I didn't laugh for a little while, until I thought, "Having Charlie is better than having a ring, anyway." So I laughed, too.

What he had really bought when he went shopping was a set of Pulpit Commentary books and some black "preaching" shoes. He used those books for more than forty years of preaching!

Later in life he talked about those beautiful books that he bought that day. They were purple, embossed with gold lettering. He would put them on the shelf in his office whenever we went to a new church and would refer to them many times as he wrote his sermons. One day, as he pulled a book down from the shelf, he noticed the beautiful purple color and gold lettering was still on the book cover, but the spine of the book, exposed to dust and light, was beginning to fade and lose its color. He was reminded of God's love that will never fade—it is always bright and lasting. So is the love we share, even after all these years.

We bought identical wedding bands at a little jewelry store in Decatur. About a year later, Charlie lost his ring one day while working in concrete. When he realized it was gone, it was under a new parking lot in Abilene, so we went back to the jewelry store in Decatur and ordered another ring just like the one I wore. We still wear those same rings today. All the detail has been worn away, but the silver and gold is still as it was.

While getting ready for our wedding which my dad would perform, I told him that I wanted him to read the passage from the book of Ruth that says, "Whither thou goest, I will go. Thy people shall be my people, and thy God my God." My dad read that at our wedding, and that was my plan from the beginning—to go wherever God called us. I just didn't know it would be in so many different places!

We were married in November of 1954, after having known each other for about six months. My maid of honor was a girl from Decatur College and Charlie's best man was his brother, George. He told me much later that on the night of our wedding, as he and George waited in a little room for the wedding to begin, George went over to the window, opened it, and called him. He said, "Come here, Charlie. Stick your head out this window and get a good breath." Puzzled, Charlie looked at him as he walked to the window. Then George went on, "That's your last breath of free air, boy! Enjoy it while you can!" (George had married before we did. I hope he didn't tell his wife of one year what he told Charlie.)

We had rented a little duplex in Decatur, and drove there after the wedding, since both of us had to be in class on Monday. On Saturday night after our wedding, we went to Fort Worth and bought an old refrigerator for $25 and moved it to our new home. On Sunday we went to church, and we were back in class on Monday morning. We didn't give any thought to the fact that there was no honeymoon trip! It has been fifty-five years now, in 2009. Who said it wouldn't last?

For this cause a man shall leave his father and mother, and the two shall become one flesh; they are no longer two, but one flesh. What God has joined together, let no man separate. Mark 10:7-9(NAS)

We joined the Pleasant Valley Baptist Church near Decatur where Cecil Foster was the pastor. I played the piano, Charlie led the hymns, and Cecil preached. We had a revival and Dr. Strickland, president of the college, was preaching. We decided to invite him and Cecil over for dinner before one of the night services.

Our kitchen was very small, with a table big enough for four people. For the first time in my life, I baked a chicken and we fixed dressing. Charlie helped a lot, because I didn't know much about cooking. I took the chicken out of the oven, placed it on a platter and spooned the dressing over it. It looked beautiful. But when Charlie tried to carve it, he found that it was as tough as a boot. As he struggled, trying to cut that chicken, there was dressing all over the table and even on the floor.

He finally took it to the counter, removed what was left of the dressing, and then carved and served the chicken, and we were able with some difficulty to eat it.

The next week in Chapel at the college, Dr. Strickland spoke on "Why Every Preacher Needs to Know How to Carve a Duck." He told us step-by-step how to carve poultry, and why we needed to know how to entertain and have hospitality in our homes.

Of course, we felt he was talking right to us, but we knew he meant to teach a timely lesson to us and to many others.

When Charlie agreed to rent the duplex where we lived, he found another student preacher and his wife to live on the other side, to share the rent. It took both of us to make the rent payment; if one of us left, the other couple was responsible for the entire payment. Jack and Christine had some problems, and they decided to move out and file for divorce, so we had to find another place to live. I was shocked when I learned about this, because in my naïve mind, I thought preachers were immune from such problems as divorce.

I have learned that all people have the same temptations, but at that idealistic time in my life, I couldn't believe it. I thought that if you decided to serve God, He would put a protective shield over you and keep all the ills of the world away. I had a lot to learn! We found an apartment in town over a garage, where we lived the rest of the time we were in Decatur.

I was still struggling with learning to cook. I had learned to cook a meatless cheese and noodle dish called Tallerina while I was in high school, so we had that about three times a week. (Even to this day, my husband hates for me to make a dish with noodles or spaghetti—he had so much of it in our early married life!) I knew how to bake cakes, because with our large family at home, that's about all I did—prepare cakes. I remember once before I was married, mother told me to look at the beans, and I lifted the lid and yelled, "What are they supposed to look like?"

In desperation for something to eat, Charlie began to teach me how to cook. He had helped his mother in the kitchen at home and had been a cook's helper in the Army. He taught me to cut up a chicken and how to make gravy. After we moved to the apartment above the garage, I decided to cook a roast, something I'd never done before. I remembered that my mother would leave the food on the table on Sunday so people could eat when they were hungry, so I left the roast in a pot on the stove. The next day we ate a little of it, but there was still some left, so I thought, "I'll just cover it up again." The next day when I took the lid off, I had to back away from the stove fast! I learned that you couldn't leave cooked meat out for three days or more. That was an expensive lesson, though, because that roast had cost some money, and we just had to throw it away!

Charlie was going to school on the G.I. Educational Bill, and he received a check every month for $120.00. I worked in the afternoons at an insurance office and earned $12.00 per week. He also worked part-time for an appliance and electronics store in downtown Decatur. Whenever they sold a television set, they would call Charlie and a friend, Richard Hollingsworth, and the two of them would install the TV antenna for the new set. Each of them made $5.00 for this work. That helped our income, but some preachers at the college thought having a TV in your home was a sin, so they had regular prayer meetings for

Charlie and Richard, that the Lord would convict them of their sin in helping people to get the evil of television into their homes.

Once near the end of the month, when neither we nor the Hollingsworths had any money left, we combined all the food in both our houses, a few cans of food for each of us, and decided to eat together until we got some more money. We poured corn and green beans and whatever else we had together, and every day we would add a little water and a few crackers, if we had them, to make a meal for the four of us.

It was during that time that the Lord provided for us in a very real and tangible way. On a Monday morning when we had no money at all and were wondering how we would survive until the G.I. check arrived, we entered the classroom building at the college, and there, on the bulletin board, was a legal-sized envelope addressed to Charlie and Juanita Nobles. We opened it to find a check for $100.00 from my dad's church, with a letter saying that they had voted to send us the money to help us! We felt that we had received a fortune! Like the woman in the Bible who found the lost coin, we were telling our friends about our wonderful windfall!

Our friend Cecil Foster, waved his arms in the air and said, "Jehovah-Jireh! The Lord will provide!" We took that money and went to the grocery store and bought T-bone steaks, potatoes, and all the trimmings. Cecil and Vada Foster, Richard and Helen Hollingsworth, and the two of us had a feast! In those days you could buy T-bone steaks for about twenty-five cents a pound. Of course, we paid some bills and bought some much-needed food, too. But the Lord had provided when we needed it most, and we were very grateful!

Cecil came to Charlie one day while I was at work and told him about a family in his church that was destitute. They had several children and needed some blankets or quilts, and he asked Charlie to help find some bedding for the family. Charlie went to our apartment and grabbed two hand-made quilts that we had received as wedding gifts—one had been made by my grandmother and the other by his mother, and he and Cecil took them to the family. When I got home later and he told me what he had done, I said, "Oh, no, not my quilts!" I went to the cedar chest and got out some new blankets, still in their wrappings, and said, "Take these two nice, new blankets to the family and bring back my quilts."

But he wouldn't do it. He said he had seen those children when he gave them the quilts and he would not take them away from them. He didn't realize what a treasure family quilts are. I guess if I had seen the children and how much they appreciated the quilts, I would have felt the same way— but if it had been me, I would have taken the new blankets in the first place, not the quilts.

My grandmother never made us another quilt. After Charlie's mother died, we got one of the quilt tops that she had made and I quilted it and then learned to make quilts. When Charlie saw how much work it takes to make a quilt, he realized that quilts are a treasure and a family heirloom.

I learned to drive in Decatur. My dad had not allowed me to learn to drive before I was married, so Charlie taught me. He had a beautiful little powder blue 1952 Chevrolet, and he was really proud of that car! He let me drive it on country roads until I was pretty sure of myself, then I had to take the driver's test three times before I passed it because I had so much trouble with parallel parking.

One day while we lived in the duplex after I had earned my driver's license, I backed out of the driveway and ran into the only tree in the yard. When the front fender hit the tree, I stopped, put the car in drive, and went forward. I leaned out, looked at Charlie and said, "I think I hit that tree!" Then I backed up and hit it again! Our friend, Richard Hollingsworth, was there and he was laughing so hard he was rolling on the ground! But Charlie was not laughing. He was thinking, "My beautiful little car!"

Years later, we saw Cecil Foster, and he said, "Juanita, do you remember hitting every tree in Decatur with Charlie's pretty little car?" It was only one tree, I reminded him; I just hit it a couple of times!

One of the classes Charlie had to take to get his Associate's Degree at DBC was Trigonometry, and he was having a very difficult time with it. He didn't think he would be able to pass the final exam, so he went to the professor, Gilbert Voyles, and asked him if he could get some special help.

Gilbert happened to have an old car that needed a new transmission. Charlie said that he would put it in for him, and Gilbert agreed to tutor him privately in exchange for his work. So one night, shortly before the exam, Gilbert brought his old car to our apartment. Charlie and Jack, our neighbor, changed the transmission, over a period of several evenings.

After the job was done, Gilbert came to our apartment for a tutoring session in the evening with Charlie and Jack. As they talked, I heard Gilbert say, "Now, I can't tell you exactly what will be on the exam, but you need to know how to do a problem like this." And he proceeded to show them how to work each problem.

When the tutoring session was over, I served my famous banana nut cake with coffee, and the next day, Charlie passed the exam. I could bake really good cakes, even if I didn't know much about cooking regular meals.

I must admit, when I got married I had a lot of growing up to do. I had my dreams about what marriage was, and they were not reality. I think I must have thought marriage was like the old nursery rhyme about the girl whose husband sat her on a cushion and gave her strawberries and cream to eat, and made her the center of the universe. I was to learn that all my dreams were pretty childish, and that life was not like that.

Once while we were in Decatur, Charlie did something that made me mad, and I said, "I'll just go home to my mother!"

To my great surprise, he went to the bus station, bought me a ticket, and put me on the bus! What a revolting development that was! I thought he would apologize and beg me to stay, but no, he sent me back home!

When I got to Dallas, I called Mother to pick me up at the bus station. When she got there, she asked me what happened. I told her about Charlie making me so mad that I had just come home. Lo, and behold, she bought a ticket and sent me back! She said, "You're married now and you will have to learn to live with your husband. That's where you belong!" She did let me stay one night, but I was on the bus the next day, going back to Decatur. So reality began to dawn. I was going to have to grow up.

When I got back to Decatur, Charlie picked me up at the bus station. I never threatened to leave again. I learned my lesson! A preacher needed a wife who would stand by him, not run off at the least inclination!

For this reason a man will leave his father and mother
and be united to his wife, and they will become one flesh.
(Genesis 2:24)NAS

Marvin and Juanita were married on
November 27, 1954

6
A PASTOR IN WEST TEXAS

When the time came to graduate from Decatur, a two-year school, we had to decide where to go next so that Charlie could finish his degree. I had already decided that I would work until he finished his degree, and then maybe I would go back to school later. At that time, I thought **Mrs.** before my name was all I would ever need, anyway.

We went to Plainview, Texas, with a friend to look at Wayland Baptist College. We were there during a fierce sandstorm, which gave us an idea of what it would be like to live in West Texas. Charlie was sitting at the table drinking coffee with his friend Robert Hensley. Robert's mom wiped off the table to get rid of the sand, filled the cups and then set them on the table. As Charlie pulled his cup toward him, he could feel and hear the sand that had already settled there, in just a couple of seconds. The sand was so thick when the wind blew that you could hardly see. I washed Charlie's white shirt and hung it out to dry and it turned to mud. We pretty much crossed that one off our list.

We settled on Hardin-Simmons University, a Baptist college in Abilene. It was about 150 miles from Fort Worth, so we could get home to see our parents fairly often, we thought. We packed our furniture into a little trailer and started out. As we drove through one of the little towns in West Texas, our coffee table fell off in the middle of the street and we had to stop, pick it up, and load it again on the trailer, while traffic was stopped all around. That was pretty embarrassing!

We got to Abilene, found a house to rent, moved our things in, and then went to the grocery store. When we got to the checkout stand, we didn't have enough money to pay for the groceries. We started picking things to put back when the clerk said, "Don't you know anybody in town who can loan you a little money so you can take all your groceries home?" We knew Cecil Foster, who had told us about Hardin-Simmons, so we went to him, borrowed a little money, and then went back to the store to get our groceries.

Charlie found a part-time job with a glass company similar to Pittsburgh Plate Glass where he had worked in Fort Worth before he went to the Army. I walked into an insurance and loan company, the kind of job I had before going to college, and asked if they needed any office help. The owner, James Cassle, told me he was just preparing an ad for the paper because they needed another secretary. I learned that he was a deacon at First Baptist Church in Abilene and when I told him I was the wife of a student preacher, he gave me the job. I worked with VA, FHA, and Conventional loans on houses and had a great experience there.

When Charlie went to enroll at the college on Monday morning, they could not find his name. We didn't know you were supposed to pre-register! Since we were already there, had moved into a house, and both of us had jobs, they let him enroll.

While Charlie worked part-time for the glass company in Abilene, one day they were setting glass in a building way out, far away from the city. Another company was laying pipe for water to go to the building. They laid the pipe for twenty miles, then they turned on the water and nothing happened. There was no pressure. No water would flow through the pipes.

They checked extensively to see what was wrong, but they could not find any reason for the water not to flow. Finally they started digging up the pipes to try to find a way to fix the problem. When they got about ten miles out, about halfway from town to the new building, somebody found a big piece of wood, as big as the pipe, stuck inside one of the sections of pipe. It was blocking the flow of water and not letting it get through.

That gave him a good sermon illustration. He would tell this story and say, "That pipe is like our pipeline to God. If we let something get into our lives that blocks our fellowship with God, we need to get it out so that our prayers can go through and the blessings can come back to us. Nothing should block our pipeline to God."

*I urge you, brethren, by the mercies of God, to present
your bodies a living and holy sacrifice, acceptable to God,
which is your spiritual service of worship.
Romans 12:1(NAS)*

Another time he was working on a building for the glass company, and all morning he kept hearing a man down the hall using terrible language, cursing and swearing with almost every word. When lunchtime came, he said to his partner, "I'm going to find out about that man down the hall." So he went down there, stuck his head in the door where the man was eating lunch, and said, "Say, can I join you for lunch?"

"Well, *****, sure, come on in", the man said in his very offensive language. As they conversed, Charlie asked the man if he went to church anywhere. Continuing with his colorful language, he told Charlie that he was a member of First Baptist Church in Abilene, the same church we attended!

They continued talking and as they ate, Charlie told him that he was a Baptist preacher. Then they both went back to work, and Charlie did not hear another curse word all afternoon!

He said, "Isn't it strange how that man respected me enough not to curse when he knew I was a preacher, but he didn't respect God enough not to use His name in vain?"

*You shall not take the name of the Lord your God in
vain, for the Lord will not leave him unpunished who
takes His name in vain. Exodus 20:7 (NAS)*

It was just a short time after we moved to Abilene when Charlie told me he had been asked to preach at Johnson Chapel Baptist Church in Aspermont, Texas. Aspermont was about sixty miles from Abilene, a long way, but it was a place to preach, so we were excited about it. Charlie said, "This could be the start of a whole new life for us!" And we were to find out how true those words were!

Johnson Chapel was a little rough looking building out in a cotton field with no houses nearby. After the morning service, we asked what time the evening services would start and one of the men said, "Oh, about dark." So, at about dark, we went back. Sure enough, a few people came, and they called Charlie as pastor. There were less than thirty people in that church, but since the building was so small, it seemed full. Charlie preached and led the singing and taught the men's Bible class. I played the piano and taught the women's Sunday School lesson.

But the thing I remember most about that church was the wasps.

The building was very old with cracks and small openings in the ceiling. Wasps had made nests in the space between the ceiling and the roof and when winter came and heat began to warm up the building, the wasps would come through the cracks and fly around all over the church! I can't stand bugs, so the first time this happened, I almost ran out of there!

Once I was playing the piano and had my coat over my shoulders, because the weather had begun to get cold. The heat was on, but it was still cold in the building. As the heat began to waft through the building, so did the wasps. They were circling here and there; it seemed they were everywhere in the building and my attention was on them instead of the sermon, the music, or anything else! Some of the wasps came down and settled on my faux fur coat collar as I played the invitation. I just quietly slipped the coat off and continued playing. I didn't want to disrupt the invitation, but my main purpose was to get those wasps away from me.

Charlie was a hand-shaker, and very good with people. One morning he was shaking hands and he leaned into the pew to greet a young lady, and just as he got up close to her, he saw that she was nursing a baby, without any covering over herself. He backed up quickly, but still shook her hand. He was a little embarrassed at that.

Charlie was ordained to the gospel ministry at Johnson Chapel exactly one year and one day after our wedding, on November 28, 1955.

The small building was packed. Many of our friends and family came. There were some wasps there, too! His first wedding was for a young couple whose parents belonged to that church, but it was conducted in a larger church in Aspermont, and there were no wasps at that church!

We didn't stay long at Johnson Chapel. We heard of another church that was closer to Abilene, the Denton Valley Baptist Church, about 30 miles from Abilene, that needed a pastor. Charlie preached for them, and we were called there as pastor.

I remember Leroy and Eunice Crawford and their five daughters. We would go to their house most of the time after church on Sundays, so that we wouldn't have to drive back to Abilene until after the evening service. Leroy didn't believe in any version of the Bible except the King James. He would adamantly say, "That's the way I read it because that's the way God wrote it!"

Leroy didn't believe in any modern conveniences, either. They had no electricity and no running water in their house. When we ate at their house on Sunday, we had to bring in water in a bucket and heat it on the stove to cook with and to wash the dishes.

I always liked to stay busy and had a hard time just sitting during the afternoon, so one Sunday I took along my embroidery. After lunch, while we were sitting around, I went to the car and got out my needlework and began to sew. Pretty soon, one of the daughters got up and got her sewing.

Eunice said, "Now, daughter, you know we don't believe in sewing on Sunday."

I began to feel a little uneasy. The daughter looked at me and said, "The preacher's wife is doing it."

I thought, "Oops!" and I put my sewing away. I learned that the preacher's wife can't always do what she might like to do best. What was it Paul said in one of his letters? – "If eating meat offends my brother, I will eat no meat." So I used no needle on Sunday.

It is good not to eat meat or to drink wine, or to do
anything by which your brother stumbles.
Romans 14:21 (NAS)

While Charlie was pastor at Denton Valley, we continued to live in our house in Abilene and drive out to the church field on Sundays. When I learned that I was pregnant, we decided to move into an old farmhouse on the church field. A few months earlier I had miscarried our first child, and I thought that if I quit my job and stayed at home, I'd have a better chance at completing my pregnancy.

It was a big farmhouse, but we blocked off some of the rooms so that we wouldn't have such a high heating bill and lived in only the kitchen and one of the bedrooms at the back of the house.

One afternoon Charlie began to develop a terrible toothache. He took some medicine to stop the pain, and it made him sleepy, but the pain didn't stop. When the pain became almost unbearable, he took more medicine and got very sleepy. When he realized that the pain was not going to stop, he said I would have to drive him to the dentist, where he had an office in his home.

I was not very experienced in driving, but I carefully drove to the dentist's house. The dentist asked him which tooth was hurting and he pointed to the one he thought was the right one. "I think it's this one," he said. Evidently there was no equipment to x-ray and find out which tooth it was, so the dentist deadened the tooth Charlie pointed to, and pulled it out. He gave him more pain medicine, and he was really out of it by this time.

During the night Charlie woke me up and said, "That dentist pulled the wrong tooth!" It was hurting worse than ever. And besides that, he was dizzy and groggy from the medicine. His speech was slurred and he was acting funny, and was very unsteady on his feet. He said, "You'll have to take me back to the dentist, honey, because that medicine has made me drunk."

He stumbled around and got dressed and I was really getting scared. I said, "I've never been around a drunk person. You're scaring me!"

He said, "Issssh all right, honey, I've been drunk before."

I drove back to the dentist's home, knocked on the door and woke him up, and he pulled the tooth next to the one he had pulled that afternoon!

While we were out visiting one day, we came to the home of an elderly lady who was unable to get out and come to church very often. We decided to stop and visit with her.

She invited us in, saying, "Bro. And Mrs. Nobles, come on in. I've just been studying my Sunday School lesson." Even though she didn't get to go to church every week, she liked to read her Bible and keep up with the lessons.

We looked at the table beside her chair and saw her large print Bible and her Sunday School quarterly. On top of it was the largest magnifying glass we had ever seen. It was about six inches in diameter. When Charlie picked it up and held it over the Bible, he saw that only two or three letters were visible at a time because of the large print.

We have often remembered our visit to that lady. She could barely see, yet she painstakingly read her Bible and Sunday School lesson, only a few letters at a time, so that the Lord could speak to her. How many of us have good eyesight and sometimes more than one Bible in our homes, and yet we don't take the time to read from the Word?

I was always active in music, playing the piano when I could at the churches where we went as pastor. I remember the music at Denton Valley. We had an older man, Mr. Dryman, who loved to sing, but he could not stay with the rhythm. No matter what the hymn, when we finished, Mr. Dryman had about three or four more syllables to sing, and he always finished out the hymn in his loud voice! Once, during the sermon, while he was sitting on the front row he went to sleep and dropped his hymnal. It fell loudly and woke him up!

One of the best things that happened while we were at Denton Valley involved a young family who were members of the church, but had not attended for a long time. Cal and Iva Britton had five children, all under the age of eight or nine. We began visiting with them and they started coming to church. It was such a blessing to see a family who had not been in church become so involved again. Cal was even ordained a Deacon while we were there.

I enjoyed visiting with Iva, since she was a young mother and I was about to become one. She helped me learn many things. She even helped me learn a little about cooking, since she had to do so much of it with her big family. Cal worked in Abilene and he would sometimes take us out to lunch during the week before we moved out to the old farmhouse, something we didn't get to do very often.

A young girl in the community, the daughter of a man who was thought to be the meanest man in the area, came to church and made a profession of faith. Charlie and Cal made plans to talk to the man, to see if he would give his permission for the girl to be baptized. Cal told us that this man usually would not let a preacher come on his place. He sometimes shot at people who came to talk to him about church, and he had been known to run people off with his gun. But they knew they had to go and talk to him in order for his daughter to be baptized.

They drove up to the man's land, and both of them were pretty scared. When they were almost to the house, Cal said, "I think we'd better stop and pray." So they got out of the car and knelt down under an old mesquite tree beside the road and asked God to help them as they went to see this man.

When they arrived at the house, the man, his wife, and his daughter were all there. Charlie had told the girl, when she came forward in church, to go home and tell her parents about her decision to become a Christian. After greeting each other, Charlie looked at the girl and said, "Did you tell your parents about what happened Sunday at church?"

"I sure did," the girl said with a big smile. Cal and Charlie could see that the girl's mother was thrilled about the decision her daughter had made. The father didn't say anything. He just sat there with a scowl on his face, and Cal and Charlie continued to worry about what he would do.

They talked a little about her decision, and that she wanted to be baptized, but the father continued sitting silently, never saying a thing. Finally Charlie turned to him and said, "Would that be all right with you?"

"Yep." said the father, "If that's what she wants, it will be fine with me."

Both Cal and Charlie experienced a feeling of relief, and were glad they had prayed on the way to the house, because God sure took care of that situation!

7
BACK HOME AGAIN

Before he could graduate from Hardin-Simmons, Charlie was asked to return to Fort Worth to pastor his home church, Elm Grove Baptist Church, where he had preached his first sermon in 1953. So in 1957, we returned to Fort Worth and Charlie became pastor of the church where all his family members and people he had known all his life attended. He did his last year of college in Fort Worth at a Methodist School, Texas Wesleyan University, and graduated in 1959 with a Bachelor of Science degree.

We lived in the parsonage next door to the church and enjoyed being with people that knew us—at least they knew him. I learned to know them and enjoy them, too, while we waited for the birth of our first child.

I asked one of the members of the church to recommend a gynecologist and she told me about a doctor in Azle, a nearby town, who practiced medicine at a small hospital there. As it got closer to the time for our baby to be born, Charlie started backing the car into the driveway when he came home. He wanted to be ready to take off fast to get me to the hospital.

When I went into labor, we went to the little hospital and the doctor was drunk! I didn't even realize it, because I had never been around drunk people, and Charlie had not gone into the inner office with me. The doctor's voice was very slurred as he said, "Your baby is just about ready to come. You go home and wait." I went out and told Charlie what he said, and he looked quizzically at me—but we did what the doctor said, we headed back home. When we got there, I was in such pain that I couldn't get out of the car. We turned around and went back to the hospital and found the nurses trying to sober up the doctor with black coffee!

It was late at night in April, 1957, when I was admitted, and our son, Stephen Carl Nobles was born at about 7:00 the next morning. My parents drove to the hospital from Dallas, and my mother fainted twice during that long night!

A young girl was in labor the same time I was and I heard her say several times, "Mom, I changed my mind. Let's go home and forget all about this!" But that's one thing that is not going to stop once it has started. You have to see it through.

Later I asked the lady in our church why she had recommended a doctor who drank. She said, "Why, he's the best doctor in Azle when he's sober!" (Too bad he wasn't sober the night I needed him most.)

Charlie pastored the church, attended college, and occasionally he had an extra job at a chicken factory that one of our church members owned—he was a chicken catcher! When the owner of the factory called him and some other men, they would go in the middle of the night while the chickens were asleep and turn on a light that made the chickens sort of hypnotized. The men would grab their feet, two chickens in each hand, and try to get as many as they could before the chickens actually woke up and started flying around. Then they put them in crates and took them to the market where they were packaged and sold to grocery stores. Charlie didn't get much sleep on those nights, but the extra money was a big help.

Arthur Brewer, Charlie's first pastor, came to preach a revival at Elm Grove. Special emphases were planned for each evening, to build up interest and increase attendance. One of the nights was called "Casual Night". Charlie said, "Anybody who wears a tie to church on that night will get it cut off!" He got his scissors and went to church early.

Kyle O'Donald, his friend since they were little boys, was a member of Elm Grove, and he liked to play tricks on Charlie. He went over to our house after we had left for church (still we felt no need to lock our house), got one of Charlie's best ties, and put it on. When he came in, Charlie saw him and started toward him with his scissors. Too late, he realized that it was his own tie Kyle was wearing—and it was a new one, at that! Everybody was watching, so he had to cut his own tie off his friend! That was not a pleasant experience, because he knew he would have to buy another tie!

Kyle's daughter, Pat, was quite a tomboy. She liked to climb trees and would get up as high as she could in the tree near her house, jump off onto the roof of the garage and play there, then jump back into the tree when she wanted to get down.

Kyle said, "Pat, I don't want you jumping on the roof. You can get hurt badly." But she continued to do it, until one day Charlie got a call from Pat's mother. Pat had fallen off the roof and Kyle was at work, so Charlie drove Pat and her mother to the hospital. Pat's arm was broken badly and she had several weeks of pain and months of inactivity as she healed.

Charlie used to tell this story and he would remind us that God often tells his children not to do things, but often we disregard his admonishment, and when we do, God sends his punishment. Just as Pat had to endure the pain, we have to endure the results of our sin when we disobey.

When Steve was three months old, we had an unexpected financial crisis. Charlie had to have his tonsils removed, and after it was done, we found out that our insurance company had cancelled our health insurance and we had to pay the whole bill. So I went to work for the Fort Worth and Denver Railway Company doing a clerical job like I had done before.

One of the men who worked at a desk near mine struck up a conversation with me and soon we were chatting regularly. I learned that he was a member of another denomination, one that believes quite differently than we do about the security of a person's soul. He believed that one had to belong to his denomination to be assured of going to Heaven.

I worked there for about a year and a half and when I left, this man said something to me that expressed his genuine concern. He said, "Juanita, you are a really nice person and I have enjoyed knowing you. I hope someday you get saved and I can see you in Heaven." I told him I was sure I would be there, but that didn't change his opinion.

I was reminded of the old story of the people who died and went to Heaven. St. Peter was showing them around, but he kept avoiding a certain corner where there was a closed door. When the new saints asked what was over there, St. Peter said, "Shhhh, the people behind that door think they are the only ones here!"

A few years later, after we moved from Elm Grove, we went back to visit Charlie's parents and attended church there. We had three children then, they were all small, and they all made a lot of noise. There was no nursery, so we did the best we could.

After the service, J. L. King, a good friend of the Nobles family, came up to Charlie, slapped him on the back, and said, "Well, one thing I can say, Charlie. When you raise 'em, you raise 'em *LOUD!*"

We lived in Fort Worth, only a short drive from the Southwestern Baptist Theological Seminary. It had been in existence for many years, and most preachers in that area went there to further their education. So I assumed that was where Charlie would go next, and that we would continue to live in the Dallas/Fort Worth area near both sets of parents and other relatives.

However, our friend Richard Hollingsworth from Decatur College had learned of a new seminary that was to be built in Kansas City—the Midwestern Baptist Theological Seminary. He and his wife went there to be in the first class in 1959, and he thought we should go there, too. Richard excitedly called to tell Charlie about this wonderful new seminary and how historic it would be to graduate with the first class in that place. So we drove to Kansas City to check it out.

The building was under construction and the students were to study in temporary facilities in one of the Baptist churches. When college officials learned that Charlie knew something about carpentry, they encouraged him to come and help remodel the church so that it could be used for classrooms, and to be in that first class.

After some prayer and consideration, we decided to move to Kansas City. Steve was not even eighteen months old, and another baby was on the way. My parents could not believe that we would move so far away! Now, years later, I can understand their anxiety, but then, I didn't think twice. I wanted to go where Charlie thought the Lord wanted us to be. I knew the Lord had called me to be a preacher's wife, and I felt this was part of the calling.

My mother's words were coming true. She had said, "I believe Juanita would follow Charlie Nobles anywhere in the world!"

Yes, that was my plan.

8
ONCE A TEXAN, NOW A MISSOURIAN

We moved into a small house in Kansas City, but didn't stay long because we couldn't afford it. We found an apartment where the amount of rent was based on the income of the tenant, so we moved there, into a second-floor apartment. We were close to the Laundromat, but I didn't drive while we were in Kansas City. Charlie would take his Greek textbook and all the diapers and drive to the Laundromat at night and study while he washed, dried, and folded all the diapers.

Charlie got started at the seminary, learning lots of new things, and I stayed at home with Steve, while waiting for Debbie to make her appearance. Of course, we didn't know in those days whether the baby would be a boy or a girl; we had to wait until the baby appeared to make that determination!

On December 19, 1958, after Charlie left for school, I went into labor. I called the seminary and asked that someone would tell him to come back home. He said that as he drove up, one of his professors was on the second floor balcony, watching for him, and as soon as he drove up, the professor yelled, "Marvin, go home!"

I had told the doctor in Kansas City about my experience giving birth to Steve, and he had assured me that he would be there, and that I would be anesthetized for the birth. One of the nurses stayed with me, checked me, and said, "She's a long way from delivery," and left to get a sandwich.

But I was not like everybody else. Charlie was sitting with me in the room and he heard me moan. He looked over at the bed, the cover had fallen away, and he could see the baby coming! He ran into the hall, yelling for a nurse. The nurse looked into the room, said, "Oh, my God!" and ran for a gurney. They got me to the delivery room, and then they had to call for the doctor.

They might as well not have given me any anesthetic, since the baby was almost born, but they did, and I was pretty groggy when I woke up. I looked around and said, "Oh, look, somebody had a baby while I was asleep!"

The nurse said, "It's your baby, and it's a girl."

I said, "Oh, no, it's not a girl. The Nobles boys don't have girls. You'd better look again,"

Well, it was a girl, a beautiful little girl with a head full of dark hair. Her hair was so long and thick, it curled up on her neck. There was no problem putting a ribbon on that baby to show she was a girl! And before I woke up, Charlie called everybody in the family to tell them that our baby was here, and her name was Deborah Jane! All our family in Texas knew about it before I did. She was the first female to be born in the Nobles family in two generations.

Six weeks before Debbie's birth, Charlie's grandmother Nobles died, so we drove all those miles to go home to the funeral. When we got there, I could barely walk to get into the house. Six weeks after her birth, Charlie's grandmother Hendrix passed away, so we made the trip again.

We drove at night so Steve and Debbie would sleep. Once during the trip Debbie woke up and was crying. I was feeding her with bottles and we were on the road, and there was not a place to warm a bottle. We saw an old tavern, so in the middle of the night Charlie stopped and I took a baby bottle in and asked the lady at the bar to please warm the milk for me. She took the bottle, placed it in a pan of water, warmed it, then shook out some of the milk on her arm to test it, and handed it back. That lady may have been tending a bar, but she knew what was needed to get a bottle ready for a baby!

We arrived at Bill & Thula's house late, but Ed and Jo and George and JoAnn were there. They wanted to see if Debbie really was a girl! It was exciting to finally have a girl after all those boys. Ed had three boys, George had two, and we had one at that time.

9
CARROLL COUNTY CHURCHES

Our first Sunday in Kansas City was the only one that Charlie didn't preach. The second Sunday he preached as supply for a church in Kansas City, and the third led to our first pastorate in Missouri. He was called to pastor Bosworth Baptist Church, a half-time church, and the next Sunday he was called to Wakenda Baptist Church, another half-time church not very far from Bosworth. We felt that God was assuring us we had done the right thing, by allowing us to serve so soon after moving to Missouri.

The Bosworth and Wakenda churches were in Carroll County, about one hundred miles from Kansas City. So we lived in two places, making the long drive every weekend. But what's a drive of one hundred miles, after you've driven eight hundred to move to Missouri from Texas?

We rented a small apartment in Bosworth, and bought bunk beds, leaving one in the Kansas City apartment and putting one in the Bosworth apartment for Steve. Some people in the church loaned us a baby bed and some furniture. So every weekend we would pack up our two babies, lots of baby stuff—clothes, diapers, bottles and sterilizers, toys, and whatever else I thought we would need for three days, and go to Bosworth. We stayed there from Friday night until Monday, when we would pack everything up again and drive back to Kansas City, and carry everything back up to the second floor of the apartment building. We went to the Bosworth church on the first and third Sundays, and spent the second and fourth Sundays at Wakenda. On the Sundays when they didn't have a preacher, each church met for Sunday School only. Fifth Sundays were always at Bosworth.

One night while we were sleeping in the Bosworth apartment, Debbie woke up and cried. I got up and put her bottle in a pan of water and turned on the stove to warm it up, then laid back down to wait for her to cry again. But she went back to sleep and so did I.

Suddenly we heard a loud POP that sounded like a gunshot! Charlie says he remembers jumping up and thinking, "This is the end. Somebody is shooting at us!" He went into the kitchen and found that the water in the pan had boiled away and the baby bottle had become so hot that it exploded. There was milk and glass everywhere. We spent a lot of the next day cleaning up the mess! But we were safe. Nobody was shooting at us!

One of the families in the church, the Penningtons, owned a large dairy farm. On Mondays before we went back to the city, they would load our car with fresh meat, milk, and cream, to help supplement the salary the church paid. We didn't get paid much, but lots of people helped us in ways such as this through the years.

•

An unforgettable moment in that church was while the offering plate was being passed, and one of the wealthiest men in the church put in some money, then reached back in to get change. The usher reached for the plate at the same time, and the result was spilled money all over the church floor! The quiet music during the offertory was definitely disrupted that time, as coins rolled everywhere. Everybody in the church helped to pick up the money, then the service went on.

A doctor and his wife who had lived in Bosworth had been killed in an auto accident a short time before we arrived on the scene, and their son allowed us to rent the big farmhouse where his parents had lived. So we moved to Bosworth. He said, "Use anything you want in the house." The living room was filled with wicker furniture, there was a large dining room set and cabinet in the dining room, and the attic was full of old books and treasures. We spent lots of time up there just looking through the things they had stored. Charlie found an old cookbook that was printed in the 1930's and that became his treasured possession. Any time we needed to know how to cook something, Charlie pulled out that old book. I also had a modern cookbook that I had received as a wedding gift, and I learned to cook what we needed.

We made a garden, and grew corn, beans, okra, squash, and tomatoes. As I learned to can and preserve food, I got a pressure canner and put up many quarts of the crisp, fresh vegetables. With the wild grapes growing on the old fence that bordered the farm, I made grape jelly that my children loved to eat after it had been spread on bread with peanut butter.

My dad sent me a recipe for goulash and I learned to can it too. I would cook the tomatoes, squash, and okra, put it in the jars, then seal it in the pressure cooker so it could be used later. It was quite an accomplishment to look at the shelves loaded with colorful jars of canned and preserved food and think how good they would be when the winter winds blew.

All the women in our church were canners, putting up the fresh vegetables that were grown in their gardens. One family invited us over for dinner occasionally. A man, his wife, and his brother lived in the house. At every meal, the lady of the house would open a quart jar of home-canned green beans and place it beside the plate for both her husband and his brother. The two men each ate a whole quart of green beans at every meal, directly out of the jar! She didn't even heat the beans.

Charlie continued to drive the one hundred miles to attend seminary every Tuesday morning, coming home on Wednesday night for church; then he would leave again on Thursday morning and come back on Friday nights to perform his duties at the church on the weekend. On the nights that he stayed in Kansas City, he was a night watchman at the seminary. He had a little cot in the furnace room where he slept, but he got up every hour or so to walk around the campus to check for any problems. He took home-canned tomatoes or beans or the okra goulash so he would have something to eat on the nights he stayed there. We were living at poverty level, I'm sure, during that time.

I went to everything I could, even when I had to take my babies. We attended all-day associational meetings. I would sit near the back, spread a quilt on the floor, and let my babies play under the benches. If there was a need to take them out, I was close to the exit.

In those days, the associational meeting was a big highlight of the year. It was a two day meeting with lots of good fellowship, good preaching and singing, and I didn't want to miss it.

I also tried to go to women's meetings. Of course, there was no nursery. We were at a lady's house for the Women's Missionary Meeting and I went with my two little ones. I held Debbie on my lap and tried to supervise Steve, but he was an active two-year-old. Like all little ones, he was curious. He knocked over some African violet plants and got dirt all over the floor. The meeting was paused while all that was cleaned up. Then he started walking around again, and I decided that when I got home that day, I would not be able to attend meetings like that again. It was just too hard to supervise two little ones in the church members' small houses.

Another time we were visiting a family in the evening at their house. Steve was outside and I didn't think he could get into any trouble. It was a big farm, far away from the road, and I thought he would be all right. I would get up and look out and check on him pretty often.

But when he came marching up to the door, holding some flowers, the lady of the house gasped and said, "Oh, my tulips!"

Steve had picked the heads off all the tulips that were growing in a row across the front of the yard and he held them up to me proudly. It was early in the spring, so that poor lady didn't get to enjoy her tulips that year.

That winter there was more snow that usual, even for north Missouri. Steve was almost three and Debbie was a toddler. We got her a little red snowsuit, since it was our first winter in that cold country! The snow was piled up about two feet. It was so bad on the roads that they had only one lane opened and you could not see over the snow banks on either side. If two cars met, one would have to back up.   I still remember one night we had the TV on, listening to the news, and the announcer said, "Spring will be a little late!" It was late March or early April and we still had snow!

Once we took the kids outside and Debbie couldn't even walk. All we could see was her little red hat and part of her upper body. We made a snowman and went back inside.

Quite a welcome to Missouri for a Texas couple!

We were living in the big farmhouse when I called my parents to tell them that I was pregnant *AGAIN*. And I'll never forget my dad's reply: He said, "Well, you know what the Bible says, 'Children are like arrows to the Lord, and blessed is the man whose quiver is full of them!'" I felt that my quiver was too full at that moment!

Sons are a heritage from the Lord, children a reward from
Him. Like arrows in the hands of a warrior are sons born in
one's youth. Blessed is the man whose quiver is full of them.
—Psalm 127:3-5(NAS

The big farmhouse was huge; I think the living room must have been twenty-five feet long. One day, I was in the kitchen and Steve was riding his tricycle. He would go across the living room, into the hall, back through the bedrooms into the kitchen, and then around again. I didn't hear him for awhile and I called, "Stevie, where are you?" A little voice far away said, "I don't kno-ooo-ow!"

The house was on the edge of town, across from the highway department where there were lots of big trucks and equipment. In those days it was safe for children to play alone outside so I let Steve and Debbie play alone in the yard a lot. They were both really little when one day I heard them yelling and crying. I looked out and they were on the highway department lot and they couldn't move! I quickly ran over there and found them stuck in some tar that was on the asphalt. I had to unfasten their shoes and leave them stuck there in order to get my kids out of that mess! My neighbor and her husband, a retired couple, came over to help me. We got gasoline and washed the tar off them, then washed the children in soapy water. Their clothes had to be thrown away! My neighbor called them "the tar babies" after that.

Charlie led the Bosworth church to go full-time, so we resigned from Wakenda and spent all our time with the Bosworth church. Our little church didn't have a nursery, so I had to take care of my two little ones myself while trying to listen to the sermon and be the model preacher's wife. As a result, whenever we went to church, I took the diaper bag with diapers and bottles for Debbie, extra clothes for Steve in case we needed them, a jar of milk and some peanut butter crackers for Steve, a pillow for Steve to lie down on when he got tired, my Bible, and anything else I thought we might need to get through 2 hours of Sunday School and church. Whenever Steve got irritable, I would get the peanut butter crackers, open the milk, and hand him his snack.

Delbert Smith, one of the deacons, told me, "You really made me hungry today with that peanut butter. It's hard to listen to the sermon when I knew Stevie was getting to eat dinner early." Our church was very small and I hadn't thought about the aromas wafting through the building at about 11:30 when people are ready for lunch anyway.

One Sunday morning, the kids were such a problem that I took them out and sat in the car, waiting for church to be over so we wouldn't be a great disturbance. It was close to the time for David to be born, and my stomach was pretty big. Debbie was sliding up and down my stomach and laughing while Steve sat in the back seat, eating his peanut butter crackers and drinking his milk. I was upset.

An older lady came out when church was over and tried to console me. She said, "Well, you know, honey, we all raised our children without a nursery. I guess you can, too!" For some reason, I was not comforted by her words!

I sometimes wonder how we made it through those days. We were not making enough money to live on. We had to take out a loan to buy heating oil to heat that big house in Bosworth where we lived and to buy gasoline for the car. Charlie would go to the seminary and stay two days without even a quarter to buy a cup of coffee. We really got ourselves into debt, charging gasoline to go to the seminary, charging to pay for things we needed.

Charlie said that sometimes he wondered what he would find when he came home, because I was having so many problems coping with life. I began to experience depression and anxiety, especially during the nights that Charlie was away.

Judy Cooper would come after school to help with Steve and Debbie when Charlie was away, because I was pregnant with David and I always was very sick in the evenings. I've always been different—I had evening sickness instead of morning sickness during my pregnancies. Sometimes during the day, Mattie Jane Smith would come by and say, "Let me take Debbie and play with her while you get a little rest." Steve played by himself while Mattie Jane had Debbie, and I appreciated her help very much.

I had not learned to handle big problems like we had. The insecurity, not knowing how we would make it from day to day with two babies, was very hard. And being so far from our family was hard, too, for a girl who had been sheltered from life as I had been.

God was faithful, though, and He loved us and sustained us. He carried us through.

David O'Dell, our third child, was born on September 20, 1960 in Carrollton, Missouri. This time I went to a doctor who had converted a house into a medical clinic, since there was no hospital in the town. I stayed in a bedroom in the back part of the house until time for the baby to come, then I was to walk down the hall to the kitchen, which had been converted into the delivery/operating room.

The doctor thought we had a while to wait, so he lay down to take a nap. But, as before when Debbie came, when I was ready to have the baby, I was really ready! The nurse called the doctor and he began to prepare for the birth. I tried to sit up in bed, and the baby began to come. Of course I couldn't walk to the delivery room. The doctor said, "There's a table down in the delivery room. Nurse, you go get it! Reverend, you go help her!"

They brought the table and the doctor said, "I'll get her feet. Reverend, you get her head, and we'll get her on this table." Of course, I was awake and aware of everything that was going on because there had been no time for anything else. They got me on the table and it was over almost as soon as it had started. David was born in the early morning. He was a happy baby and he slept in a bassinet next to my bed while I was there in the clinic.

After his birth, I was still lying on the delivery table and the doctor and nurse were working on the baby when suddenly I was overcome with the wonder of giving birth. Charlie was standing near my head and I said, "Honey, what did you think when you got to see your son being born?" He had not been in the room when I had given birth before. I must admit, after several years of growing up, I was still a hopeless romantic. I expected him to drop to his knees, take my hand in his, kiss me gently, stroke my hair and say, "Oh, my darling, it was the most wonderful experience of my life to see my own son born!" But that's not what he did.

Standing by the bed, he looked at me and said, "Oh, it was all right. I've delivered lots of calves!" I was looking for a Romeo, but what I got was an old cowboy.

While we were in Bosworth, Charlie encouraged the people to build some more space. We were reaching lots of people, but didn't have room for more Sunday School classes. It became a problem because they just didn't want to spend the money it would take to do the job. People began to get upset with him because of his focus on building and reaching more people. Things got sort of sticky as people began to pull away. When another church called and asked Charlie to consider being their pastor, he decided to do it, so we moved to Bogard, Missouri, in the same association and not too far from Bosworth.

We went back to Bosworth many years later when Charlie was asked to preach a revival there, and I played the keyboard and led the music. They had built a small addition onto the church for Sunday School space and were reaching people, but the small auditorium was still the same one we had used in the late 1950's. Many of those who were kids when we were there were now the leaders of the church. We renewed acquaintances with those who remembered us, and met some others as we had services each night.

We are so thankful to see God's work as it keeps on going. We are glad to live in America where this is possible and pray that it will always remain so.

David, 9 months; Debbie, 2; Steve, 3 ½

10
THE TRAIN RIDE

It was a long way to Texas from Missouri. We made that trip many, many times in a car, but when I would get homesick to see my parents, and Charlie was unable to go, sometimes we would buy a train ticket and I would take the children and ride the train to go to Dallas. I would leave at night so that the children would sleep, and arrive in the morning, then spend a week or two with my parents, my brother, and two sisters, and of course, all the grandparents. This was a cheap way to travel because the children rode free and we only had to buy one ticket.

My little sister, Julie, was only four years older than Steve, so they had a great time playing together. When they grew a little older, they loved to make up plays and perform them for all the family to watch. Julie and all my children grew up to perform publicly. Steve and Debbie were chosen to be in South Pacific at the high school in Sedalia when they were in grades four and six. They went on to be in all kinds of plays. All four of the kids were in musical plays as well as in drama. Debbie performed opera while in college at Baylor, and David did drama in Community Theater even after he was grown and worked as an attorney. My sister Julie performs on the saxophone along with her husband who plays the guitar. Three of our children are professional musicians—Steve is a pianist and does performances in Germany and Europe, Debbie and Cindy both teach elementary music in the public schools and sing professionally, and David is a Minister to

Singles at a church in Texas. His singles group performs melodramas occasionally at their church in Midland. So their early training in plays and performances paid off well for them.

Once Steve was performing in Germany and he said, "My parents are both public speakers—my dad is a preacher and my mother is a teacher. My brother was an attorney before he became a church pastor, both my sisters are teachers and sing professionally, I sing and play professionally—We have all figured out how to get people to pay us to sing or talk!"

But back to the time when we rode the train. Steve and Debbie were very young and I was expecting David when this event happened. We were on the train, going back to Missouri. Mother had made me a navy blue maternity dress, which I was wearing proudly.

The children woke up before 6:00 a.m. and the train was not scheduled to arrive until about 8:00, so it was quite a distance to Kansas City. One of the children had a fuzzy blanket, which had shed all over my new dress. I was trying to keep them quiet so as not to disturb all the other passengers, but an 18-month-old and a 3-year-old are hard to keep still. I was still having nervous depression at times, and tears came easily when I was unable to cope with life.

I sat there, crying, while my kids ran up and down the aisles, and a man with a clerical collar came by and said, "Ma'am, I'm a chaplain. Can I help you?"

I answered, "Sir, I'm a preacher's wife, and I don't think you can."

Finally, at about 8:00 a.m. the train reached the station at Kansas City, "At last," I thought, "Charlie will be here to help with these babies!" But when I went into the station with my bags and babies, he was nowhere to be found!

I called the seminary to see if he was there. He wasn't. I talked to Ed Evans, a friend of Charlie's and told him that I was at the train station with my two little ones and that Charlie was not there to pick us up. He said to call back if he could help. But I needed to find Charlie.

In Bosworth, where we lived, the telephone system had a central operator who connected you to the number you were trying to call. The girl working the phone system was Judy Cooper, who often helped me with the children. So she knew where I was when she connected me to Charlie. When he answered at our house, I said, "I'm at the train station. Why aren't you here to pick me up?"

"Oh, no," he said. "I thought you were coming at 8:00 tonight, not 8:00 this morning!" He is usually an early riser, but I could tell by his voice that I had awakened him.

He told me he would be there as quickly as possible, but Bosworth is one hundred miles from Kansas City, and I knew it would take him a couple of hours just to drive it. I called Ed Evans back and he said he would pick us up and take us to his house to wait. I thought I had told Charlie about talking to Ed, but I knew I couldn't stay in that train station for two hours or more with my two little children running around all over the place.

Ed came and got us and took us to his house, where we stayed with his wife and children while we waited for Charlie to come for us. I had never met Ed's wife and I felt strange taking my two little ones and just showing up at her house. But the children played with her children, we talked a little, and everything was all right as we waited to hear from Charlie.

We waited, and waited, and waited. It was mid-afternoon and he still had not come. I was very anxious, wondering what had happened.

Meanwhile, Charlie had arrived at the train station to get us. When he didn't find us anywhere, he asked the ticket agent about a pregnant woman with two small children. The ticket agent said he had not seen us. He called the hospitals. No one with our description had been admitted. He even went into the women's restroom at the train station, looking for us. The startled women looked around for us when he gave a description, but, of course, we were not there.

He went to the police station to inquire about us and was told that he would have to wait 24 hours to report us missing. He later said they probably thought it was a case of a woman trying to get away from an abusive husband, so they would not tell him much. He even called the morgue, to see if a woman and two children had been admitted!

He frantically searched and then searched again, thinking the worst had happened to his family. Everywhere he turned, he found nothing! It seemed we had just dropped off the face of the earth without a trace!

Finally, he called back to Bosworth to try to find out something about us. When his call was connected, Judy listened in on the call because a short while before, I had called Bosworth to see if anyone had heard anything about *him*. When Judy heard his frantic voice, she broke in on the line and said, "Bro. Nobles, your wife is at the home of Ed Evans in Kansas City."

By this time, it was about 6:00 in the evening. I had been in Kansas City since 8:00 a.m., wondering where he was, and he had been searching for the children and me for almost eight hours.

Charlie called Ed's house as soon as he knew where we were and said he was on the way to get us. I was waiting outside when he drove up, and what a reunion that was! His sweet kisses and his arms around me gave me all the relief I needed. All the worrying and crying was over because we were together again. For all those hours we had been lost to each other, thinking the other one would never be found again. What a joy to find someone you thought was lost forever!

Charlie used to tell this story in one of his sermons. He compared the concern he felt because he thought his family was lost to the concern we should feel when we know someone is lost in sin and away from God. Charlie looked in every place he could think of, exhausted every lead that came up, and kept on looking until he found us.

He emphasized that we should try to do all we can to bring those who are lost from God's kingdom into fellowship with Him. Then both the lost and the seekers can share the happiness of knowing we are home with Him.

All we like sheep have gone astray; we have turned every one to our own way; and the Lord hath laid on Him the iniquity of us all. —Isaiah 53:6 (NAS)

11
BOGARD—A FARMING COMMUNITY

We moved to Bogard, Missouri, when our third child, David, was a week old. My mother had come when David was born. The day we moved into the parsonage, mother and the ladies of the church fixed up the house while I stayed at the home of another church member with my new baby. That was the easiest move I ever made. When I got to the house, curtains were up, dishes were put away, and everything was done!

We moved into the parsonage shortly before Halloween. On Halloween night some kids played a prank on us by turning off the propane tank outside. So when I got up in the night to warm a bottle for David, there was no way to do it. Also it was cold in the house. That was a little disconcerting, but Charlie fixed it. By the next day everything was all right again.

Vernon and Dorothy Kuhlman were faithful members of the church there and we have a lot of memories of them and their family. They had several children, but Mary, their youngest, was the one who took care of our children sometime. She was about thirteen, and Charlie would always say to her, "Mary, Mary, quite contrary, how does your garden grow?" She would come back with, "I put it in the soil bank, and live on government dough!" Vernon, the song leader, was a faithful supporter and helper to Charlie. All the Kuhlman children were musical and their family was very faithful and dependable.

Vernon's sister and her husband were also members of our church. Charlie learned an important lesson because this lady had always wanted to be a mother, but had been unable to have any children. Always, on Mother's Day, the mothers were recognized and were given flowers and plants, but this lady was always in the background.

One day she said to Charlie, "I would have loved to be a mother, but I never could have any babies." He began to realize the heartbreak of infertility.

Years later, one of our daughters experienced infertility, and would not even go to church on Mothers Day because of the heartbreak she felt as mothers were being praised and honored. There are many women who would have been mothers, if only they could, and this lady taught my husband to empathize with women like this. Every Mother's Day since we were at Bogard, he made mention of women who were barren, while he was talking about mothers.

Mrs. Edith Hayes, a widow, lived in the house just behind ours, separated only by a large garden plot where we planted lots of vegetable seeds every summer. She had taught the "beginners" (4 and 5 years olds) for many years and loved the little ones. She loved our children, too, and Steve was in her class. Steve would go over to her house and say, "Mrs. Hayes, do you have any bread?"

"Yes," Mrs. Hayes would say.

"Do you have any butter?" Steve would ask.

"Yes, I do," Mrs. Hayes would tell him.

"Do you have any sugar?" Steve would continue.

"Yes," Mrs. Hayes would reply.

"That's what I want," Steve would tell her.

So she would fix him bread, butter, and sugar and he would sit at her table and visit with her while he ate it.

Once Steve went to Mrs. Hayes' house and asked for bread, butter, and sugar, and then proceeded to tell her that all we had in our house was mustard!

Steve started to school in Bogard, in a class where the teacher taught both first and second grades. He would listen to the teacher and do the first grade work, then listen to the second grade instruction and do that too. The next year, when he was in second grade, he had to do it all over again.

In this school, the superintendent would call Charlie and say, "We are setting up our calendar for the year, and we don't want to do anything that would interfere with the church activities. What do you have planned for…."

They would talk together and make plans so that the church and school did not interfere with each other's plans. The school administrator in Bogard in the early 1960's was careful not to plan any school events on Sundays or Wednesdays.

We had been married only a short time and lived in Abilene when I wanted to buy a television set. Charlie said we could not afford it, and I suggested that we go to the bank and borrow the money to buy it.

He said, "You go to the bank and if you can borrow the money, we'll buy a television set." Of course, he thought that a woman could not accomplish this task.

I went to the bank, told them I had a job, filled out the papers, and they loaned me the money to buy the TV. Then I went back to a shocked husband and told him that we could pick out our TV set. We bought a console TV that sat in our living room for many years. We made several moves with it. This story happened in Bogard, involving that very same television set.

By the time we got to Bogard, there were lots of things wrong with that TV set. You sometimes had to hit it on the side to get the picture to come on. Another problem was that the channel-changing dial was broken. That was long before the days of remote control. You had to actually get up and turn a knob to change the channels. When the dial broke, we would hold on to the little peg the dial had been on and change the channel with our fingers. But after a while, as it continued to wear down, that didn't work either. So Charlie got a pair of pliers and put them on top of the TV and said, "I don't want anyone moving these pliers. This is the only way we can change the channel, so don't carry them off anywhere." So our kids learned to change the channel with the pliers and to keep the pliers on top of the TV.

One day, while visiting one of the church members, I noticed that Steve was walking around, looking at things in a quizzical manner. He got to the television set and looked back at me, puzzled.

"Mommy," he said, "how do they change their TV? Where are their pliers?"

We were sitting at the table in Bogard, and Debbie spilled her milk. Charlie jumped up and grabbed a rag to clean it up. No sooner had he seated himself than David spilled *his* milk. Exasperated, he jumped up again and was trying to mop up the second glass of spilled milk as it ran all over the table and onto the floor. He looked at Steve and exclaimed, "Well, Steve, pour yours out too!"

Steve, ever the one to try to please, looked up at his dad and with his trusting eyes on his dad's face, he quietly poured his milk on the table.

That broke us up. We have often remembered this and wondered what Steve must have been thinking while he carefully obeyed his dad!

Charlie worked with Royal Ambassadors (a southern Baptist organization for school-age boys) and every year he would spend a week or two at Windermere, our state Baptist conference center, counseling the boys at R.A. camp. I enjoyed going to Windermere, too, but I liked to go to Music Week. During that week, a well-known musician would lead us through several pieces of music, we would have conferences on church music, and we would culminate the week with a concert, showcasing the music we had learned.

One summer we decided to take our vacation at Windermere during Music Week. We could all enjoy the beauty there, I could get some music training, and Charlie and the kids could have fun together while I was in the various sessions.

The music director that week was head of the music department at Oklahoma Baptist University. He said, "I can teach anybody to sing."

Charlie had sometimes led music at church, and he loved to sing around the house, but he could never get on the tone and he made up his own tunes to everything. Once while we were at Elm Grove church, he had promised that if we had a certain number in a revival service, he would sing a solo.

We reached the goal, so he got up and sang his solo. Then the visiting revival preacher got up to preach. He said, "You know, sometimes we want something to just go on forever. And other times, we're glad when it is over." Charlie never tried to sing a solo again.

So when this music professor said he could teach anybody to sing, I said, "I want you to meet my husband."

We went together to meet with him at a time given by the clinician, and were the only ones there. The man sat down at the piano, played a note, and said, "Sing this note," Charlie sang, but it was not that note! The clinician tried a few more notes, then he gave him a hymnbook opened to "America" and said, "Sing this for me."

Charlie opened his mouth and loudly sang the first verse of the song, but it was not the correct tune. After he finished, the clinician looked at him and said, "Well, I might be able to teach you to sing, but it would take more than a week, and that's all we've got." So Charlie didn't get to learn to sing that week.

Charlie's singing has long been a source of comment. Later, at another church, he was given a little sand bucket, a child's toy, filled with Styrofoam cutout notes. The person who gave it to him said, "Here, now you can hold you head up high, because you can carry a tune just like the rest of your family."

In the late 1980's, while Charlie was a Director of Missions, our state Baptist Music Director, Bob Wooley, began a singing group called "Missouri D.O.M. Choir". He invited every Director of Missions in the state to join.

They met several times to practice, they all bought matching suits and ties, and Bob found some great places for them to sing. The 40+ men looked very dignified, standing on the stage to sing. They did special music during some of the state conventions and they even performed once for the Southern Baptist Convention.

Before that big convention, though, Bob gave special instructions to Charlie. He said, "Now Marvin, I want you in this choir. I want you on the front row because you make us look good. But Marvin, please don't sing!"

When we get to heaven, I can imagine him singing in perfect harmony along with all those wonderful singers from time immortal, because now, at the age of 80, after all those years in church listening to and participating in the music, if it is a familiar song, he can pretty much stay on tune and sing as good as anyone else.

In the early and mid 1960's, Southern Baptists had what we called "simultaneous revivals," when Southern Baptist churches were encouraged to have revivals at about the same time, to make an impact on communities everywhere.

Earlier, we had a revival at Bosworth with a minister from the First Baptist Church of Carrollton, Missouri, whose name was Bro. Fountain. In our youth and naivety, we thought he was much older, though as we think back, we realize he couldn't have been over fifty. He was a frail man, small of stature, and mild-mannered, and we thought he was pretty old.

He came to our house one night for supper before the revival meeting. After the meal, he and Charlie stepped into a bedroom to pray, while I got the dishes off the table and tried to get the children ready to go to church. Charlie said they knelt down beside the bed and began to pray. Both of them had prayed, and when Charlie finished, he jumped up and had the doorknob in his hand when he realized that Bro. Fountain was still on his knees, almost prostrate on the floor. He looked back at him, and thought, "We need to hurry, church is about to start." Charlie has always liked to get to church early.

Then he heard Bro. Fountain groan lightly, and Charlie thought, "He's going to have a heart attack right here and I'm going to have to preach tonight!" Bro. Fountain still did not move. Charlie stood with the doorknob in his hand and suddenly realized, "We have prayed, and now this preacher is waiting for God to speak to him." He quietly took his hand off the doorknob and knelt beside the revival preacher, who remained on the floor, making small utterances and praying silently. He learned a lesson that night—you are not finished praying until God has spoken to you.

While we were in Bogard, we had a revival at our church with a young man who was really a dynamic preacher, but he was not a "people person." After the services, he would leave by the back door or just walk by people without speaking.

One day he ate lunch with us, so after lunch I sat down and "straightened him out." I told him that if he wanted to be a good preacher, he had to care about people—he needed to talk to the people, acknowledge them, smile at them, and be interested in them. I thought I was just helping him, but in later years Charlie reminded me of the encounter, and said I had really laid him out—telling him how he should act.

He is still a pastor in Missouri. Years later, Charlie preached and I sang for his congregation. He never mentioned the incident, but every time I see him now I remember it. Sometimes I guess I was too intense, but I wanted all preachers to be like the one who was my father and the one I married. They really cared about people and loved them, and I thought they were the best!

One night we heard the church bell ringing. It was late, the church was locked, so how could the bell be ringing? Inside the church there was a long rope that was tied to the handle of the bell in the bell tower. A person had to pull that rope to ring the bell. So Charlie went over to the church, which was next door to the parsonage, unlocked the church and went inside. Sure enough, the bell was ringing but nobody was around. The bell stopped ringing, so he went back home.

A little later, after he was settled back in the house, the bell started ringing again. So off he trekked, back to the church. He unlocked the door, turned on the lights, and looked up into the bell tower. The bell was going from side to side, ringing loudly, but not a soul was anywhere around! This was a real mystery.

Some time later, he found out what had happened. The teen-aged Kuhlman boys had climbed to the roof of the church and tied a rope to the handle on the bell in the bell tower, then they had gone across the street and climbed up on top of the school. With the other end of the rope, they could pull it at any time and make the bell ring. They were sitting there on the roof of the school, ringing the bell and laughing as they watched the preacher go from the house to the church and back again. Larry and Danny Kuhlman had a good laugh out of that one.

Bill and Jean Lake and their children were members of our church in Bogard. Bill farmed a lot of land and we became really good friends. Our kids got along well together, and Jean was a very good cook, so Charlie liked to sit at her table as often as he could!

Bill always got up around 5:00 a.m. to start his day. He would call our house very early if he wanted to get a message to Charlie. Whenever Charlie would sleepily answer the phone, Bill would say, "Oh, did I wake you up? I thought everybody got up this early." And he would laugh and then go on and give Charlie his message.

So Charlie decided to put a stop to that! One night he was studying at about 11:00 p.m. and he called Bill. When Bill sleepily answered the phone, Charlie said, "Oh, were you already in bed? I thought everybody stayed up this late!" Bill stopped calling him early in the morning.

One year we had a particularly wet autumn, and before the fields dried from the rain, the snows began. Fields of corn and grain were covered with heavy snow, and because of the wet ground, the farmers could not get their heavy machinery into the fields to harvest their crops. Everyone was hurting and it looked like the farmers would lose everything they had worked for. So Bill bought a team of horses and a wagon, and handpicked as much corn as he could get from his large acreage. It was hard work, muddy work, but Bill knew he would lose everything if he didn't take drastic measures to harvest what he could. By handpicking, he was able to get enough corn to keep his animals fed until he could plant again the next season.

Charlie used this as a sermon illustration, stating the extent to which some farmers would go to get a crop—then saying, "How much trouble will we go to in order to get the crop of souls that God has left here for us?"

Bill and Jean's children were older than ours. Cheryl, the oldest daughter, did some baby-sitting for us and even went with me to Texas one year when I drove by myself to visit my family there, so she could help with the children.

One night we went to their house for homemade ice cream, one of Charlie's all-time favorites. When he asked for another refill in his bowl, Kathy, the youngest daughter, said, "Brother Nobles, you've already had eight scoops!"

Another of our members was a pig farmer. As you drove close to John and Eva Cobb's farm, you could smell the pigs. The nearer you came, the more aromatic the smell! If anybody said anything to him about it, he would say, "Doesn't smell like pigs to me, it just smells like money!"

Friends came over after church one night to the parsonage, and as I was preparing refreshments and talking to some of the ladies, one of the kids came in the kitchen and said, "Where's Debbie?"

We looked around and realized we had left her at church! Charlie went over there, unlocked the door, and found her asleep on a pew! I'm so glad she didn't wake up while the lights were off and nobody was there.

After that, we made sure we had all our children when we headed home from church.

While we lived in Bogard, a door-to-door salesman came through, selling Necchi sewing machines. He brought the machine in and demonstrated the fancy stitches, a buttonhole maker, and all the "frills" of that wondrous machine.

I had been sewing since I was 15 when my grandmother taught me to make some school clothes. I had made all my children's clothes, my clothes, curtains, and other household items. I enjoyed sewing and did a lot of it. Much of it was because it was just a cheaper way to get clothes, but I did enjoy it. I had an old Singer and all it would do was a straight stitch.

I thought about how wonderful it would be to have one of those fancy sewing machines. And I rationalized, "I really deserve to have one of these machines. I've worked hard while Charlie has been in seminary. It is only right that I have this sewing machine."

Charlie was away at seminary. I decided that I would buy that machine, but I didn't have any money for a down payment. The salesman set it up on monthly payments, and he asked, "Well, what do you have that you could use for a down payment?" I said that all I had was lots of canned corn, beans, and tomatoes. It was near the end of summer and I had worked all summer putting up food so we would have it in the winter. So the salesman boxed up the food and took it as a down payment, leaving me with that wonderful fancy sewing machine!

That weekend when Charlie came home from the seminary, I showed him the machine and told him what I had done—how I had signed the agreement to buy the machine and had given the salesman our canned goods as a down payment, and agreed to make monthly payments for two years.

Through all these years, there have not been many times when Charlie got mad, but this was one of those times. He informed me that I was to call that man and have him bring our food back and pick up the sewing machine. We did not have the money to make monthly payments. We could not afford the wonderful sewing machine. No amount of pleading or rationalizing did any good.

So I called the salesman, who had left me his card. He brought back the canned vegetables and picked up the sewing machine.

I continued to sew on my old Singer machine, and many years later I was able to buy a fancy sewing machine, even fancier than the one I had to send back! Now I make quilts, and even have an embroidery machine as well as a sewing machine!

Cindy was born on March 19, 1963, at the new hospital in Carrollton. She was the hardest one to get here. I was in labor a long time. The doctor told me to walk, and maybe the baby would come sooner. Once while I was walking, I saw Charlie lying on my bed trying to get a little rest. I was not very understanding when I saw that! I yelled at him to get up and walk with me. A young woman about to give birth to her fourth child in less than six years can be a little irritable, especially in a situation such as that! But now, I can see that his walking with me didn't help me have that baby one minute sooner. Cynthia Allene Nobles was born at about 10:30 in the morning. We had been at the hospital since early the night before.

We had used a Bible name and a grandparent's name for each of our children. Stephen Carl was named for my dad, Coy Carl Wier. Debbie was named Deborah Jane, for Charlie's mom, Thula Jane Nobles. David O'Dell was named for Charlie's dad, William O'Dell Nobles. When Cindy was on the way, we tried to come up with a Bible name, but didn't find any we liked. If she had been a boy we were going to name her Timothy Ray, after Charlie's brother Raymond. We needed to use a part of my mother's name if she was a girl. Her name was Juanita Allene. What could go with Allene? We were at a loss. We were on the road on one of our trips either to or from Texas, when the light dawned. I liked the name Cynthia, and it kind of went with Allene all right, so I said, "If it's a girl, let's name her Cindy—Sin is in the Bible!" So she is Cynthia Allene.

We were working at the church with Bill and Jean Lake one day when Cindy was a baby, doing a little painting and cleaning up. It was November 22, 1963. Steve was at school, and Debbie and David played as we four adults worked. Suddenly, someone came in and told us to go home and turn on the TV. President Kennedy had just been shot! We went home, turned on the TV, and watched in horror as we saw each event unfold. We saw it all on black-and-white TV, using the pliers to change the channels!

A new family moved to Bogard after we did. Earl and Kathryn Thye had nine children—six girls and three boys. They were members of a different denomination, but there was not a church of their faith in Bogard, so they joined the Baptist church. They said that when they became Baptists they had to buy a bookshelf just so they would have a place for everybody's Bible and church literature. All the kids were active in Sunday School, Training Union, G.A.s and R.As, and of course each child had his or her own quarterly or book for each of the different organizations. (G.A. was a Baptist mission organization for school-age girls. It stands for "Girls' Auxiliary".)

They had kids close in age to ours and we became good friends. Their daughter, Kathy, was Debbie's age and a son, Dale, was close to Steve's age. Curtis was their youngest, close to the age of our Cindy. All the other Thye kids were able to take care of the younger ones. They were a wonderful family and we had some great times together, even if one of them was when Steve and Dale tried out smoking behind their barn.

Charlie asked me to take some papers over to an office in Carrollton, the county seat town, so I got the kids in the car and drove over there. Of course, there were no seatbelts required at that time, so I had Cindy in the punkin seat in the front so I could restrain her with my hand if I had to make an unexpected stop, and the three other kids were in the back.

I arrived at the office, parked, and picked up the punkin seat and the papers. I carefully got all my beautiful kids out and instructed them to hold on as we crossed the street. David held onto my skirt on one side, Debbie held my skirt on the other side, and Steve held Debbie's hand as I carried Cindy in her punkin set and we crossed the street and went into the office. I was really proud of all my beautiful children as I walked in, set the punkin seat on the counter, and waited for the lady to come and talk to me.

But before I could get all my business done, she had the audacity to say to me, "You know, you really ought to move to Illinois. They have free birth control there!"

I stood, amazed, unable to think of a thing to say! But after I left, I thought of some things. That was about the rudest thing that ever happened to me.

The emotional problems that I had earlier began to occur again. One morning I woke up and fainted, then was very weak, so Charlie didn't go to the seminary that day. He had to drop out that year and take care of me. Dirt, dishes, diapers, and debt had taken over and I couldn't handle it. I spent a lot of time in tears and depression at this point in my life, and missed a lot of precious time with my children.

I stayed at the home of Mrs. Hayes and slept for days. Church members took care of the children because I just could not cope with life. The doctor prescribed large amounts of Valium, and I remember the ceiling dancing around, because of the heavy medication, as I lay in bed at our neighbor's home.

Charlie went to the doctor with me one day and said, "Doc, she is just not getting any better. This Valium and other medicines are knocking her out and not helping her. What can be done?"

The doctor said, "Rev. Nobles, what she needs, you can't afford."

Charlie said, "Well, tell me what she needs and we'll see if I can afford it."

Dr. Vinyard said, "She needs extensive counseling for a long period of time, and that is a very costly treatment."

So Charlie set out to try to find a way to get that treatment for me. His psychology professor at Midwestern Seminary had introduced him to some material on counseling, so he went to see this professor to ask his advice. When he arrived at the seminary that professor was not there, but an associate, Dr. Everett Reneer, was.

Charlie talked to him, telling him about our problem, and asked him if anything could be done to help me. Understanding the desperate plea for help, the professor set up a time when he would be in Carrollton, the county seat town near Bogard, and asked Charlie to arrange for a room in the First Baptist Church. He told him to bring me there and he would see if he could help me.

Dr. Reneer gave me a personality inventory and then discussed the problem with us. He told Charlie that I had a severe disorder at that time, and was in dire need of counseling. He arranged to be in Carrollton, or for us to be in Kansas City, every week for several months for personal counseling sessions.

This kind man helped me so much! He talked with me and helped me work out problems that I just couldn't handle by myself. He talked with Charlie to help him understand my problems. At one time, he told us that I was so insecure and dependent that I was cowering on the edge of life, while Charlie was standing on top of a hill in his shirt sleeves, saying "Bring it on, I'm ready!"

117

But the thing that really cured me was when I finally realized that this problem was caused by Satan. He was making me unhappy. I was discontent, being so far away from family members, and I was making it worse by worrying about money, and everything else. When I finally prayed, "Lord Jesus, please take this problem and make me content where I am," He did it. I could not have reached that point without Dr. Reneer's help, but Jesus finally took the problems away.

Charlie was eventually able to resume his seminary studies, and graduated in 1965 with his Master of Divinity degree. It took him seven years to complete his seminary degree at Midwestern Baptist Seminary, but when he walked out of his last exam, his shout could be heard for miles around! He had finally accomplished what he set out to do! Praise the Lord and thanks to Him for His care and blessing.

The Nobles family in 1965
Children are ages 2, 4, 6, and 8

12
MOVIN' ON UP—TO THE CITY

After Charlie's seminary graduation, we were called to the New Hope Baptist Church in Sedalia. Our children were two, four, six, and eight. I was a stay-at-home mom, but needed to find a way to make a little extra money, so I started teaching private piano lessons. I had taught a few lessons in Bogard, but in Sedalia, I had quite a few more students. In addition to several children, I taught a couple of preachers' wives who wanted to learn to play so they could play for church.

Steve was eight and was already playing the piano. When he was five, I noticed he had an interest in the piano, so I taught him a few letters of the alphabet and began teaching him to play before he even started to school. He was a natural and had a thirst for music, and he went on to learn more and more. When we got to Sedalia, we found a teacher for him so he could really excel and become more accomplished. By the time he was in sixth grade, he was helping the music teachers at school by playing for them. He went on to accompany choirs in high school. When we moved to Hannibal, he found my old piano books from college and taught himself Bach and Mozart, and he went on to become an accomplished pianist and accompanist. He lives in Germany now and plays concerts, accompanies singers, and writes music. He has written an operetta and performs on the piano regularly.

During the time we were in Sedalia, we felt that God wanted us to be missionaries in Africa. Charlie was reading in the <u>Word and Way</u> (our state Baptist paper at that time) about the need for a man to set up and implement a program for Baptist Men and RAs in Nigeria. We volunteered to go there and began all the preparatory work for being missionaries. I had felt that God wanted me to be a missionary when I was a young girl, and Charlie was willing to do whatever God had for him, so now seemed to be the ideal time for us to do this.

We filled out all the papers, wrote our life stories, got physical and psychiatric examinations, and did everything we had to do. At one point during this process, Charlie had not finished his life story and it needed to be turned in, but there seemed to be no time to get it done. He got sick with the flu and had to stay home a few days, and was even in bed part of the time. He said the Lord gave him the flu so he would have time to think and get that paper written.

We worked on the process of becoming a missionary for nine months. I knew I had to have more college hours so that I could home-school my children while living in a foreign country. I drove to Warrensburg, about 30 miles away, and took enough classes at Central Missouri State University to qualify as a missionary wife.

But the Mission Board did not approve us. Because of the serious emotional problems I had experienced, the Board was afraid I could not handle the stress of being in another culture. There was a war going on in Africa at that time, the Biafran conflict, and the Board thought that if they sent us there, they might have to send us back home again. In fact, they told us that they had recently appointed some missionaries with similar problems and they had been sent home because of the stress of situations on a foreign field.

When the Foreign Mission Board did not approve us, I decided to continue in college and finish my degree. A very wise person had counseled me at Central Missouri State University. My plans were to just take random classes so that I could qualify as a missionary wife, but the counselor had said, "Suppose this missionary appointment does not work out. Is there anything else you might want to do with your life?" I told her I had always thought I might like to be a teacher, so she advised me to take classes that would count toward a degree in education. Since

I had completed twelve hours, I thought this was a pretty good start toward finishing my degree.

Our children were three, five, seven, and nine when I went back to school full-time. I was also teaching piano lessons to twelve students each week and working in the church. So I was a busy lady. Charlie asked me what he could do to help, and I said, "Do breakfast." So he did, and he continued to "do breakfast" until all the kids were out of school. He came up with unusual things for breakfast, like cut-up wieners on leftover biscuits, broiled in the oven with cheese on top. The kids were always wondering what dad would have for them next.

I finished my degree in education when the children were in grades one, three, five, and seven. We had some good times reading the Newberry books while I was going to school and learning about children's literature. I was also taking college piano lessons, and I would practice at night. Steve told me he really enjoyed listening to me practice while he was lying in bed, before going to sleep every night.

When Steve was in fourth grade, they were studying homonyms in school and he was making a list of these words. He had a list of homonyms that he had folded and put in his jeans pocket so he could work on it any time he thought of another set, such as beat, beet, or through, threw.

One night after the kids went to bed, I picked up their clothes and put a load in the wash. The next morning Steve was looking for his jeans. "Mom," he said, "where are my pants I left here on the floor last night?"

"They're in the wash," I said.

"Oh, no!" Steve cried. "You washed my homonyms!"

I retrieved his wet jeans from the washer, and sure enough, folded in the pocket, were the soaked papers with all his words written on them.

That was when I learned that he had 300 sets of homonyms and they were to be turned in that day to see who won the contest with the most homonyms! He was certain he was going to win—but not now!

There was no way he could write all those homonyms again, and even though I wrote a note to the teacher, he lost the contest. It was a long time before he forgot about mom washing his homonyms.

Debbie was sitting in class, doing her work in fourth grade, and humming softly to herself. "Debbie," the teacher said, "stop that humming."

"Oh," Debbie said, "I didn't know I was humming."

The teacher didn't believe her and gave her a hard time about humming and then pretending she was unaware of it. She has always remembered this, because I always hummed at home while I was doing my work, and so did her dad.

So I began to wonder, "Why do I hum all the time?" and I remembered my dad humming. There was never a time when he was working, that he was not humming. He whistled, too, and I tried to learn to do that, but never seemed to get it right, so my grandmother would console me by saying, "A whistlin' girl and a crowin' hen will always come to some bad end."

Charlie says that sometimes his mother would hear a hen crow on their place, and if she did, she killed that chicken and cooked it for dinner. She said, "I won't have a crowing hen on the place." So that's the "bad end" for the hen—I didn't find out what it was for a whistling girl.

Charlie started whistling a lot while we were in Sedalia. Our youth group was trying to earn money for a mission trip to Galveston, Texas, one summer. Many of them had never seen the ocean, so plans were made to take them all the way to the Texas coast and to do some mission work there. Our church janitor had recently resigned, so the whole youth group was hired to clean the church and care for the grounds, and all their earnings were put in a special fund to go toward their trip.

Of course, with lots of hormonal teen-agers around, Charlie was always finding a couple of them locked in an embrace. So as he walked around the church, he began whistling loudly; then the teen-agers would know he was coming, and they could get ready for his appearance, so they wouldn't be embarrassed when he showed up around the corner.

Our grandchildren also picked up this humming/whistling habit. When Jensen, Debbie's daughter, was about seven, she started whistling all the time. Sarah, David's daughter, sings and performs in plays. Marissa, Cindy's daughter is never without her I-Pod, singing along. Chachi, Cindy's son, always has a tune in his head and a hum in his voice. Not only does he hum, but also he makes the sounds of the drums and other instruments in the off beats of the song he's thinking about in his head!

The high school in Sedalia was preparing to present the play <u>South Pacific,</u> and they needed two children to be in the production. So they sent a note to all the elementary music teachers, asking them to recommend two children, preferably a fourth grade girl and a sixth grade boy, who could sing and act, to be in the play. Steve and Debbie were already singing together in church. They would stand on a little platform behind the pulpit so their faces could be seen, and sing in two-part harmony!

Therefore, the music teacher at Whittier School recommended Steve and Debbie. They were musical, they were in the same family, they were the right age—fourth and sixth grade—and she thought they would be perfect for the roles of the children.

We were asked if they could be in the play and we agreed. I went with them to rehearsals, which were very long and frequent. I did what studies I could do for college while sitting in the auditorium waiting for the children to be called to do their parts. They learned their roles well and did a great job. This was the first of their many performances in plays throughout their lives.

Charlie got a little upset with the grueling schedule, and he continued to be that way about performances at schools. But we learned that if you are in drama or music, that's the way it is in public schools, so we dealt with it.

The year David would have started school, he missed it by five days because of the cut-off date for the schools in Sedalia. To start school, a child had to have a birthdate of September 15, and he was born on September 20, so he had to wait a year to start.

Even after waiting a year to mature, David never cared much for school. He could "take it or leave it" but it was not his great interest. He would rather play than study.

Then came the year for him to be in third grade. He went into the room the first day, and there was a young, pretty teacher. He had always had older women as teachers before, and he was really surprised to see this young lady who was going to actually be his teacher. It was her first year to teach, and she was excited and full of enthusiasm and fresh, new ideas.

But the thing that really impressed him was the day she came to school, early in the year, wearing a backless sundress with a jacket over it. As the day progressed, so did the heat. Since there was no air-conditioning in the schools in those days, and the rooms could get pretty hot, this teacher took off her jacket and continued teaching. When the kids saw her backless sundress, all of them took notice.

David came home and said, "Mom, all the boys fell out of their seats today when Mrs. Friedly wore a backless dress!"

From that day on, David liked school. Beginning in third grade, he learned to enjoy learning and studying, thanks to a pretty, young teacher with a nice figure and a backless dress!

Choose my instruction instead of silver, knowledge rather than choice gold, for wisdom is more precious than rubies, and nothing you desire can compare with her.
Psalm 8:10-11(NAS)

Steve, Debbie, and David got a paper route in Sedalia. Steve and Debbie, with their dad's help, would fold the papers and deliver them on weekends, with a little help from David. Of course, Cindy wanted to help, too, but she was too little. Every time she would try to fold the papers, Steve would have to do them over, which made a lot of extra work for him. It was always hectic at our house on Sunday mornings, and that was when they had to fold lots of papers.

After they were folded, their dad would drive them on their route to deliver them.

They always took the papers to Steve's room in the basement to fold them, and every Sunday morning Cindy would go down there to "help".

Steve was exasperated with her, so he came up with a perfect plan. He paid Cindy a quarter every Sunday morning if she would NOT help. Cindy thought this was fine, so every Sunday morning she was up bright and early, and trekked downstairs to collect her quarter and watch, while the other kids folded the papers.

I had learned to cook most everything, so I decided at Sedalia to branch out and learn to do yeast rolls for Sunday dinner. While the kids folded the papers, I was in the kitchen mixing up the ingredients, pounding the dough down, and doing all the things the recipe said to do. Then I would roll out the dough, cut out the rolls, and set them on a pan to rise until after church. I would come home, get the roast out of the oven, pop in the pan of rolls and wait as that wonderful aroma of homemade rolls wafted through the kitchen.

But one day as I set the rolls on the table, my loving husband said, "Is this a new brand of canned biscuits? They are really good!" I decided to just buy the canned biscuits after that, and I saved myself a lot of work. My career as a baker of rolls was very short.

After we arrived on the church field, someone told Charlie about a lady who had been diagnosed with cancer and had been given only a short time to live. He went to see her and sat down next to her bed to talk with her. In the midst of the conversation, he said, "How long have you had this cancer?"

The lady sat straight up in bed and pointed her finger in his face and said, "I do not have cancer! I don't want to hear that word!" She was so agitated that he didn't stay very long for that visit.

The lady did have cancer, and her life from that time was very short, but she refused to acknowledge it.

In one of Charlie's sermon, he told about this lady. He would say, "We may deny our sins, just as that lady denied her cancer, but they continue to fester and grow in our lives, until we acknowledge and confess them."

Shortly after moving to Sedalia, we were introduced to Jim and Juanita Crystal. Juanita had been paralyzed in an accident several years earlier and had spent her life in a wheelchair. She had four young children, and was more active that most people who walk on two legs with no handicaps. In fact, one of her children was born after her accident. The doctors thought that having a baby might shock her body into responding again, but it didn't.

Somebody told Charlie he should go and visit Juanita, and cheer her up. However, any time anyone went to see that lady, she was the one who did the cheering up!

Juanita never let her handicap stop her from doing anything. After her accident, her house was remodeled so that she could reach all her kitchen appliances and do all her work herself. I went to her house one day and saw her busily working at refinishing a piano! If she wanted something done, she would figure out a way to do it.

One cold day she rolled up to our church on East Sixteenth Street and the front doors were closed. She could not get up the steps to the doors and could not get anyone's attention. So she wheeled her chair around until she found a long stick and used it to beat on the door until someone came to open it and help her up the steps in her wheelchair. She drove a specially equipped car and was very independent. For years, she worked with her husband in his tire shop, keeping the books and keeping everyone who worked there in line!

Once during testimony time at church, Charlie said, "If you would like to give a testimony, just stand up and do it."

We saw this arm waving. Juanita Crystal said, "I can't stand, but I can speak for Jesus. Today marks the anniversary of the day I hung up my shoes and took up my wheels and I want to thank God for it. If that had not happened to me, I would not know Jesus as I know Him today."

Juanita was instrumental in getting "handicapped" access in downtown Sedalia. For many years, wheelchairs could not cross streets or enter many of the buildings in the downtown area. Because of her efforts, now there are ramps at every corner, and buildings have handicapped entrances. She was prayer chairman for many revival meetings, even an area-wide Billy Graham meeting, and she taught an adult Sunday School class in New Hope Baptist Church for many years. Juanita has gone on to glory now, but her influence lives on.

One of the men in our community was an alcoholic. His wife and family were members of the church, so Charlie began to work with him and witness to him, trying to win him to the Lord. The man would call on the telephone and keep Charlie on the phone for hours, discussing things he was concerned about.

One night he called, very despondent. During the conversation he asked, "If I tell you something, will you promise not to call the police, not to call anybody, not to come out here until morning?"

Charlie asked him if his family was at home, and was told that they were away at her mother's home. So Charlie said, "Yes, I promise." Then he heard a loud gunshot, and the phone went dead.

He was afraid the man had shot himself, but he had promised not to do anything, so he didn't. He did not sleep that night. He prayed and worried about that man, and what effect his actions would have on his family.

When morning came, Charlie decided it had been long enough; he could go and check on what had happened. So he drove to the man's house, expecting to find him dead. But there he was sitting on his couch. He had shot a hole in the floor of his living room, and then had gone to bed. It seems he just wanted to see if that preacher would keep his word. He never was reached for the Lord.

Bill and Evelyn Watson had some friends who liked to play music and sing. Bill played the guitar, I played a little ukulele, the other man played his banjo, and we enjoyed singing together. They would come to our house and we'd spend an evening visiting and playing music, usually doing old country songs. We even performed together once at a local barbecue restaurant.

The couple became better friends as we saw them more frequently. We talked about the Lord with them, and had a very good time. We prayed for them diligently but they did not attend church, even though we kept inviting them to attend.

One day the man told Bill, "We are not going to come around to that preacher's house any more. I married my wife because I like her the way she is, and the more time she spends with you all and the preacher and his wife, the more I can see that she wants to come to church. If she comes to church, she will change, and I want her to be the way she is now."

He knew her life would change if Jesus came into it. I hope this couple made a decision later to come to know the Lord, but if they did, I don't know about it.

Mrs. Glasscock was an older member of our church who was there every time the doors were opened. She did lots of things around the church and loved to be involved. But she became ill and had to have surgery, so Charlie went to the hospital to be with her daughters during the surgery.

After awhile, the doctor came out and told the daughters, "Your mother is completely eaten up with cancer. I did not even do the surgery. I just sewed her back up because the cancer is so invasive. She will live only a few weeks, if that long."

Of course, the sisters were devastated, and Charlie was glad he had gone to be with them. They decided not to tell their mother about it, but to let her live worry-free, as long as possible. They had prayer, and he drove back to the church.

When he got there, he saw that the ladies group, Women's Missionary Union, was meeting. He felt impressed to go in there and say, "Ladies, if I tell you something, will you promise me you won't talk about it to *anybody* except the Lord?" The women agreed, and he told them about Mrs. Glasscock and the prognosis that had been given by the doctors.

They had prayer and the ladies went home. Each lady continued to pray for Mrs. Glasscock in their daily devotions, as they had promised.

After a short period of time, Mrs. Glasscock went back to the doctor; he did a blood test, and there was no cancer! She lived for fifteen more years and had a happy, productive life.

Looking back, we recall that three of the ladies in that group who prayed for Mrs. Glasscock lost their husbands to cancer, and two of them died to cancer themselves—all before Mrs. G was taken home to be with the Lord! It's hard to understand why some are healed and others are not. It's all in God's hands.

Sedalia is the home of the Missouri State Fair, and every year in August hordes of people come to Sedalia to take part in or to visit the fair. Many people take in boarders and sometimes tents are set up on lawns to provide housing for the many people.

One summer while we were in Sedalia, some teen-agers called "hippies" came to the fair. Some of them attended our church, and it was hard for some of the older people to accept those who came in ragged jeans and tie-dyed shirts, or with long hair and with their bodies pierced in unusual places. This was in the late 1960's when the "hippie" movement was gaining momentum.

When the fair was over, some of the kids stayed and joined our youth group. Edna Mae Abney was working with the teen-agers as they prepared to perform a musical that they had written during Vacation Bible School. Some of these kids were playing guitars as they participated in the music. Charlie came through the church auditorium one day as they were rehearsing and saw what was going on. Edna Mae saw him coming, his lips in a thin line, and she knew he was displeased about something! He called her aside privately and said, "There won't be any guitar playing in this church!"

Edna Mae had a big decision to make. She had promised the kids that they could do the musical as they wanted and that they could play their guitars, and some of the kids had come without parental involvement. She knew that if she told those kids they couldn't play their guitars, they would stop coming and possibly not come to know Jesus as Savior.

The kids did their musical, and there *was* guitar playing in the church. Charlie was able to live with it, since many of those kids came to know the Lord. The times were beginning to change, and we learned that methods change along with them, as we continue to seek those who need to know Jesus.

Another time, Charlie went to visit Edna Mae to ask her to be the WMU President. She was in her living room, ironing, and wearing a very thin, very worn, old nightgown. It was hot, the doors were open, so when Charlie got there, he tapped on the door and walked in. We were good friends; we walked into each other's houses all the time. But Edna was very self-conscious as she stood there, and her main thought was to get him out of there. She agreed quickly to do the job he asked her to do, just so he would hurry up and leave. She said later that was her "most embarrassing moment"!

Charlie had a friend who had been in Seminary with him. They had been prayer partners for several years when he was called to pastor his first church in a little town near Sedalia. He would come over and he and Charlie would sit at our dining room table and talk together, discussing problems and how to do things.

When he had his first wedding, he came to our house and Charlie helped him plan it.

This preacher was Gary Taylor. He later became pastor of the Tower Grove Church in St. Louis and the First Baptist Church of O'Fallon, Missouri. Gary has become well known in our convention, and he serves now with the state organization as Evangelism Chairman.

New Hope Baptist Church was like a family to us during the years 1965 to 1970. Many friends from that time remain friends today. But wait till you see how God revealed Himself to us next.

The things he did to bring us to Hannibal were truly unbelievable!

13
THOSE HANNIBAL HILLS

During the summer of 1970 while we were living in Sedalia we decided to visit the Mark Twain attractions in Hannibal, Missouri, for our vacation. One of our church members loaned us his big purple bus that had been made into a camper, and as we traveled through towns along the road, it would make horrible popping sounds. It was so loud that people would stop and stare at this large, purple bus as it backfired and exploded through every small town from Sedalia to Hannibal. Debbie had a friend along with her, so we had five kids in the bus. We had a good time on the bus as we drove, and we went to some of the Missouri State campgrounds in that part of the state.

I remember thinking about Hannibal, "It seems like a giant mole got loose in this town. There are big hills everywhere. I would *never* want to live in Hannibal!"

Guess where the Lord called us next? Hannibal!!

After I completed my teaching degree at Central Missouri State University in December of 1969, I taught a half-year at Otterville, Missouri, a little town near Sedalia. During the summer, I took some courses in reading, received my Reading Specialist certificate, and signed a contract to set up a reading lab in the high school in Sedalia in September, and teach remedial reading. There were no openings in the elementary schools for fourth grade, which was what I really wanted to teach. But during the last few weeks of summer, the pulpit committee from the Calvary Baptist Church in Hannibal called and asked us if we would talk with them about coming there as pastor.

We always tried to be open to what the Lord wanted, so Charlie agreed to talk with the committee, even though we didn't really want to move. We were happy in Sedalia, our church was responding well, and we saw no reason to leave. But it was his opinion that if the Lord sent a committee to talk to us, we needed to at least investigate so as not to make a mistake. We knew that as the Lord moves to do things in our lives, we may not be aware of His plans for our lives.

The committee came to hear him preach, and then took us out to lunch. During lunch, one of the committee members said, "When can you come and preach in view of a call?" They didn't even have a consultation. The person who had asked the question was not the chairman of the committee, but she looked at the others on the committee and said, "He is the one we want, isn't he?" The chairman, said, "Yes, I think so." So we arranged a date.

The weekend we were to be in Hannibal, we prayed really hard. We did not want to move to Hannibal. So we asked the Lord to do some things to let us know for sure whether we should go or not. We "laid out the fleece" several times before making out decision.

I needed a job. I had wanted to teach fourth grade, but there were no fourth grade openings in Sedalia, so I asked the Lord to get me a job if He wanted us to move to Hannibal. And I was specific—I asked for a position in the elementary school, preferably in the fourth grade, since there had been no openings in elementary schools in Sedalia.

We looked at the house that was Calvary's parsonage and we thought that we just could not live there. It was an old house, not big enough for our family, and not arranged well. We said, "Lord, we'll have to have a different house if we move here."

On that weekend, I went to talk with the administrators at the school in Hannibal. The only opening in the elementary grades was a fourth grade class in Eugene Field School! The lady in the office who was interviewing me said, when she found out I was an elementary teacher, "You just might be the answer to our prayers!"

After looking at the house again, and telling the committee that we didn't think we could live there, one of the members said, "Maybe we can buy you another house if you will come. We realize we've been needing to update the parsonage." We couldn't believe it!

It seemed the Lord was taking care of all the problems. It looked like we might have to move to Hannibal. So, that night in the motel, we prayed once more. We said, "Lord, if you really want us to move to Hannibal, let somebody come forward during the invitation on Sunday morning."

After the sermon the next morning, the chairman of the pulpit committee, Howard Hinds, came forward and rededicated his life! And between Sunday School and the worship service, even before they heard Charlie preach, the committee met with others in the church, and they all agreed to buy another house for us to live in if we would come there. They said, "That house was too old, anyway. We need to buy a new house."

We were amazed and awed with what God had done. He had answered all our questions; He had provided for every need. There was no room for doubt. We had to say, "This must be what God wants us to do."

I had to resign my teaching job in Sedalia before it even started, and we moved to Hannibal in September of 1970. We lived in a fairly new house at the end of a dead-end road, right next to the woods. Our kids enjoyed playing in those woods.

When we left Sedalia, our final service was like a funeral. It was really hard to leave that church where we had made so many friends and our children had grown so much. New Hope Church had been like a family for five years, and we really hated to leave, but we knew without a doubt that we were following God's will for our lives. Everything we had asked had been done; we could not argue with the Lord.

When we got to Hannibal, we found that there were a few problems. In 1959 they had averaged almost 600 in Sunday School, but since that time, the Sunday School attendance had been going down steadily. Another problem was a bus that had been bought and it was not being used very much. Some people thought it should be sold, others wanted to keep it; so it was a bone of contention. Charlie decided to find out about the bus ministry and see if the bus could be used in a positive way. He learned about a bus conference in Hammond, Indiana, and he began talking to some men about taking a trip there to see what the bus ministry was all about.

One of the men on the pulpit committee, Bob Stone, was the most vocal about getting rid of the bus. So he talked to Bob and Howard Hinds and they went with him to the bus conference. People couldn't believe that Bob Stone would go along with this; he had been one of the leaders in the movement to sell the bus, but God had a plan, and He was beginning to work it out.

After that conference, people began to get excited about beginning a bus ministry. Three buses were purchased, reconditioned and painted, and workers were enlisted. A driver and three workers were on each bus. The crew did a program on the bus, singing and keeping the kids in the seats, and getting all the riders to the correct classes and church and back to the bus before delivering them back to their homes.

Because of the community where the church was located, most of the kids that were brought in on the bus were black, and that had been a problem at Hannibal in past years. They had actually voted one year to not allow the local Baptist college choir to sing in the church because one of the choir members was black! So race was definitely a problem. When all these black children began coming to the church, the issue was faced and dealt with, and blacks were welcomed in the church.

The church eventually bought two more buses, bringing the total to five, with a total of about 175 per week riding the buses. Other churches heard about the bus ministry at Calvary Church and began coming to see what it was all about. Twelve other churches started bus ministries in their churches after visiting Calvary and seeing what was being done there.

The church grew in numbers and in spirit. There was a concern for others, not only for the children but for the parents. Children took materials from the church to their parents, and some of these parents were reached for the Lord. Some families were reunited because of the bus ministry. Two alcoholics were reached and became dry because of the bus ministry. In eighteen months there were 104 baptisms; 25% of these were adults. There were thirty-seven by letter; twenty-six of these were adults. The bus ministry was one of the high points in the life of Calvary Baptist Church.

When we began bringing in all those children on the buses, we opened the balcony so we would have more room for seating.

The bus kids liked to sit up in the balcony of the church. One Sunday morning, a little boy was making airplanes out of bulletins and sailing them down into the main part of the auditorium. One of them sailed down and the point hit a man on the head, right on his bald spot!

That man, Joe Smith, became the Junior Church pastor. He was an ordained minister and he decided we needed something besides the regular church service for the kids, so the Junior Church was begun. He said the Lord sent him a very "pointed" message when He called him to that job!

Every Saturday the bus workers would go out, park the big bus on the road, and then knock on doors, inviting people to ride the bus and go to church the next day. As Charlie walked up to one door, he saw a large pile of dirt in the yard, and a little black girl about eight or nine years old was standing on top of it. He said, "Would you like to ride that bus and come to church tomorrow?"

She looked at the bus with its big letters proclaiming the name of the church, and said, "Mistuh, are you from the Bap-a-tist church?"

"He said, "Yes, and we would like for you to ride that bus and come to Sunday School and church with us tomorrow."

She put her hands on her hips and said very adamantly, "Mistuh, you ain't a-gonna bap-a-tize *me*!"

Well, he did bap-a-tize her and many others in that community.

One of the teen-aged girls who rode the bus was Vanessa. She was about fourteen and had never been to church or been around Christian people. One day, Charlie was talking to a group of people where Vanessa happened to be, and as he talked, he placed his hand on her shoulder. She immediately jumped, shook off his hand, and said, "Don't you touch me!" He began to find out about Vanessa.

He learned that several men had sexually abused her in her young life and by this time, she would not let a man touch her. The bus captain began taking Vanessa home with her, talking to her, helping her to understand about God's love, and the love of Christian people for her. Before we left that church, Vanessa gave my husband a hug and her picture! She had learned that not all men were bad, and she had accepted Jesus as her Savior.

While we were in Hannibal, Charlie did things that were unusual and different. He never wanted to do "church as usual" but wanted people in the community to notice the church. Our first winter there, we had a revival with Charles Massegee, a full-time evangelist he had met at Hardin-Simmons University in Abilene.

Actually, he had scheduled the revival for Sedalia, but when we moved, he asked Charles and his team to come to Hannibal and go ahead with the revival as planned.

It was January, and the week the revival was scheduled, we had a big snow. Everybody said the meeting would be a failure. They said nobody in Hannibal would brave those snow-covered hills to come to church during the week in a snowstorm.

But they did! Charles had some special emphases and one of them was a program for kids called "Jewels for Jesus". The kids each got a crown and every night when they came or if they brought a friend, Charles or one of the others in the team would punch holes in the crowns. The "jewels" were the holes and the child with the most would win a prize.   One of the kids said, "This isn't 'Jewels for Jesus', I think it's 'Holes for Jesus'!"

The people came and packed the church. We had chairs in the aisles, kids sitting on the platform, the choir was filled to capacity, and the auditorium and balcony were overflowing.

A professional photographer came to take pictures of the crowd. He couldn't believe what he saw. He shook his head and said, "I didn't know people came to church like this any more." It was truly a landmark for that church. During the week, about ninety people made professions of faith! Nothing like that had ever happened before in Hannibal during a snowy January!

Then the Bus Ministry started on Easter Sunday, 1971, with 75 new riders. There were so many kids, we couldn't find places to put them all. Calvary was in a mixed neighborhood, with both white and black population. Many of the kids had never been to church before. As they began attending our church, we had to make lots of adjustments in space and how we did things.

One little boy was named Andrew, the most hyper-active child we had ever seen. One of the bus workers had to sit with him and actually hold on to him to keep him still. If the worker ever let go of him, "Zipppppp", just like that he would be under the pew and gone. Then he would be seen popping up several pews away, and one of the workers would try to catch him. We had to keep our eyes and our hands on Andrew!

The changes at Calvary Baptist Church even caught the attention of the Hannibal City Council. They noticed an evident change for the better in the community around our church, and were wondering what had caused it.

They called my husband and asked him to come to a meeting and tell them what was happening at the Baptist church on the corner of Hope and Willow Streets. So he went to the City Council meeting and told them about the things that happened—the revival, the beginnings of the bus ministry, and how lives were being changed as people came to know the Lord and others came to know Him more closely.

Whenever we went to a new church, we always joined the church on our first Sunday there. The kids hated to have to stand in line and shake hands with all the people. So when we joined the Calvary church at Hannibal, David was at the end of the line, and as soon as he could, he slipped out. As a result, several of the people didn't even know we had a son his age. They met Steve, Debbie, and Cindy, but didn't get to meet David.

One day a woman at church said to me, "I think you might have some problems at your house. Are you locking your doors?"

I assured her that I was locking the doors when I went to work. Then I said, "Why do you ask?"

She said, "Well, I was driving by your house the other day and I saw a strange little boy going in your side door. I knew he wasn't yours, because we met all your children when you joined the church, and we didn't meet him."

That was David. He was the strange little boy.

David had a paper route in Hannibal, and one week he went with his dad to R.A. camp at Windermere, so Debbie said she would do his paper route for him. She fell down one of those many hills in Hannibal and broke her leg.

Debbie's leg was encased in a "walking cast". We went to the Lake of the Ozarks State Park on our vacation that first summer, and every day Debbie would walk so much that her cast would be soft on the bottom of her foot. Every night Charlie would mix up a bunch of Plaster of Paris and repair her cast. The next day she would do it all over again! That broken leg didn't keep her down! Times had changed since I broke my leg. Now she was as mobile as anyone and she had a really good time!

During that same trip, we went to Six Flags Over Mid-America near St. Louis. Every time we went on a ride, the people running the ride would say to Debbie, "You can go around again. You don't have to stand in line and wait for another turn because of your broken leg."

When Steve and David found that out, they wanted to wait in line with Debbie so that they could get on with her, and have double rides. Because they were protective of her broken leg, they got the same benefits she received. As I think back, I wonder if that was true brotherly love—I think the boys just wanted double rides, too!

Just before that vacation, one of the young ladies who had grown up with our children in Sedalia came to see us in Hannibal. Gianna Snyder and her mother and brother were faithful friends in Sedalia, and I helped Gianna to get started singing solos in church. Her beautiful voice just needed to be used, in my opinion, so on her twelfth birthday she sang her first solo. After that, music became an important part of her life. She says now that she cannot imagine living with God and music.

She had just graduated from high school and wanted to go on a trip, so her mother encouraged her to visit us. She called and said she was coming, and when she arrived, we were just a few days from the time we would leave on our vacation. The day before we were to leave, our car broke down and Gianna heard us discussing the problem. We didn't have the large amount of money it would take to fix the car, but we had a guest and it was lunch time, so Charlie went to get hamburgers for everybody. Gianna, having overheard our discussion about money, wanted to pay for the hamburgers, but Charlie smiled and said, "God will take care of this. Don't you worry," and he wouldn't let her pay. He said to her, "God has always provided for us, and I would be ashamed to not serve Him and thank Him for His goodness."

By the end of the day, a member of our church offered us his car so that we could go on our vacation as planned.

It was in Hannibal that Cindy started to love Donny Osmond, and collect his records and memorabilia, and David started to love football. Cindy collected Barbie dolls and I think she had about 34 of them— including Kens and Skippers and all the rest. David collected hot-wheels cars and I don't know how many he had. It was a number too high to count!

One of the families in our church got a transfer with the husband's job that year, and their daughter was a senior in high school. She stayed with us so that she could graduate and moved into Debbie's room, so Debbie got her own room in the basement. She said she loved that basement room, even if it had concrete walls, because it was hers alone. She always wanted her own room, and very seldom got it!

Our house was on a hill, so we had an entrance in the basement, and we kept the piano down there. Steve practiced a lot and taught himself while we were in Hannibal, and he kept on learning more. He found some of my college music books and practiced Bach exercises on his own. His thirst for learning music was insatiable. He practiced hours on his own. Nobody ever had to remind him to practice!

The year that I taught fourth grade in Hannibal, I had only seventeen students. One day a little girl in my class whose family attended our church came up to my desk while everyone was working and said, "Mrs. Nobles, how do you become a Christian?"

I had my Bible there, so I got it out and led Rhonda Haskins to the Lord at my desk. She prayed to receive Christ right there in the classroom. That night, I called her mother and told her about it, and Rhonda went forward in church the next Sunday to make her public profession of faith, and was later baptized.

Years later, while we were living in DeSoto, I got a letter from Rhonda. She had married a preacher and wanted to thank me for leading her to the Lord in that fourth grade classroom.

We very seldom went to movies, but during the early 1970's a movie came out that we thought we might all enjoy. There was a lot of hype about it, so when _Patton_ came to a theater in Hannibal, we decided to take the whole family and go. We got there, got our popcorn and sodas and entered the theater after the lights had been turned off, so we didn't see anybody who was there.

The opening scene was full of expletives as George C. Scott lambasted all the young men in his command, using very colorful language. We were embarrassed that we had taken our children to hear something like that. During the first half of the movie, we sank lower in our seats as the language continued to flow. Both of us were thinking, "Hope nobody we know is at this movie."

Intermission came and all the lights were turned on. There in the theater sat four or five couples, deacons and their wives, from our church. Each one of us sheepishly looked at each other, shrugged, and sat through the rest of the movie.

Joe was a member of Calvary and a Sunday School teacher when we arrived on the scene. Joe was an alcoholic, but he was dry and had been for several years before we got there. As we learned about Joe, we learned that while he was drinking, he would get mean. He would beat his wife, tear up the furniture, and cause trouble in town.

So he and his wife made a pact. They agreed that whenever Joe started drinking and his wife realized that he was on a binge, (and she could recognize those times), she would put him in the bathroom and lock him in. They had special locks installed on the doors so there was no way for him to get out. They had a little hole cut into the bottom of the door so that she could slide food in for him. He could sleep in the bathtub, and he had everything else he needed.

Before she locked him in, she would check the bathroom and get all the liquor out, because he would hide liquor in there while he was sober so that he could stay drunk longer. But no matter what amount of crying and pleading he did, she would not open the bathroom door and let him out until he was stone cold sober.

Then, one day, a miracle happened. There was a revival at the church and Joe agreed to go with his wife, and he got saved. But he didn't just get saved, he got delivered from alcohol at the same time! When we arrived in Hannibal, Joe was living a Christian life, teaching a Sunday School class and helping alcoholics to kick the habit. He told Charlie, "Any time you have an alcoholic call you, you just call me and I'll come. Day or night, any time, I have an arrangement with my boss, and he'll let me come to talk with any alcoholic who needs help to get off the stuff."

Joe was always giving money to send a child to camp or to help in some other way. He also helped to counsel many men who were hooked on alcohol.

Charlie used to say in one of his sermons, "If God could save Joe and deliver him from alcohol at the same time, He can do anything for anybody, if we will just let Him." Joe is gone now, but for several years he was an example to us and to the people of Calvary Baptist Church.

Calvary Baptist was the first church we served where Charlie was called on to help a church that was having a serious problem, and had lost some of their membership. This was the beginning of his ministry to churches in need of revitalization.

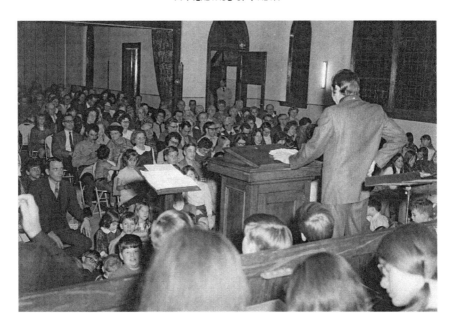

The big revival in Hannibal

Revival in Hannibal

14
SUNNY FLORIDA

We had been in Hannibal about two years when Charlie got a call from Luther Dyer, a friend and pastor in Miami, Florida, asking him to consider coming to the Wayside Baptist Church in Miami to direct the bus ministry. The church in Hannibal was growing and doing well, and the bus ministry was also growing. But the thought of "sunny Miami" was something to think about!

Charlie talked with some of his friends about the church in Miami, and they advised him to stay where he was because of the success he was having and the excitement of the people in the church. But the glamour of life in Miami got to both of us. We both were very excited about the prospect of living and serving in Miami, Florida!

Wayside flew our whole family to Miami and as Charlie met with various people and committees, we became more excited, thinking about the possibility of life in Miami. The people wanted to do everything they could for us to make it easy for us to accept the position of Minister of Evangelism. They took us out to fine restaurants, showed us the beautiful city, found us a place to live, and introduced us to wonderful people who loved the Lord.

We both thought it was where we should be, because we wanted to be there. It was cold in Missouri and it was warm in Florida, the Sunshine State. We thought, "We will be continuing our service with the bus ministry, so surely the Lord is in this."

A short time later, we moved to Miami and Charlie became Minister of Evangelism for the Wayside Baptist Church.

I'm sure it was not easy for our children to leave familiar surroundings and go to new places as often as we did. Before moving to Miami, we had been in Hannibal only two years. Cindy had become good friends with two little girls, children of deacons who took part in many church activities. She, Laurie, and Beth enjoyed playing together and visiting at each other's homes.

We left Hannibal on a Sunday night after a reception. Our furniture had already been packed and taken by the movers. We drove about three hours, then stopped at a motel, and the next day we started out again. When we stopped for lunch on Monday, we noticed that Cindy was really drooping. Her head was hanging low and she looked very, very sad.

Charlie put his arm around her shoulders and said, "What's the matter, Cindy?"

She looked up at him, her eyes filled with tears, and she said, "I've just left every friend I have in the world!"

Our hearts broke for our youngest, our little eight-year-old. We were excited about the glamour of Miami and the promise of new things ahead, but she had nothing but the unknown to look to. All she knew was that her best friends were left behind.

It wasn't long after we arrived when we realized we had made a mistake. We had tried to be careful and open to the Lord's will, but this time the glamour of the place caused us to make the wrong decision. However, while we were not in His perfect will, we felt we were in His permissive will, because the Lord used us.

Our kids made friends and went to school and were happy.

I taught at The Academy of Learning, a school for boys and girls with all kinds of reading problems. I wrote a special reading program and was given an award for Excellence in Teaching for writing and implementing that program in the school. Children in my reading classes were second graders through high school age.

Charlie won people to the Lord and baptized people every Sunday at Wayside. He said he could go out on any night of the week, make three visits, and win a family to the Lord. He did almost all the baptizing at Wayside, about 225 people per year. So God definitely used us.

But there was a longing in our hearts that showed us we were in the wrong place. He wanted to preach.

Charlie wrote a letter to the Calvary Church where we had been, admitting his mistake, and asking that they reconsider him as pastor again, but the Pulpit Committee thought it best to leave things as they were. So we continued to serve in Miami, doing the things we needed to do, but putting out resumes to churches in Texas and Missouri, letting people know that we wanted to get back in the pastorate.

The Lord left us there two years as we waited to get back into the pastorate. We made the most of it, and had lots of good experiences.

Steve and Debbie were in the Youth Department at Wayside. They sang in the Youth Choir, played in the handbell choir and went on mission trips. Once their handbell group played The Star Spangled Banner at the Orange Bowl before one of the Miami Dolphin football games. They had the opportunity to be in a large youth group and do lots of things they had never done before.

David and Cindy were in elementary school and enjoyed many activities at the church with lots of kids, something they had not had before. They took part in plays and choir events at the church and made friends with many of the kids.

We lived in a house next to the church with a swimming pool in the back yard. Many of the people there had pools in their houses or their yards, and we were in many beautiful homes with the members of Wayside. The people were tremendous and treated us like royalty.

Miami schools there were overcrowded and all of them had "split-shifts." Some kids went to school from 7:00 a.m. to noon, others went from noon to 5:00 p.m., and others were on the regular 9:00 to 3:30 shift. David left our house at 7:00 to get his bus, Debbie started her shift at noon, and Cindy was on the regular time schedule, as was I.

Steve also had the afternoon shift. It took a lot of planning just to get everybody to school.

During the summer after we arrived at Wayside, Charlie and I were sponsors for a youth tour. We were to ride the bus with the kids and chaperone them as they played handbells and performed a musical for several churches. The big, over-the-road bus was packed with about 70 kids, and our two oldest were among the group for their first really big mission trip!

We stopped for gas, and all the kids piled off the bus. After we re-loaded, we drove on. We had not gone far, when we saw a man at a gas station waving his hands, trying to flag us down. The bus pulled over, opened the door, and the driver said, "Is there a problem?"

"There sure is!" the man said. "You left a couple of kids back at the service station you just came from." We began looking around to see who was missing, and one of the missing girls was our own daughter, Debbie! She and another girl had been in the bathroom when the bus left, and somebody didn't count all the kids. We turned around, picked them up, and continued on our way. After that, somebody counted every kid as they got on after every stop!

Charlie began to get frequent calls from the nurse at Cindy's school. She was sick and had to be picked up, but it seemed that every time this occurred, it was at the same time of the day. After picking her up and bringing her home several times, he began to wonder about her sickness.

When the nurse called the next time, he said, "What class does Cindy have during this time?"

The nurse turned to Cindy and said, "What's your next class?"

Cindy said, "Reading, and I *love* reading."

The nurse relayed the message and Charlie said, "Would you check with the office and see what her next class is and call me back?"

The nurse looked at Cindy and said, "I'm going to check with the office about your next class." Then Cindy *really* began to look sick.

The office records showed that Cindy was to be in Math class during the next period, so the nurse called Charlie and told him.

He said, "Send her back to class."

The jig was up. She was trying to get out of math class because she had so much difficulty with math. So she didn't get sick at that time again. She knew her dad had caught her!

Bob McClain, one of our bus captains, came by our house one day and said, "Marvin, come go with me. I have something I'd like you to help me do." He took him to J.C. Penney's and bought him three new suits, shirts, and ties to match. Charlie had been wearing the old clothes he had—double knit pants that were a little too small, and other things that were slightly out of style. Bob decided to get him dressed up right!

Bob was a precious man who liked to give to others. He had a great hobby, too. He liked to take raw minerals, cut and polish them, and make them into beautiful jewelry. He was always making some beautiful pin or ring to give to someone.

Another of our bus captains came to Charlie one day and said, "I have a family that I want you to visit." So one evening Charlie went to see Angel and Maria Melero. He was invited in and led to the beautiful "Florida room" in the back of the house, a large, window-lined room decorated with tropical plants. After they were seated at a table, Angel Melero said, "Mr. Nobles, we know there is a God. Tell us what else we need to know."

Charlie started at the beginning, telling Angel and Maria about the creation story and the way God led throughout the Old Testament to bring His Son into the world as recorded in the New Testament. Three hours later, Angel and Maria both accepted Jesus as their Savior.

Angel told him, "Our kids started riding that church bus and when they came home they would be happy and singing church songs. So I said to my wife, 'That church is getting to our kids. You'd better go and find out about it.' So she rode the bus and when she came home she said to me, '*You'd* better go and see what that church is doing with our kids.' So I rode the bus and then I wanted to know more."

After the Meleros became members at Wayside, the church began a ministry to Spanish-speaking people. Angel translated the messages from English to Spanish in a little room off the sanctuary. More and more Spanish-speaking people came and many of them accepted Christ as their Savior. One Sunday night Maria gave her testimony about the bus ministry and how she and her family came to know the Lord. Her Spanish accent and her sincere thankfulness to God moved many people to tears, as they listened. During that time many Cubans and Spanish people were entering the United States and settling in and around Miami.

Another time, Charlie visited a Cuban woman who had attended Wayside. He went into her apartment complex, past a guard at the gate, through several locked entrances, and into her apartment. She had recently been divorced and had moved to Miami with her daughter, who rode the bus to Sunday School.

As Charlie talked with her, listening to her story, he said, "God loves you."

The woman, startled, jumped a little. She looked at him and said, "God loves me?"

"Yes," he said, "God loves you and cares about you."

The woman began weeping. "Mr. Nobles," she said, "nobody has ever told me that God loves me. The church I grew up in always taught that God would 'get' me if I was not good and that He would punish me. I have divorced my husband and left my country, and I have been told that God does not want me to do those things. I have always thought of God as someone to fear. Nobody ever said He loves me."

Charlie assured her that God did love her and led her to the Lord. She and her daughter were baptized and became regular in attendance at Wayside, along with many others.

Cindy and I went to the grocery store one day, and on the way back she said, "Mom, why do they give you all your money back when you go to the store?"

I said, "They don't. We have to pay for what we buy."

She looked puzzled, then she said, "But when they give you back your change, they count it all out, and then say, and that's $10.00 or whatever you gave them. So aren't they giving you back all your money?"

It would be interesting to think with a child's mind, and try to figure it all out, wouldn't it?

I was on the little porch that people there call the "Florida Room" one afternoon. No one else was in the house, and I was enjoying the quiet and working on some sewing. David, about age eleven, and his friend, Ed Wood, rode their bikes outside as they played together.

Suddenly David came bursting in and fell down into a chair by the sewing machine. "Mom," he said, "I want you to tell me how babies get here."

I swallowed a couple of times, and said, "David, your dad will be home in a little while, and I really think he ought to talk to you about that."

He leaned forward and looked right in my face. "Mom," he said, "I want you to tell me right now." I tried a couple more times to put him off for a little while and finally he said, "Mom, I'm not getting out of this chair until you tell me how babies get here." David was to become an attorney later in life, and his tenacious search for the facts was already evident!

I swallowed again. Then I told him the whole story, from beginning to end. I didn't leave anything out. He got the whole load.

When I finished, he sat there a minute, a thoughtful look on his face. "That's what Ed told me," he said, "but I didn't believe it."

Debbie met Martha at school and they became good friends. Martha attended church with Debbie some of the time, but I don't think she was a member there. Her parents were doctors and very well fixed financially. They were planning to send Martha to Europe during the summer for a bicycle tour of some of the European countries.

Martha began talking to Debbie about going with her, so they came to talk with us. We couldn't afford the cost of the trip.

Martha talked with her parents, and they offered to pay the cost for Debbie, so she had the privilege of visiting Europe that second summer in Miami, riding her bicycle over the beautiful countryside and visiting many beautiful places.

The tour people had a large van, and any time the kids could not ride, they carried their bikes and let them ride in the van for a while to give them breaks. It was a once-in-a-lifetime thing for Debbie, to be given this special trip at age fifteen.

One of the special emphases that Wayside did every year was a "fish fry" where the men caught and cooked fish and everybody was invited. Several men in our church had large fishing boats. They would go deep-sea fishing for several weekends and catch enough fish to feed 2,000 or more people. Then they would set up chairs and public address equipment in the courtyard of the church, a large grassy area between the buildings, and many people would come, eat a free fish dinner, and be introduced to our church as they attended a large outdoor worship service.

Charlie had a big responsibility during that time. Besides fishing all night, his duties went right on. He had to service and gas up twelve buses one Saturday right after returning from a long fishing trip.

A young Spanish man worked at the service station where Charlie always went to gas up the buses, and he had tried to witness to him several times. The young man was always too busy and did not have time to listen, or didn't care to. On that particular Saturday, Charlie was sitting in the driver's seat of one of the buses, waiting for the young man to finish with the gas, when he stepped on the bus and said, "Well, how are you doing today?"

Charlie was so tired. He had fished all night on Friday, and then had spent Saturday morning with the bus crew, going out to invite people to ride the bus. It was Saturday afternoon, and he thought,

"Lord, not now. I just can't witness to this man now. I'm just too tired." So he didn't say much to the man, thinking he would come back later and talk with him. The man finished with the gas, and Charlie drove away.

The very next week, that young man left Miami and he was never seen again. Many times in sermons, I've heard Charlie tell that story. He would say, "The Lord gave me a wide open opportunity to tell him about Jesus, and I was just too tired."

He has often wondered what happened to that man, where he went, and if anyone ever told him about Jesus. He used this story to illustrate that we need to take advantage of the opportunities that are given to us by God to tell others about Him. And he said, "Use those opportunities. Don't let one pass you by."

Pray also for me, that whenever I open my mouth, words may be given to me so that I will fearlessly make known the mystery of the gospel. Ephesians 6:19(NAS)

We decided to take our kids on tour when we went on our next vacation. We thought we would go back to every church where we had served as pastor, and present a program. We contacted the churches and worked out the dates, and I bought a whole bolt of fabric and made matching dresses for Debbie, Cindy, and me, and shirts for Charlie and the boys.

We worked up a program of music and preaching. Steve played the piano, and he and the girls and I sang. During one of the songs, David played a xylophone that we borrowed from the school music department, and then he gave a little testimony. Charlie wrapped it up with a devotional.

We visited several churches we had served in the past and some other churches along our route where we could get an invitation from people we knew. We enjoyed working together, doing our own private tour. That was one of the highlights of our lives, and one of our favorite memories, having our own singing group and going "on tour".

Wayside was averaging 400 riders every Sunday on 12 buses, and seven junior churches were coordinated and directed every Sunday morning by my husband. The bus ministry and junior church had about 90 volunteers who served weekly on the buses or in the various children's worship groups, presenting the gospel. About 1200 people came to church on Sunday mornings, attending two Sunday Schools and three worship services. It was an exciting place to be.

The little children loved Charlie. They would hug him, and one little boy would often hold him around the leg and look up and say, "I wish you were my daddy."

Ishmael Del Gado came to him one day, held out a little bag filled with coins, and said, "Will you take my grandpa's money?"

After talking with him awhile, Charlie learned that his grandfather had died, and Ishmael had been given the small bag with coins that had belonged to his grandfather. He wanted to give it to Jesus, so he grabbed it before he got on the bus and brought it to the man in charge of the bus ministry.

Charlie called the boy's mother and explained what Ishmael had done. She agreed that if he wanted to give the money to God, she had no problem with it. So Ishmael brought his grandpa's money and gave it to God. It was a very small amount of money, but Ishmael got a blessing by doing what he did.

One of the men who worked in the bus ministry, Dick Graves, knew about a church in Texas where they needed a pastor. His parents were members there, so he recommended us to the Highland Park Baptist Church in Texarkana, Texas.

After being called to Highland Park in 1974, we made plans to go back to Texas. The moving van picked up our furniture and we drove to Texas with our four children and three cars.

I was driving one car with Debbie, David, and Cindy, and Charlie and Steve were in the other car, towing a small green car we had bought for Steve when he turned sixteen.

We didn't have CBs or cell phones, or any way to communicate with each other, so we just tried to stay in each other's sight. The large car that I was driving used a lot of gasoline, so at one point, I drove around Charlie and signaled that I had to get gas at the next town. Then I went on in front, and pulled in at a service station. Charlie had not caught up with me yet, but while I was inside in the bathroom, he pulled in to a service station across the street from where we were.

If I had looked up, I would have seen his car. It would have been hard to miss a big car towing a little green car, but I missed it. I was thinking that he had continued to go on, so I assumed he was in front of me. I got the gas, rushed to get the kids in the car, and took off, trying to catch him.

At the gas station across the street, Steve and Charlie went to the bathroom, and when they came out, my car was gone.

Charlie thought, "Maybe she went into town. She might have needed to get something from the store."

So he drove around the town, looking for me. Meanwhile, I was driving as fast as I could down the road, trying to catch up with him! When he finally realized that I had gone on ahead, he tried to catch me.

Debbie was in the front seat with me and Cindy and David were in the back seat doing their usual "back seat" thing. Whenever they were together in a confined space, David would start to aggravate Cindy, she would start yelling, and pretty soon Mom would be crazy! Add to all this the frustration of not knowing where Charlie and Steve were, and you can see why I stopped along the road, got a switch, and spanked two kids. Debbie was so embarrassed that her mother would create such a scene!

After what seemed like a couple of hours, the kids began to get worried, too, and began asking questions that added to my frustration.

"Mommy, what will we do tonight if we don't find Daddy?"

"Do we have any money?"

"Where is Daddy? How are we going to find him?"

I was getting more and more upset, so I stopped at a telephone booth and called the Highway Patrol. I told them what had happened and where I was, I gave them a description of the other car, and asked them to search for my husband and tell him where I was. The officer on the phone could probably tell by my voice that I was really upset. He tried to calm me down and told me to go to a designated place and stay there. He assured me they would find my husband, or they would come to that spot and let me know something.

There was a terrible rainstorm, but I kept on driving as fast as I could, thinking that I would catch up to Charlie and Steve if I went faster. It never occurred to me that they might be behind me. So I went to the place they had told me to go, parked the car, and waited—my tears were coming down about as fast as the rain!

Meanwhile, Charlie had figured out what had happened. Knowing me as he did, he assumed I was in front, racing to catch him. So he called the Highway Patrol. As soon as he said, "This is Marvin Nobles"— the officer said, "Well, Mr. Nobles! I've just been talking to your wife!"

The officer told him what he had told me and where I would be waiting. Charlie drove on and we finally got together again!

I made sure that he didn't get out of my sight after that little incident!

The bus ministry in Miami

15
TEXARKANA, TEXAS

The Highland Park Baptist Church had been losing members for several years before we went there. They had a very big church plant, a beautiful sanctuary, lots of rooms, and not enough people to fill it up. The average attendance was about 250 when we went there, and about 400 when we left. People responded to the things that were done, and the Lord blessed. It was another place where the Lord used Marvin Nobles to get people to love each other again. He would often say to the people, "If you want to fight, you called the wrong man. I'm a lover, not a fighter."

When we moved to Texarkana Steve was a senior in high school, so he only went to school one year there. Debbie was a sophomore and was able to attend Texas High for three years until she graduated. Steve and Debbie were both in school plays. Debbie was Daisy Mae in Li'l Abner and Steve was in Carousel and Mash. Debbie also was a finalist in the Miss Texas beauty contest while we were there. David's focus was journalism and he worked on the school paper, but he was in plays, too, after he started to High School. He also joined the Swim Team and began a life of physical activity—swimming, running, bicycling, which he continues to this day.

David became a good friend of Marty, a boy who worked on the school paper with him. On one occasion, David was driving his car with a bunch of his friends. Marty and the other guys had cups with ice and cold drinks. As they rode, they were trying to drop the cups out of the back window and see how long they would stand up before they fell over and spilled. One of the cups skidded and hit the wheels of another car, which startled the driver and caused him to have a little trouble steering. He took down the license plate number and called the police and reported David, the driver of the car, for vandalism.

The police chief was a member of our church, so he called Charlie and told him what had happened. He wanted to stop the action before David had to be called to the police station and booked for vandalism. The police chief said he thought if David would go to the man and apologize, he would drop the charges. So Charlie told David he had to go to the man and apologize.

David didn't want to do it, because he thought he had not done anything wrong. He insisted that they were only having fun, but Charlie insisted harder, so David reluctantly apologized. The man dropped the charges, and it didn't go any farther. That's the closest we ever came to a run-in with the law.

Cindy met Tricia in fifth or sixth grade when we moved to Texarkana. They are still good friends today, even though Tricia lives in New York. They were both in love with Donny Osmond. They would get together and listen to his records and read magazines about the Osmonds. They collected all kinds of Donny Osmond memorabilia.

Once the Osmonds came to Shreveport, which was not too far from Texarkana. Cindy talked Debbie and her boyfriend into taking her and Tricia to the concert. She was so excited to get to go and see the Osmonds! She thought she had died and gone to Heaven!

The next Sunday night in church, Charlie asked for testimonies. He said, "Has the Lord done anything good for you this week?"

Eleven-year-old Cindy was the first person to stand up and speak. She jumped up and said, "This week the Lord brought the Osmonds to Shreveport, and I got to go and see them!"

One day Charlie heard on the news that Donny Osmond had gotten married. He said to himself, "I've got to tell Cindy about this. She can't hear this on the news."

So he went to school and picked up Cindy and Tricia, who were both in sixth grade at the time, and comforted them as they cried over the loss of Donny.

While I was looking around in the music room at church one day, I found a set of handbells. They had not been used for a long time, so I got them out and cleaned them and began a handbell choir. Then I started another one. We had one for youth and one for adults. I started making musical arrangements for the bells, and working with the bell choirs to perfect and perform them.

The youth bell choir would go and play for other churches or for nursing homes, or anywhere I could take them. Once we were playing at a reception and while we played, people were milling around and talking and there was a lot of noise.

One of the youth, a big, husky boy named Chip, felt that the people were being rude and not paying us enough attention. As soon as there was a break in the music, he came up to me, and whispered loudly, "Mrs. Nobles, do you want me to get them quiet for you?"

He could have done it, too. He was a football player and a pretty big boy!

I said, "No, that's all right. They'll hear enough." Later I tried to explain to him about playing for receptions, and that the people were not totally quiet. But he still thought I should have let him take over and make them listen to us! After all, we had practiced for hours to play for them and Chip thought we deserved their full and undivided attention!

(Our son Steve is a musical entertainer, and he jokingly calls playing for receptions "music to ignore" which is probably a true statement, but one that Chip had not yet learned about.)

One of our elderly deacons, Mr. Groseclose, was a great encourager to Charlie. He would put his arm around him whenever he thought he might be down or discouraged and say, "Now, pastor, we must be doing something right. We still have people coming down the aisles." Charlie could always count on this wonderful man of God to be a great encourager.

Mr. and Mrs. Carpenter were wonderful senior adults. They were always in attendance, and they always tried to help and encourage. They would go the church office once a month and pick up the "newcomer" cards that were sent by the Chamber of Commerce in town. Then they would go out and visit these people who had moved into Texarkana and tell them about our church and invite them to come. Many of the people they contacted came to visit our church and some became members.

The Crystals and the Abneys from Sedalia have remained good friends through all these years. They came to visit us in Texarkana, bringing their camper and all their children. With the Crystals' four, the Abneys' three, and the four of ours, we had wall-to-wall children at our house!

All us adults decided to do a little touring. Since the children were so much older, we left them to their own desires for a while. But something unexpected came up. Craig Crystal began having very bad stomach pains. Our daughter Debbie, about 14 years old at the time, decided she knew what to do. He just needed a little laxative! So she gave him some Ex-Lax. She was unsure of how much to give him, and she wanted to be sure he got over his stomach ache, so she told him to eat about half a package of the chocolate medicine.

When we got back home, he was in a much worse state than he had been before. Jim and Juanita Crystal had to take Craig to the emergency room at the hospital, where he was tested and hospital staff members thought he had been taking drugs! It was a while before Craig recovered from the remedy Dr. Debbie had given him!

During the year Steve was a high school senior, we looked at several colleges, and he decided he wanted to go to Baylor University, a Baptist school in Waco, Texas. Since Baylor was very expensive, we tried to get him to consider another school. But Steve was determined. He and his dad filled out papers for loans, grants, and scholarships, and this became a possibility for him. He was a journalism major in Baylor, as he had been in high school, and was active on the Baylor school paper. He had worked in Miami with a man who helped him to write feature articles for the newspaper, and he was getting pretty good at it.

Two years later, Charlie and Debbie began filling out papers and the process began again. After months of forms and papers, Debbie made her application to Baylor and was accepted. She was in the drama department; she acted in operas and majored in music. It was not easy, having two children in college. Of course, they had to work and after graduation, they had to pay back loans, but they were both able to graduate from Baylor.

When David was a senior, we were living in a different place, but the process began again. David and his dad filled out lots of papers, and he, too, was accepted at Baylor. And David went on to get his law degree from Baylor, also.

When it was time for Debbie to leave for college, she really needed a car so that she could come home from time to time. There was no way we could afford to buy her a car. So we began looking at various options, wondering how we could come up with a car for her.

Debbie had met Lisa at a Christian camp, and they had become good friends. Lisa attended another Baptist church in town. Her family lived on the Arkansas side of Texarkana and we lived on the Texas side. Debbie shared with her the fact that she really needed a car, so Debbie and Lisa began to pray about the situation. Lisa went home and told her parents and they prayed about it, too.

Lisa's parents had bought her a new car and she had an older car, a 1977 Monte Carlo, that she needed to sell or dispose of in some way, but she had not done it yet.

One day Lisa said to her dad, "I know what to do about my car."

Her dad said, "I do, too."

"What do you think?" Lisa asked her dad.

"You tell me what you think first," he said.

"I think I should give Debbie my car," Lisa said.

Her dad said, "That's what the Lord told me, too, and I was going to tell you about it tonight."

So Lisa went to see Debbie and told her about that conversation. They came to us and told us, and we went into shock. But that is how Debbie got her car to drive back and forth from Baylor.

She drove that Monte Carlo for several years.

One weekend Debbie came home and brought a strange young man with her. She said he was a hitchhiker that she had picked up on the way home. He needed a place to stay for the night, so she just brought him home! We were pretty alarmed! This young man had a big pack that he was carrying on his back. He came in, deposited his pack, and spent the night in David's room, sleeping on Steve's bed.

We were pretty scared, because for all we knew he could have had knives or anything in that pack!

The next morning, Debbie took him out to the highway and he went on his way, hitching a ride.

On another weekend Debbie started out from Baylor to come home to Texarkana. She was well on the way when she realized that she had no money and she was almost out of gas in the car. She had some checks, but gas stations won't take checks, and she did not have a credit card.

As she drove into Dallas, she saw two men who looked like they were about twenty years old, standing by their car. She stopped, asked them if they needed help, and they said they were out of gas.

It was really a risky thing to do, for a girl to stop and offer a ride to two men she didn't know. But the Lord was watching out for her, I guess. She took them to where they were going and they gave her five dollars. She got five dollars worth of gasoline and that was enough for her to get to Texarkana.

Debbie says now, that the Lord has given her the gift of being able to think ahead and plan, but He hadn't given her that gift yet when this happened.

Charlie began having problems with high blood pressure and after quite a bit of "encouragement" from me, he agreed to go to a doctor to have it checked. But when he would go to the doctor's office, he would have to sit and wait, and that caused his blood pressure to go up higher. He had work to do, too, and sitting in a doctor's office just made him think of all the time he was wasting. He went to the desk and asked about it, and was told that the doctor was a busy man, and sometimes he was late due to things that were unexpected.

At one of these appointments, he went to the desk and said, "Look, I've been sitting here an hour and a half waiting to see the doctor. I know he is a busy man, but I am a busy man, too. I am pastor of a church just a few blocks from here. I'm going back to my office and when the doctor is ready for me, you call and I'll be here in five minutes."

The startled receptionist had probably not heard this before, but she said, "Yes, Rev. Nobles, we will call you."

He went back to the church office and when the receptionist called, he drove to the doctor's office and had his appointment with him. He made the follow-up appointment and when the time came for that, he called the office and said, "My appointment is for 10:00 and I'd like to know if the doctor is in and if he is on time."

From then on, the receptionist would call him when the doctor was ready, and he didn't have to sit and wait any more. He said to me, "Doctors need to know they are not the only busy people in the world!"

One of the young ladies in our church was an RN and worked at the local hospital. She called Charlie one day and said he needed to get to the hospital fast. As soon as he got to the intensive care floor, he heard a woman wailing and crying loudly, "He's lost! He's dying! He's going to Hell, and it's my fault!" He walked on down to the waiting room and there was a lady who attended our church. Her grandson had recently been baptized and she had started attending with him. She continued sobbing and crying over and over, "He's lost! He's dying! He's going to Hell, and it's my fault." Charlie had visited in her home and had tried to witness to her husband, but every time he went in the front door of their house, the husband went out the back door to his shop. He would not stay to talk to the preacher. He would say, "If I wanted to talk to that preacher, I would go and talk to him. I don't want to talk to him."

As Charlie sat in the hospital room talking to the lady, she told him this story: "When we were married, I knew my husband was not a Christian, and I tried to get him to go to church with me. He would get mad, so I finally just stopped going and stayed home to avoid arguments. Our children came along, then our grandchildren, and one day one of our grandsons went to your church and made a profession of faith. I went to see him baptized and decided I was just going to be faithful and go to church every Sunday. I would ask my husband to go, but he would get upset, so I would just go without saying any more about it. I knew I needed to witness to him, but I didn't.

"Then today he began having trouble with his heart. I was riding in the ambulance with him and I thought—I need to witness to him—but I didn't want him to get upset and die before we got to the hospital. Then they took him into the operating room and I thought—I need to witness to him before he goes in—but I didn't want him to get upset and maybe have another heart attack before they could help him. So I waited, and now he has lost consciousness. I know he's lost, he's dying, he's going to Hell, and it's my fault!"

The man did not gain consciousness and he died. What a tragedy for his wife, who had lived with him for over fifty years!

During our tenure at Highland Park in Texarkana, from 1974 to 1978, we did several "big" things. We had a couple of revivals with Charles Massegee and his team, we had a revival with James Robinson, and we had Bob Harrington, "the Chaplain of Bourbon Street" in our church. For that meeting, Charlie put a large ad in the newspaper, announcing that Bob Harrington would be speaking.

The church was packed for this meeting. Many people not associated with our church came because they saw the advertisement about the service in the local newspaper.

A man in our town who was not a Christian read the ad. He had always said, "If I ever get to hear Bob Harrington, I'm going to get saved." When he saw that ad, his fate was fixed. He came to our church that night, accepted Jesus as his Savior, and is still serving faithfully at Highland Park Baptist Church. There were many decisions that night, but R. H. Caplinger's was the most memorable.

16
A SHORT STAY IN JOPLIN

Charlie was called to pastor the North Main Baptist Church in Joplin in 1978, and between the time that we were called to the church and when we arrived, almost half the people left the church. There was a big split and Charlie spent a lot of time building them back up again. God used him again to heal a rift among the people. This had become his ministry—to go to a church that was hurting and help them to love again. He used the bus ministry to bring people in, as he had done in the past. The church bought a couple of used school buses, painted them, and began a program like the ones Charlie had led before.

Steve and Debbie were in college at Baylor, and David and Cindy attended school at Webb City, while I taught reading at Carl Junction. Webb City and Carl Junction are two little towns near Joplin.

David was a high school senior during that year. He joined the swim team and participated in their swim meets. He was still active in journalism and worked on the school paper, as he had in Texarkana. He also took park in the drama department and had a lead role in the school production of <u>Mash,</u> the same play Steve had been in while we were in Texarkana, but in a different role. David earned a lot of recognition, even though he entered the school in his senior year. He told us later that he had a whole list of girls he had planned to date at Texas High during his senior year, but that was all ruined when we moved to Joplin. But he found there were girls in Joplin, too, and he dated a nice girl that year.

Also, during that year, Steve graduated from Baylor University. He asked us for a special graduation present, a ticket to ride a plane to ten different cities in the United States. With this special three hundred dollar ticket a person could get on and off the plane ten times and visit any big city that he wanted to see. Steve had always said he wanted to travel, so we got him the ticket.

He went to Dallas, New York City, Chicago, Miami, Mexico City, and several other cities. But when he got to Los Angeles, he called us and said, "I'm going to stay here," and asked us to ship his clothes to him. It was a sad night for us when we packed up his clothes and the other things he wanted, and mailed them to him in Los Angeles.

He worked with an advertising agency for a couple of years. Then he moved to Cologne, Germany, where he taught English as a second language, and began working as a pianist and songwriter. He wrote an operetta and he has business relationships with several singers who perform with him regularly. He has become very fluent in German and has lived and worked in Cologne since 1982. He also works as a translator, using his language skills to translate documents from German to English or vice-versa, for many products. When you buy something and see the directions written in German, it might be something Steve has done! In addition to written documents for products, he has done several voice demos, and had built up a pretty good business with people who depend on him for this service.

Our year at Joplin was a traumatic time. Shortly before moving to Joplin, we learned that our son, Steve, was gay. That summer, Steve was living and working in San Antonio and we drove there to visit him. Cindy was thirteen, and she was walking around his apartment looking at things on his shelves when she found a notebook lying on top, so she picked it up and began to read. In it, Steve outlined some of his feelings. She brought the notebook to me and said, "Mom, what does this mean?" I read a few paragraphs, then took it to Charlie and as we read it, we realized that Steve was gay. I think he left that notebook lying there so we would find it, so we would know.

It was the furthest thing from our minds to even suspect that this might be a possibility. We knew he had been unhappy at times, but never imagined that his sexuality was a problem for him. He enjoyed things that most boys didn't—he loved to play the piano and to read, he loved drama, he even liked to cook, and he never liked to play sports, but in spite of all this, we had really never thought of his being gay.

He had been struggling with this knowledge for several years. We learned that the youth director at the church in Miami and some of his best friends in the youth group had ostracized him. When he was struggling the hardest, he went to his youth director for help, and was turned away and rejected by those he trusted. He did not come to us. At one point in his life, while we were in Texarkana, he went to a trusted friend, Beverly Massegee, and confided in her, but he asked her not to tell us, so we did not know.

So we learned that his graduation trip had been a time when he wanted to "see the world" and decide which city he wanted to live in as a gay man. While he lived in California, he met some people from Germany. He learned German on his own and decided to move to Europe, where the gay lifestyle is accepted more than it is in America.

He was open with us and answered any questions we had after we learned that he was gay. We talked together a lot as we worked through that difficult time. As we served in Joplin that year, sometimes while driving we would see a child that reminded us of Steve, and both of us would break down and cry.

He told us that one of his deepest regrets was that he would never be a dad. He loves children and they love him. All the nieces and nephews look forward to seeing him when he is in the states.

We love him and accept him for who he is. We know he was saved as a little boy, and we feel that his salvation is real. He attended church in Los Angeles and played the piano for church until the pastor told him he could no longer do it because of his gay lifestyle. That was another rejection he had to deal with.

We have been able to visit him in Germany twice and he has been back home several times. We talk with him on the phone and communicate by email to keep in touch. He is our son and we love him. He has a good relationship with his brother and sisters. We regret that he felt he had to go away from our family because of his gay lifestyle.

Steve is well known and accepted by people in Europe, and has made a name for himself there as a musician. He plays concerts and accompanies singers. Many of the people he works with are people he has worked with for years.

One day, Debbie called her dad at the church office in Joplin. She was having a particularly upsetting time and she wanted us to come to see her. Charlie could not go, but he said, "Mom can come." He came to my school and told me I needed to leave right then and go to see Debbie. It was about eleven o'clock in the morning. I went to the office, told them I needed to leave, went home and packed some clothes, and was on the road by noon, heading for Waco.

Before I left, Charlie had given me special instructions. He said, "I don't want you to get lost. If you will just stay on I-35 south, you can make it. Don't get off 35 South." So the last thing on my mind and the only thing I thought about was 35-South.

I arrived at Debbie's at about 11:30 that night. It was her senior year in college, she and her boyfriend had just broken up, and she was having a difficult time. We visited and I fixed some food for her freezer while she went to class. When she was feeling better, I decided to head back home so I could be back to work on Monday.

When I started to leave, it was in the evening. I was going to go to my parents' house in Dallas, spend the night, and go on to Missouri the next morning. I remembered Charlie telling me to stay on 35-South, so I went out to the interstate and got on 35-South.

After about an hour of driving, I began to notice that I had not seen any signs about Dallas. So I pulled into a service station and asked, "How far is it from here to Dallas?"

"Lady, which way are you going?" the attendant asked.

"I'm on 35-South," I said.

"Well, lady," he said, "you're heading for Austin. If you want to get to Dallas, you'll have to turn around and take 35-North."

I said, "But my husband told me to take 35-South."

He just shrugged and said, "You can go south if you want to, but Dallas is north of here."

So I turned around and went the other way. Sure enough, I got to Dallas.

During our time in Joplin, Charlie continued to do the things he had done in other churches. When we came and found that half the people had left, the church had a big debt. They had just finished an educational building. So he helped them to get a debt consolidation so their expense would be smaller.

The bus ministry was used to bring people in, our friends, Charles and Beverly Masssegee came to do a revival, and decisions were made for Christ.

We had a World Missions Conference at our church in Joplin, which is sort of like a revival meeting with missionaries speaking about their life and work, a different one each night. One of our missionary friends came to preach at one of the meetings.

He knew of a church that needed a pastor in DeSoto, Missouri, so he asked Charlie if he could recommend him for that position.

Charlie agreed, and after the committee came to hear him preach, they asked him to come to First Baptist Church, DeSoto, Missouri, in view of a call.

We drove to DeSoto, near St. Louis, a little "bedroom community" as Jim Wilkins called it, to talk to the committee and to preach.

During the meeting, one of the men in the church came in and said, "Bro. Nobles, I want to ask you a question. Do you think drinking a beer once in a while will send you to Hell?"

Charlie said, "No, but it will make you

smell like it." Jack Gannon thought that was a perfect answer and from that time, he has been a supporter of Marvin Nobles.

The railroad was in the center of town, the largest employer there. Lots of people in DeSoto drove to St. Louis to work; hence, the name, "bedroom community." Jefferson County was about forty-five minutes south of the city. We were to learn much about Jefferson County, because DeSoto came to be the place where we stayed the longest. That's where we still live. We moved to DeSoto in July, 1979.

Our son, Steve

17
EMPTY NEST

During the first business meeting after we arrived at First Baptist Church, DeSoto, we granted church letters to one hundred thirty-five people. There had been a huge problem with the former pastor and all those people went to start another church in town. We learned that people had been leaving for a couple of years prior to the big exodus that happened in 1979.

First Baptist Church was in need of healing, and Marvin Nobles was the man God called and used to get the job done.

At every service he would say, while we were welcoming visitors, "Turn to somebody near you and tell them you love them. Give them a hug and really mean it!" For some of the people, that was a hard thing to do because they were hurting. Many friends were gone and there was bitterness among the people because so many of their friends had gone to other churches.

Several years later, when we got to know the people better, one of our good friends said to my husband, "You wanted us to hug people and say we loved them and we didn't want to love them! We were hurt and mad and we wanted to stay that way!"

I used to wonder why the Lord kept sending us to churches that were in decline, churches where the people were mad and hurting. I came to realize that the calm, caring, loving personality of Marvin

Nobles was what was needed to turn them around. So that was why God sent us there.

God led Charlie to cause the people to start loving again. Even now, people talk about the change that came to First Baptist Church DeSoto while Marvin Nobles was pastor, from 1979 to 1984.

David had graduated from high school in Webb City, so he started to Baylor the September after we moved to DeSoto in July. A journalism major, he worked on the University newspaper while Debbie continued to take part in productions done by the opera department at Baylor. Cindy attended DeSoto High School for three years. She acted and sang in school plays, Annie Get Your Gun and Oklahoma being the most memorable.

We had lots of good times at DeSoto. I led a youth Bible study at our home right after we moved there, and we had lots of kids coming. Some of the kids who came are still active in our church. A couple of the young men who were youth then are serving as Deacons now.

I also taught a young adult Sunday School class that started with only eight people and grew to around 35 when we divided the class. Charlie's belief about church growth with Sunday school was "you divide a class to grow it bigger". So when a class reached a high number, he wanted to make two classes out of it to reach more people.

Some of the people in that class are leaders in First Baptist DeSoto today. Others from that class have moved their membership and are serving in various churches in our county. Several made decisions to accept Jesus as their Savior. Jacque Charlton was one of the first ones in the class to make that decision. She remains a good friend, and sends us a note on her "spiritual birthday", thanking us for introducing her to her Savior, Jesus.

Mary Jo Linhorst and her husband were members at another Baptist Church, but they came to the couple's class and joined First Baptist by letter. Mary Jo's mother had been a worker with Child Evangelism Fellowship, so Mary Jo had worked with children all her life. Gradually she began working with the children in First Baptist DeSoto. As the years went on, Charlie encouraged her to listen to the Lord and she surrendered her life to full-time Christian service. She was able to get most of her seminary work done and has been on staff at First Baptist as Children's Director for many years. She told Charlie, "thank you for pushing me gently to become who I am today."

Mary Jo began making some big changes, which is when the big attendance in Vacation Bible School began. We began having more and more in VBS. The attendance for the summer Bible program grew to about 700 at one time. Children from all over town come to Vacation Bible School at First DeSoto.

An annual citywide revival was begun. Several of the Baptist churches in and near DeSoto went together, rented a tent and erected it in a central location in town. All the pastors worked together to reach people for Jesus. Many decisions were made because of these meetings.

We had several full-time evangelists who preached and did music for the citywide revivals. Some of them were Brad and Becky Ramsey, Bob Elliott, Jack Stanton, Jerry Spencer, Clifford Palmer, and Charles and Beverly Massegee. The pastors in town continued the group revivals for a few years after Charlie was no longer the pastor of First Baptist Church.

One of the most effective things that was done during Charlie's tenure at DeSoto was a program of enrolling people in Sunday School wherever they happened to be. This was the *ACTION* plan for Sunday School, developed by Andy Anderson when he was a pastor in Florida. He later went to the Sunday School Board and made it available for all churches in the convention to use.

Because Charlie believed in getting the town's attention with the church, he wanted to send out occasional mailings to everybody in town to let them know what was going on. One of the members of the church who was a retired mail carrier came to an outreach committee meeting. He looked at a street map and told the committee the name of every family in town and where they lived. Darrell Girardier's memory helped us get the news out to every family about things that were going on at First Baptist Church.

Cards were filled out for each family. Then when people went out to visit, they would take the card with that person's name on it, go to the house, and ask if they attended church regularly anywhere. If not, the visitor would ask if he or she could enroll them in Sunday School at First Baptist. Some of them didn't, but a lot of them did. Their names were put on the class rolls and the teachers would send them cards and go to visit them. As a result of this cultivation of the people, many of them came and made decisions to accept Jesus.

Charlie took several of the kids and adults on a mission trip to Independence, Iowa to help a church there. They continued the work in that town for several summers, doing backyard Bible clubs, taking a religious census, and performing puppet shows for the children. They also did a worship program every night, inviting people from all over the town to attend.

Charlie divided the volunteers into four groups and sent each one to a different park in the town, where they did a Backyard Bible club and visited in the community. It was very hot during the summer when they were doing this. One of the men, Ted Francis, said, "We were in that hot park working, and Marvin got to drive around in his air-conditioned car bringing us cold drinks. I think he got the best job!"

Janis, a young lady who had grown up in DeSoto, came back home with her two children, after divorcing her husband, and began attending church regularly. Later her ex-husband came to town, to try to win her back. Charlie counseled them and eventually he officiated when they were remarried, reuniting their family. But before that, he won the man to the Lord.

It was a day we won't forget when Rich Terry came down the aisle, weeping, sobbing, giving his heart and life to Jesus. He knelt at the front pew and poured out his heart as he accepted Jesus into his life.

One Wednesday night, Charlie and Cindy went to church early. I planned to drive down to church a little later, but as I stood on the porch watching them drive away, I noticed the sky was murky and green and the wind began blowing pretty hard.

Before they could get there, which was only a few minutes drive, the wind got pretty fierce. Upon arriving at the church, they decided to wait awhile in the car, since the wind was worse and limbs were falling all around.

When a tree fell over on the top of car and then went down over the top of the hood, blocking the windshield, they became alarmed. Thinking it must be a tornado, Charlie told Cindy to lie down in the seat and he placed his body over hers to protect her as much as possible. Trees continued to fall and the wind whistled. Her little car rocked as the wind blew, making them even more alarmed.

After the wind stopped, there were trees on each side of the car and large limbs covered the top and windshield, which caused them to have a hard time opening the doors. They went into the church and discovered that part of the roof was gone.

We learned later that it *had* been a tornado. It went over the church and down a hill, where it hit one of the buildings in town. A man who was working inside was killed, and a lot of things in town were torn up. Our home, high on a hill where the tornado didn't hit, was unharmed. The church roof was damaged and some other repairs had to be done to the church as a result of the dangerous weather.

The winter of 1982 was most memorable. On the morning of January 30, the town of DeSoto woke up to twenty-four inches of snow! We had never seen anything like that!

It was Sunday morning and time for church, and the roads were impassable. We lived only a few blocks from church, so I put on my high boots (the snow was deeper than the height of my boots) and we dressed as warmly as we could, and walked to the church. Our music director and his wife, Marvil and Melba Hawkins, managed to get there in their car.

Our church had a radio ministry, so we went to the sound booth and did a broadcast from there. People who remembered to tune in could hear the Sunday morning service that day, even if we were not able to assemble together.

School was closed the next day, and the next, and for many days. I set up my quilting frame in the front bedroom and hand quilted almost a whole quilt before we were able to go back to school!

Cindy and her dad were always kidding each other while she was in high school. One day while they were in the kitchen, Charlie said, "Cindy, get me some coffee."

Cindy looked at him mischievously and said, "No!"

Charlie came back with, "If you loved me, you'd do it."

Cindy, a twinkle in her eye, said, "Uh-uh! My mama taught me not to fall for that line!"

One summer while Debbie was staying with us between semesters at Baylor, she got a role in a play at Jefferson College. She was driving to a rehearsal, about fifteen miles from DeSoto. Her car had Texas license plates, and as she drove through Hillsboro, a little too fast, a patrolman stopped her. He walked up to her car and said, "Young lady, I see you are from Texas."

"Yes, sir," Debbie said politely.

"Well, tell me, then," the officer went on, "do they have speed limits in Texas?"

"Yes, sir, they do," she replied.

"And do you obey the speed limits when you are driving in Texas?" he continued.

"Yes, sir, I try to," Debbie said respectfully.

"Well, please, if it would not be too much trouble," he continued, "would you try to obey the speed limits while you are in Missouri, too?"

She assured him that she would try, and he did not give her a ticket.

After Cindy graduated from DeSoto High School, she attended Baylor for one year. Debbie and David were attending Baylor, too, so we had three kids there. Steve had already graduated.

That was really hard for me—to see my last child leave home. I had to stay at home because school was starting at Hillsboro School where I taught, so Charlie drove Cindy to Texas with all her belongings to get her settled. I was crying when they left. I worked in the yard all day, and kept on crying. The tears just wouldn't stop.

Later that afternoon I had to go to the bank for something, and I was still very emotional. The president of the bank in our little town noticed that I was very upset and spoke to me. I was still teary and I said, "Please excuse me. I just lost my daughter."

The man knew who I was because his children had attended high school with Cindy and he knew her from the school plays, but I had not met him personally. He touched my shoulder, and with a sympathetic, shocked expression on his face, he said, "Oh, I'm so sorry!"

"Yes," I said, "she just went away to college."

The next look he gave me was not so sympathetic! I'm sure he thought I was a little out of my mind, and that day, I probably was.

Debbie and Cindy lived together in an apartment in Waco, but it didn't work out too well. Cindy didn't want a boss while she was there, and she said Debbie, the big sister, wanted to tell her what to do. She only attended Baylor one year.

During her second year of college she went to Missouri Baptist in St. Louis and met Jack Scanio, and they were married. David had met Margaret Rush when he started to Baylor. They dated all through college and were married the day after their graduation from Baylor that same year.

When Debbie graduated from Baylor University, Charlie was invited to wear his Master's regalia and participate in the graduation ceremony by leading in one of the prayers. We decided that was only fair, since we had three kids in Baylor at one time, and three graduated from there. We had a lot of money invested in that school!

After Debbie's graduation from Baylor, she taught school in a small town near Austin, Texas, where she met Jeff DeGroot. They were married in 1985.

Debbie with Juanita and Charlie at her college graduation

18
A NEW DIRECTION IN MINISTRY

The Director of Missions for Jefferson County, James Enoch, had been in that position for thirty-five years. When the time came for him to retire, he asked Charlie if he could recommend him as his replacement. After some prayer and consideration, Charlie agreed. He was called as Executive Director of Missions for Jefferson County, Missouri, in 1983, where he remained until his own retirement in 1994. We were able to continue living in our home, the first time we had not had to move when Charlie went to a new position.

Someone had donated the money to build a swimming pool, so one of the first things during Charlie's tenure as D.O.M. was to build the pool and a swimming program was begun. They already had a large summer baseball program, so this added to the recreational side of Jefferson Association's assets. Computers were introduced in the office, and the secretaries learned to use them, but Charlie's goal was to retire before he had to learn how to use the computer. He had a good system with file folders, and he wanted to keep it that way.

He thought of that—keeping it that way—when he was called to help arbitrate a business meeting at one of the smaller churches in the Association. One of the men at that church said, "Ours is a little country church and we like it that way." They were not interested in learning new ways to reach people because they liked things the way they were.

We enjoyed visiting the different churches, sometimes to sit and listen, but most of the time he would preach and many times I was asked to sing. We loved the people. It was a wonderful time in our lives, one of the most blessed, to serve the association and get to be in all the churches. Charlie had one sermon called "The Victorious Christian Life" that he tried to preach in every church in the association. I marked my Bible with the date and name of the church until I ran out of room in the margin on that page.

While he was Director of Missions, Charlie was called on to preach or serve as interim pastor many times. We were at Highland Baptist Church near Hillsboro on a Sunday morning when he was to preach and I was to direct the music and sing. I made up a program of songs and planned to sing "Holy Ground" just before the sermon. I planned to say, just before the tape started, "God said, Moses, take off your shoes. You are on holy ground."

Everything went according to plan. I sang the song, the people smiled, and I sat down, and Charlie preached.

When church was over and we drove away, Charlie turned to me and said, "Hey, what did you do to old Moses this morning?"

"What do you mean?" I asked.

Charlie said, "Well, you said, 'God told Moses to take off his feet because he was standing on holy ground.'"

I refused to believe that I had said that. So that night when we went back for the evening service, I asked one of the ladies we knew pretty well, whose husband was the sound man, "Did I say 'Moses, take off your feet' this morning?"

She broke up laughing. "You sure did," she said. "And this afternoon I figured out why Moses spent so much time up on that mountain. After he took off his feet, he got his stump stuck between some rocks, and he couldn't get back down!"

While I was teaching third grade at Hillsboro, I had a little boy who had to sit with his desk right next to mine, so that he would stay on-task. He was rather hyper and distractible, to say the least! When the kids were on break to get drinks and go to the bathroom, he would sometimes hit a child on the head and slam her face into the drinking fountain or start fights in the hall. We had lots of trouble with this boy, whose name was David, but the third grade teachers understood that his home situation was very bad, and most of his problems stemmed from that. Some of the students were not so understanding, though. One day a group of boys picked him up and stuffed him in the trash can in the bathroom!

Every morning the children gathered in their home room until a bell rang, at which time all the third graders moved to different rooms for special reading groups. I was taking roll and counting lunch money and doing all the things that a homeroom teacher has to do while the children were waiting for the bell. The students were not too quiet during this period of time, even though they were supposed to be reading or doing something at their desks. This little boy just could not stay still and he was away from his desk when the bell rang.

When he heard the bell, he ran to his desk, sat down in his chair, and reached inside the desk to get his reading books. When he pulled out his books, everything in his desk fell out with a loud thud! I went to his desk to see what was wrong. Everything in his desk was glued together. All his books, papers, pencils—it was a mess!

He said, "Oh, I guess I forgot to put the top on my glue!"

Since all his belongings were on the floor, I turned his desk over, and sure enough, there was an open bottle of glue. Glue was everywhere— covering the bottom of the desk, between all the books, dripping onto the floor—it was a total mess!

I began trying to help him get his books apart and found that it was an impossible task. As I tried to get my students out to go to their reading classes, and the reading students into my room, and clean up the mess, David looked up at me and said, "Does this mean I don't have to do any work today since I can't use my books?"

Another time, early in my tenure at Hillsboro, I would have the kids recite the Pledge of Allegiance to the flag every morning. But we didn't have a flag in our classroom. So I would point to a place on the wall where I planned to put a flag when I could get one, and said, "Look up there, pretend you see the flag, put your hands over your hearts, and we will say the pledge."

This continued for a long time until one day a student looked at me and said, "Mrs. Nobles, do we have to pledge allegiance to the wall again today?" I managed to get a flag after that because I thought it was important for students to know the pledge and to love our country.

While teaching reading at Hillsboro, there were two boys in one of my classes who caused quite a bit of trouble. No matter what I did, they managed to cause a disturbance. Finally, I reached my limit. I told one boy to scoot his desk to one side of the room, and I scooted the other boy's desk to the opposite side. One of the boys went home and told his mother that I had hit him and told him to shut up.

So the mothers of the two boys came to see the principal, arguing that I had upset and injured their children. The principal called me in and I told my side of the story. He called some of the other children, and they told what they saw, which substantiated what I had said. The mothers insisted that their boys were right, and the argument continued.

Finally, I said, "Ladies, let me tell you this. I am not lying because I'm a Christian. And 'shut up' is not in my vocabulary. I may have said 'hush', but I don't use the words 'shut up'." Shortly after that, the principal sent me back to my classroom, sent the mothers of the boys home, and closed the meeting.

Later that day I began thinking about what I said, so I went to the principal's office and said, "Was I out of line when I said I was a Christian?"

He said, "You were not out of line, because that is who you are. That's all you could say and I know it is true." I appreciated the fact that he stood up for me in that situation.

During Charlie's tenure as D.O.M., he decided to do something about Bates Creek Camp, our Associational Camp for the kids. It was run-down and rough, but the time for camps like that was becoming a thing of the past. People wanted more up-to-date facilities. Some of the old cabins didn't even have bathrooms.

When Charlie became pastor at DeSoto, one of the ladies was getting ready to take the girls to Girls' Week at camp and she was asking people to bring coffee cans to her. He asked her why she needed the coffee cans, and she replied, "We don't have bathroom facilities in the DeSoto cabin, and those little girls don't need to be traipsing around at night going to the bathroom, so I want one coffee can for each girl to have at night." He was amazed at this, and the first thing he did was to get men together to build showers and install toilets and sinks in the cabin. So the second year that we were in DeSoto, when it came time for camp, at least there were bathrooms in the cabin!

The camp building at Bates Creek where visiting camp personnel stayed was jokingly called "the Tiltin' Hilton". It really needed some work. Men came to volunteer and remodeled it, providing bedroom areas so that visiting pastors or missionaries would have a nicer place to stay.

There was one general restroom with about three or four stalls each for boys or girls, so another one was built in another part of the camp, making bathrooms more accessible.

The kitchen cooking facilities were updated, and the outside of the building was refaced. The whole camp was just generally updated. Later, after he retired, people began to build bigger, more elaborate cabins, and more work was done to make it a much better place for the kids to have camp.

After the camp was updated, churches began building bigger and better cabins, providing better facilities for the kids to stay in.

DeSoto also built a new cabin; actually, it's more like a lodge than a cabin. They honored Charlie by naming it the "Nobles Cabin."

Maryville University in St. Louis started a field-based program to help teachers get their Master's Degrees. The professors came to us and we attended class on campus at Hillsboro, one night a week for several hours.

Teachers from several schools in Jefferson County came together, and it was a good way for us to continue our education. All work was completed and I got my Master of Education degree in 1986, nine years before I retired from teaching in 1995.

I taught a few Masters' classes in the next years, as I continued to teach at Hillsboro. After I retired from Hillsboro in 1995 I taught a class or two every year for Missouri Baptist College and Southwest Baptist College, field-based in Jefferson County.

The Nobles family in 1979. Our 25th anniversary

19
SUNSHINE AFTER THE RAIN

Our daughter Cindy and her husband, Jack, lost a baby early in their marriage. They had been married several years when they decided to try in earnest to have a baby. Cindy had always loved babies and felt that she wanted to be a mother, but had not become pregnant.

She had ten procedures with artificial insemination during one year, but none of them resulted in a pregnancy. The next step was in-vitro fertilization, a $10,000 project. They decided not to go through with that, because there was no guarantee that they would have a baby, even with that.

The doctor discovered that she was becoming pregnant, but she would have a spontaneous abortion every time she conceived because her body was rejecting the fetus. As soon as the fetus attached to the uterine wall, her body would begin to reject it, and she would eventually have a miscarriage every time. Once she did become pregnant and carried the baby six months, and then lost it. She knew the baby would have been a girl, and she had a name for her—Mariah.

The heartbreak was almost more than she could bear, because she so desperately wanted to be a mother. Debbie married after Cindy did, and her babies came with no problem, so Cindy longed to find out why she could not do the same thing.

Cindy wrote this after the loss of Mariah as she dealt with her grief:

"Momma loves you." I gently spoke these words to you
when they told me you were growing inside me.
I was overwhelmed by the idea of you; by my love for you; by you.
You were my reason for living.
I wanted to give everything to you, to be everything for you.

"My baby is dead." The words rang inside my head.
I didn't want to believe it. I couldn't believe it.
But it was true.
I would never be able to give you anything.
All I had to give you was this: "Momma loves you, Mariah."

They tell me that they understand. "I know how you feel."
But they don't know. They can't know.
They have their babies here, alive.

I wonder how you would have grown, Your first words, your first steps.
Daddy's eyes, or mine? I imagine you in my mind.
I think of you with ever increasing sorrow.
I have so few memories, but I treasure them all in my heart.
They are all I have of you.

They tell me that someday I'll see you in Heaven.
They talk about a joyful reunion,
But they don't know the pain that I feel now.
They don't know the suffering that cannot be comforted.
I didn't know—until I held my dead baby in my arms.

There was a struggle between life and death on that warm August day.
You were fighting to hold on to life, but death would have its way.

You would have made our lives complete, but our eyes will never see
The life that we created, the life that ceased to be.
Our minds are full of questions and dreams of what might have been,
We'll always love you, Mariah, but we pray our broken hearts He'll mend.

I used to believe that joy was to feel your movements inside me,
The precious few kicks you shared with me,
The sick feeling from eating ice cream,
The swelling from eating pizza,
Then I began to believe that joy was in your short life,
The almost six months of your growth—
The wondering if you were a girl or a boy—
The dreaming about your future.

Now that you are gone I find joy in your memory, a bittersweet joy—
A joy mixed with sadness.
Thank you for these joys.
Thank you for making me a mommy.

I didn't talk to you when you were born.
I held your limp, lifeless body
And I didn't talk to you.

Did you know how much I wanted you?
The dreams I had for you?
The special way you made me feel?

I should have told you, but it hurt too much.
I should have held you close,
Caressed you, kissed you, talked to you.
But as I looked at you all I thought about was that you were dead.
So I'm sorry I didn't tell you how much I love you.
Please forgive me.

My arms are empty.
I have a daughter, but I cannot hold her.
My heart is empty.

I heard a baby cry today;
A small baby, a newborn.
With each cry I felt a tug at my heart, with each cry I loved you more.

I am so aware of babies now.
I listen for them wherever I am.
When I hear them crying, I am mesmerized,
I become one with their beautiful sound.
The rest of the world is shut out.
Oh, how I long for your cries!
I want to see you again, to touch you.
Mariah, why were you taken from me?
Will the pain of death never fade?

No one thinks about you anymore.
But I do.
Everyone says it's time to get on with my life. What life?
Everyone says I'm "doing so well". That's what they see.
Inside I'm destroyed. I feel defeated.
If they really cared about me, wouldn't they see?
Shouldn't they be able to tell that I'm pretending?
What could they do, though?
Nothing.
It wouldn't matter.
It doesn't matter.

All my life when I had a really big problem, Daddy would fix it.
"Daddy do it," I used to say when I was a little girl.
I called Daddy yesterday.
I wanted him to say something, to do something to fix it.
Daddy can't bring my baby back.
Daddy can't ease the overwhelming pain in my heart.
Daddy doesn't even know what to say to me.
Where do you turn when Daddy can't fix it?

My mind fills with confusion as I sit beside your grave.
The questions that will never be answered grow in my mind.
Life seems so pointless.
It's not worth the struggle.
When will it end?

Memories of the way you touched me swim inside my head.
The memories I long for, the memories I dread.
Always when I think of you my heart will throb with pain;
If the pain reflects my love for you I pray it will always remain.
Realities of your life and death haunt my troubled mind.
I am plagued with sorrow.
Joy has been left behind.

In every waking moment Mariah is the theme.
Even sleep cannot console me for I see her in my dreams
Are my feelings of loneliness and love for you ever going to subside?
The pain will fade, they say, with time.
The love will never be denied.
How can I go on with life knowing Mariah is gone?
The emptiness inside me lingers, but my heart to her belongs.

All my life I've dreamed of having a family;
a husband, children, a life.
When Mariah died, my dream died.
If I never dream, I'll never fall short of my dreams,
But if I never dream, I'll never live.

So many things in this world happen without explanation.
Life goes on.
I know there's no reason.
I know no one is to blame.
But still I sit here wondering day after day.

It hurts so much to see people all around me living their lives,
While I just sit alone and cry.

The pain inside grows deeper every day.
My heart just keeps on breaking.
"Stop the hurting!" I pray.
Someday I'll realize that it doesn't hurt to think of you.
Until then I'll count the memories.
It's all that I can do.

So many things in this world happen without explanation.
People forget.
Life goes on.

It should be my baby crying in the nursery.
It should be my baby everyone is exclaiming over.
It should be my baby being dedicated to God.
It should be my baby being rocked in her mother's arms.
My baby should be bringing me immeasurable joy,
Not bringing me unbearable sorrow.

After reading this poem that Cindy wrote, one is better able to understand the deep grief that a woman goes through when she realizes that she cannot bear a child.

They decided to adopt. They registered with the Missouri Baptist Children's Home and with some other agencies for adoption, and then they waited. Several times they got a call and were told that they were next in line for a baby, but then the girl would decide to keep her baby, and the tears would begin again. One time the girl even had an abortion, which caused Cindy to have deep stress.

Once she and I were sitting in the parking lot of a grocery store when we heard a woman yelling at her child, even hitting the child, and Cindy lost it and became extremely emotional. She wept bitterly and said, "Why can other people have babies and I can't? Why can people who even mistreat their children have more babies, and God won't let me have one?"

Charlie had been on the board of a Crisis Pregnancy Center in Jefferson County, and they knew of our daughter's search for a child. One day a 32-year-old woman came to the center for a sonogram, planning to have an abortion. When she saw the baby on the screen, she said, "This baby is alive! I can't kill this baby." She asked the director if she knew anybody who wanted a baby, and the director at the Center did. She called us to tell us about it, and we called Cindy.

The birth mother affirmed that Cindy and Jack could have her baby, a little girl. She was due in February. The baby came in November, way too early, but they were able to keep her in an incubator and she grew and thrived. Marissa Nicolette Scanio was Cindy's baby, but she could not take her home until she was stable.

For three months Cindy and Jack waited, without any assurance that the baby would be theirs. The birth mother could change her mind at any time. Since she was so small, not quite four pounds, Marissa had to stay with a foster mother after her release from the hospital. This lady was also a nurse, because the baby had to wear a heart monitor and be watched very carefully. Cindy and Jack could go to see her, and they could hold her, but they could not take her home. Cindy gave the foster mother a small camera, and said, "Would you please take some pictures? If I get to keep this baby, I'll have pictures of her from the beginning. If something happens that we don't get her, give the pictures to the ones who take her." She was afraid to hope because of many disappointments in the past. She said, "I won't believe she's mine until I can take her home."

Marissa only weighed three pounds, fourteen ounces at birth, but by Feburary 1, at the age of three months, she weighed eight pounds, the size of a newborn. That's the day they got to take her home.

They had painted her room with bright, primary colors, and prepared it with everything they needed, but they knew that the birth mother could still take her back at any time before the adoption was finalized. When they went to court and Marissa was theirs, they were thrilled to take her home and be her legal parents.

Marissa quickly caught up and developed as a normal child. Cindy worked with her, read her books, gave her mind-stimulating toys; she spent every moment with her.

But six years ago, when Marissa was eight, Cindy became pregnant again. This time when she went to the doctor, they had some answers for her. She still had the condition, which caused her body to reject the fetus, but medical science had developed a method to help a woman like her carry a baby to term. She was given a medicine that tricked her body into thinking it was not really pregnant, so that the baby could continue to grow. Every three months she had to go to the hospital and stay all day, hooked up to machines, to receive the medical treatment that enabled her to continue carrying the baby.

Charles Glenn Scanio was born in August, 2003, a perfect baby. Cindy was forty when he was born, and doctors feared that something might go wrong. But God blessed and he is fine.

Little Charlie, as we call him, is such a joy. He is a fast learner, a musical child, and we thank God for him.

Truly he and Marissa are the sunshine after the rain that came in Cindy's life for so long.

Cindy, Marissa, and Chachi

20
A THOUGHT-PROVOKING QUESTION

One night in Bogard, Missouri, while Charlie was serving as pastor of the Baptist Church there, and still attending seminary, a Deacon's meeting changed the direction of his ministry.

One of the men, Bernard Cahill, raised a thought-provoking question. He said, "Suppose we all walked out of this meeting tonight, and locked the doors, and nobody ever came back to Bogard Baptist Church. How long would it be before someone in the community noticed that Bogard Baptist Church was not meeting? What are we doing to make a difference in this community?"

This is the question that my husband asked from then on, every time he went to a new place of service.

He began to be more accountable to himself. He made a personal goal of seventeen visits a week, with the intention of having one or more people ready to walk down the aisle on the next Sunday morning, to make a profession of faith, or to join the church by letter or statement.

I asked him why he chose the number seventeen, and he told me, "I kept a count of the visits I made for several weeks, then I averaged them, and that was the average. Some were hospital visits, they were not all evangelistic, but I chose that number as a goal for that reason."

He continued this commitment as long as he was pastor of a church.

Charlie always felt that the way to build a church was through the Sunday School. He would go around to all the classes and "check out" the teachers, to see if what they were teaching was doctrinally sound, and if they had an interesting teaching persona. He sometimes reorganized the Sunday School structure, making new classes, providing planning meetings for the teachers. At First Baptist DeSoto, he set up an organization of departmental coordinators for each age group, to give added help to the teachers in the classes.

A lady in the church at DeSoto was a very popular teacher, and her class was extremely large. All the ladies wanted to be in her class. So he asked Esther Cundiff to be the first Adult coordinator, helping to recruit and train the other adult teachers.

Coordinators were installed for each department of the Sunday school—Adult, Youth, Children, and Pre-school, with the teachers accountable to them. Thus, the organization was better and the Sunday School began to grow. As the Sunday School grew, so did the rest of the organizations in the church.

He had "Sunday School Revivals" where a noted leader in Sunday School work would come and preach for a series of meetings, helping teachers to learn to do a better job of teaching the Word, and making an impact in the Sunday School organization. The person doing the preaching would make a graph of the Sunday School and show the people where they were, whether they were growing and reaching people, and how to be more effective evangelistically as they taught their classes.

He used evangelists to do revival meetings that would get citywide attention. This was evident in Hannibal, Miami, Texarkana, and DeSoto, when Charles and Beverly Massegee led revivals in each of these places. A large number of decisions was made each time.

In all the churches where we served, we had revivals at least once a year, and sometimes twice. This was a large part of the evangelistic effort in Charlie's ministry.

He had Bob Harrington, the Chaplain of Bourbon Street, at our church in Texarkana, for a one-night meeting, where many decisions were made. This was something the people talked about for a long time and still remember.

Citywide summer tent meetings were held in DeSoto for several years. Pastors from nearby churches in Jefferson County all supported the meetings, and people came from all the different churches. These meetings continued for a few years after Charlie left the pastorate and became a Director of Missions. As churches worked together to have large, evangelistic meetings in DeSoto, many decisions for Christ were made.

He used the Action Plan of Growth for Sunday School, enrolling people in Sunday School wherever they happened to be. The old rule was that you had to attend Sunday School three times before you could become a member. With the new plan, a person could become a member without ever coming to church. It was up to the teacher and the people in the church to get them to come and find out what church was all about.

While Charlie was Director of Missions, he had planning meetings for church workers and for pastors. He divided the churches in our association into groups, graded by size, and had meetings for the pastors to help them in their work. Some of the pastors of small churches had not had the benefit of a seminary education, so this was a way to help them know how to handle some things they might not have learned about.

Because The Mississippi River ran through our county, he started a meeting called "Glorieta on the Mississippi" to help Sunday School teachers become better equipped to work in their churches. (Glorieta is a Southern Baptist Conference Center in Arizona where Baptists from all over the United States go to planning meetings to learn better methods and to learn about new materials.)

He had big things going for workers who wanted to avail themselves of learning opportunities. In addition to the planning meetings, worship services were scheduled where people from all the churches in the county could meet and worship together and get to know one another.

Marvin Nobles served as pastor or staff member from 1955 to 1983, when he became Director of Missions for Jefferson Baptist Association in Jefferson County, Missouri. He retired from Jefferson Association in 1994. For the next ten years, we took our camper with the BUDD builders and worked to build churches during the winter months.

Bud McBroom found the place to go, and it was our job to notify the people and get them there. About fifty couples were on the list, and we sometimes had thirty camping units parked around a church, while they were building a place for the people to worship.

Retired men who could do just about anything in the building trade came together to do this, but very few of them had ever actually worked in the building trade. We had men who had retired from teaching, from the military service, from the railroad, from the ministry, and only one or two who had actually spent their lifetime as builders.

21
SPECIAL MEMORIES

Shortly after our kids were married, before there were any grandkids, we were sitting in the home of David and Margaret in Longview, Texas, having Thanksgiving dinner. We had enjoyed a fine meal and were just talking—Charlie and me, David and Margaret, and Debbie and Jeff, who had driven up from Austin, Texas. Debbie and Jeff were experiencing a very hard time because Jeff had lost his job in Austin and, although he had tried, he couldn't seem to find another position similar to the one he had lost.

Suddenly Debbie said, "Dad, I don't think God answers prayer any more!" We were all startled by this outburst. Debbie had always had confidence in prayer, confidence in God, and we could hardly believe what we had just heard.

After a moment of shocked silence, Charlie said, "Why not?"

"Well," Debbie said, "Jeff has not found a new job. We've been praying for a job for several months now and he doesn't have one yet. And we've been praying for a baby, and there is no sign of anything there, either. I just don't think God answers our prayers any more."

We talked with her for a little while about it, and after we got back home, Charlie sat down and wrote her a letter about trusting God and having confidence in prayer. They continued to live in Austin and Jeff continued his follow-up of job leads.

In January, we got a phone call from Debbie. She said, "Dad, can you fly out to Shreveport and meet us as we drive through, and then drive our truck to North Carolina?"

"I guess I can. Why?" Charlie replied.

"Well," Debbie said, "Jeff got a job in Raleigh, North Carolina, with McDonald's hamburger chain and we are moving. He's driving a U-Haul, towing the car. I'm driving the truck, towing the boat, and I just can't drive any more because I'm sick all the time. I just found out I'm pregnant!

God really does answer prayer!

A.J. was born in 1987, Austin was born in 1989, Jensen Anne came in 1992 and Cole joined the family in 1993.

Debbie's quiver got full, too!

David and Margaret lived in Longview, Texas, with their children Daniel, who was born in 1987 and Sarah, who was born in 1992. David worked as an attorney and Margaret was a para-professional, working for a law firm doing medical research.

In 1996, David began feeling the call of God to go into the ministry. He talked with Margaret about it and they decided that he would quit his job with the law firm and go to the Seminary and prepare to be a Minister of Education.

Shortly after Daniel had learned of his parents' decision, he was sitting in the kitchen one day talking with his mother.

"Mom," he said, "when Dad is a minister, will he make as much money as a lawyer does?

"Margaret told him, "Well, after a few years, he will probably make as much as he is making right now, which is not really as much as a lawyer usually makes."

"Then we'll really be making less," Daniel said.

"That's right," Margaret told him.

Daniel thought for a minute, then said, "Well, that's all right, though, because if God wants Dad to do that, that's what we need to do. We need to do what God wants Dad to do."

Pretty good insight for a nine-year-old, I'd say!!

Early in 1997, they put a "For Sale" sign on their house and it sold in only two weeks and two days, without a realtor. David quit his job with the law firm and went to work at the First Baptist Church of Longview, as Minister to Singles and Minister of Outreach.

He got his seminary work done through Southwestern Baptist Theological Seminary in Fort Worth, doing a lot of it in field-based locations. He served next in Oklahoma City and now he is Minister to Singles at the First Baptist Church of Midland, Texas. The Lord has made them very happy with their decision to follow Him.

David worked with my dad some and learned about woodworking. He had a knack for it, so every time he got a chance, he was cutting, sawing, sanding, buying more tools, and making more things out of wood.

He has progressed to making elaborate pieces such as chests, tables, quilt racks, and even a whole bedroom suite for a man in his church.

Three grandsons were sitting at the breakfast table at our house in DeSoto on a spring morning, eating cereal. Two were seven years old and one was six. I was working at the stove, getting ready for other meals of the day, since all of them were visiting along with their parents.

Sewing, busily collecting quilt patterns and quilting a lot had recently captivated me. I had made baby quilts for each grandchild as he or she came along and was making plans to start some big quilts for them. My quilting book was lying on the table, so I said, "Boys, Grandma is going to make each of you a quilt that will be for when you grow up and get married. Would you like to look through my book and pick a pattern you like?"

Debbie's two boys, A. J., age seven, and Austin, age 6, excitedly said, "Yes, Grandma!" They went immediately to the big quilt book. First A. J. looked. He picked a big Texas Star pattern and said, as he jabbed his finger up and down on the page, "I want this one, Grandma, and I want the colors to be all pink and purple!"

Then Austin grabbed the book. He was a little more subdued as he looked through the patterns, then excitedly said, "I want this one," as he pointed to a Pinwheel pattern. "I want it in the colors right here on this page!"

I noticed that the other seven-year-old, Daniel, David's son, was quietly eating his cereal, not paying any attention to the two other boys. So I said, "Daniel, don't you want to look at Grandma's book and pick a design?"

He didn't even glance up. He just took another bite, chewed for a minute, and then looked out the window as he said, "No, I guess not. My wife will probably want flowers."

Another time, Daniel was watching me do some hand sewing. He looked puzzled, then said, "Grandma, why do you have to taste the thread before you put in the needle?"

We went to Germany to visit Steve during the summer of 1987. It was quite a venture for us. Charlie planned the trip, with a visit to London and Amsterdam along the way, because we thought we might not ever get back there. He had been in Amsterdam and Germany during the Korean conflict and wanted to revisit some of the places he had been while he was in the Army.

While we were in London, I thought the food was bad, but the coffee was really bad, in my opinion. At one restaurant I said to the waiter, "Don't you have any plain old American coffee?"

The waiter stood up straight and tall, a crisp white napkin over his arm, looked at me indignantly, and said, "Lady, you are not in America! You are in London!"

After being properly chagrined, I didn't ask again. But I sure wished for some better-tasting coffee, American or English!

I was always thirsty and looking for something cold to drink. But ice and cold drinks were nowhere to be found in Europe. And they don't drink water from the tap in Germany because they think the water is not healthy! If I ordered a coke, they would bring it without any ice at all. If I requested ice, they would put one or two small cubes in the drink and before the waiter could get it to me, the ice would be melted.

I thought I would die of thirst. I determined that if I ever went back to Germany, I would bring my water cup and I would find some way to get ice.

Five years later, in 1992, we went back to Germany. The first night we stayed in a hotel and there was a small refrigerator in our room. I thought, "Great! I can have some ice!"

I opened the freezer compartment door to see a small plastic tray about five by ten inches, with tiny cups for the water to make ice. Well, I did the best I could; I filled up the tray. The next morning I emptied the ice into my water cup, filled the cup with water, and started out. Steve was embarrassed to see me carrying my cup. He said, "Mom, don't bring that big old cup!" But I insisted, because I get so thirsty.

We visited several places, and I carried my cup everywhere. Lunchtime came and we went into a nice restaurant. I saw the waiter talking quietly to Steve, but they were speaking in German, so I went on to my seat.

Steve came to the table, thoroughly embarrassed, and said, "Mom, the waiter said to me, 'Why is she carrying that cup? Does she want us to put money in it?' He thought you were a beggar with your big old cup!"

I felt kind of bad, but not bad enough to get rid of my cup!!

After returning to the states from our second foreign trip, we were at Debbie's house telling her and her family about all the things we had seen and the places we had visited. Her two little boys, A. J. and Austin, listened as we talked. They had learned about Bible stories. They knew about Israel and the Holy Land, even though they were both pre-schoolers. Austin knew the story of David and his sling, and Phillistine giant Goliath, so he listened carefully as I told about being on the very mountain where David hid from King Saul and some of the other stories that we related.

Later that day Austin said to his mother, "I know Grandma and Grandpa saw some Israelites. Do you think they saw any Phillistines?" He was so little he could barely say the words, but he was learning about the stories!

Teach them to your children, and to your children after them. Deuteronomy 4:9(NAS)

Charlie's brother Ed and his wife went with us to Germany the second time. He took with him a map of the area where he had served during World War II because he wanted to look for some of the places where he had been during some of the battles in which he had fought so many years ago. One day we drove into Luxembourg and followed a road that was as close as we could find to the Seigfried Line where the American soldiers had been hiding, waiting to overcome the German soldiers who were hiding in bunkers along that road during a part of the war.

Steve and his friend went with us to help us try to find the place Ed was looking for. Steve drove our rented car out into the country along a road that seemed to lead nowhere, except to farms and more country. We did see several bombed out bunkers, but we could not locate the particular one that he was looking for. Ed looked around and said, "This looks familiar, but I just don't know. I guess we can't find it."

After awhile, Ed said, "Well, let's just go back. I didn't think we'd find it." As Steve began to turn around, Ed said, "Wait a minute! Up there! Go just a little further!"

We did, and Ed excitedly said, "This is it! There's the bunker."

Steve slowed and before he could get the car stopped, Ed, with his bad legs, jumped out of the car and began running in the direction of some trees. He looked around and saw the bunker was still there! The trenches where the German soldiers had placed their guns had not been filled in. There were indentions in the ground where the soldiers had stood with their guns braced. I walked down into one of the trenches and the top reached about to my shoulders. Trees had grown up on top of those trenches, which was why he could not recognize the place, but it was the very spot where he had fought during the war!

As Ed looked across the field, he said, "Right down there is a stream. That's where our company stopped and waited for the time to storm the bunker and take it over." Sure enough, there it was! He told us about some of the men hiding by the stream, sometimes submerged in the water, until they could move on up to do what they had to do—take the bunker.

Ed stood, amazed and awed, as he recalled the time he was a young man in the heat of battle, right in that very spot! As he thought about some of the men who did not get back home, he was very emotional. Tears filled all our eyes as we thought about the many young men who died on both sides of the war so many years ago.

Another of Charlie's brothers, Raymond, was working for the government at that time, stationed in Tel Aviv, Israel. So that was our next stop. We left Frankfort on an El Al Airliner and that was quite an experience! We arrived at the airport and all of the passengers on this particular flight were taken to an exit where we boarded a bus that took us out to the plane. Two armored tanks escorted the bus to the plane, and then stopped before we were allowed to disembark. The tanks rolled to a stop, guns were trained on us as we got off the bus and the tanks didn't leave until the plane took off. Everyone was subdued and a little bit scared, especially those of us who had never been to Israel before. We found out later that this is how all the El Al flights are monitored, and that they very rarely have hijackers on the plane because of their precautions.

I like to take lots of pictures, so I was rummaging through my bag to get my camera, and Charlie said, "Don't you dare get that camera out! Just get on the plane!" After we were on, I was seated next to the window and I did sneak a picture of the tanks through the glass.

We visited the Holy Land and many of the things we had read in the Bible came to life as we saw the places where Jesus and his disciples lived. Raymond took us all over and gave us a good tour of many places. We went on only one professional tour—into the Old City of Jerusalem and into Bethlehem. All the other places we went were narrated and directed by Charlie's brother.

It was the experience of a lifetime, and I am grateful that we had the opportunity to be in that place.

Charlie's brother, Raymond, is not an ordained minister, but he is very faithful in his church and in his service to God. He has been in the Military or has worked for the United States government all his life and has visited many different countries. Once, in one of the Eastern countries where Christians are not looked upon with favor, he met regularly with a group of Christians and led them in worship, under threat of being jailed. Wherever he has been, he has worked for his Lord and has been faithful to Him.

At one time his work sent him to Rwanda, Africa. Since he was there on a Sunday, he set out in his rented car to find a church so he could worship with the people. He got lost and in his efforts to find his way, he saw a radio tower on a hill. So he drove to the hill, thinking that he could look around and get his bearings.

He got out of his car, listened, and heard what he thought was Christian music. It sounded like a hymn. Even though he could not understand the language, he thought, "That must be coming from a church."

So he got in his car again and followed the sound until he came to a little church. He entered, and since the service was already in progress, he sat quietly on the back row.

A man came to him and spoke to him in English, and then the service continued. When it was over, the man who had spoken to him went to the front and said something to the people in their language. Then everyone turned and looked at Raymond, and the man said in English, "We have a visitor this morning and he is going to came and tell us about the churches in America."

Raymond stood, and as he walked to the front, he thought, "What can I say to these people?"

He remembered that in his pocket he had a little card with the basic premise of the F.A.I.T.H. outreach program that he was leading in his church. So he thought, "I'll tell them about this." (F.A.I.T.H. was a program developed for Southern Baptists meaning "Forsaking All I Trust Him." People attended classes for a number of weeks to learn this method of evangelism.)

Raymond pulled out the card and began talking about the words for which F.A.I.T.H. stood. The scriptures and facts on the card were the basic facts for the plan of salvation. So he began talking about what Baptists believe and what the Scriptures say about how to become a Christian and to be sure you are on the road to Heaven.

He gave the first point and the people nodded and seemed to be with him as the interpreter told them what he was saying. He gave the second point and the people gave him their full attention. When he was into the third point, he noticed an old man near the front, audibly crying.

Raymond thought, "I don't want to offend these people. Maybe I should stop." But something told him to continue. He went on, telling the people about how to accept Jesus and have a personal relationship with Him. More people seemed interested, so Raymond thought, "I'm going to give an invitation."

He began his plea, the pianist began to play softly as he explained how to accept Jesus as your Savior, and the people in the church began to respond. The old man who had been crying was the first to step into the aisle. Before the invitation was finished, fourteen people had accepted Christ as their Savior!

Raymond went away, not knowing what kind of church he had been in! But because of his witness, fourteen people now know Jesus personally and that church may be preaching a different message from now on.

I will exalt you, My God the King, I will praise your name forever. I will tell of your mighty acts. And I will proclaim your great deeds. Psalm 145:1, 4b, 6b(NAS)

When Debbie and her family lived in North Carolina, they had a big house surrounded by trees. On one side was a large lake and in front of the house was a long drive going out to the busy highway. In back of the house there was a large tree farm, and on another side was a place where dogs were bred and sold.

Cole, who was not quite three at the time, was supposed to be taking a nap, but he wasn't in his room and nobody could find him.

It had been a half hour or longer since anyone had seen him, and they began to worry about where he was and which way he had gone. He must have wandered away, and on every side of the house was something that could be a potential danger to a little one like him. Debbie got in the car and drove around, looking for him. The highway and the lake were especially dangerous, and everyone was running around, searching, and calling his name.

Suddenly they saw a large bearded man coming from the direction of the tree farm, carrying Cole. Thankfully Cole had gone the way of the least danger, and he was safe. God protected him and the woodsman, a modern Paul Bunyan, brought him home.

One morning Debbie was preparing breakfast, and her two youngest were not yet awake. Cole was not a year old, and Jensen was not quite two, and they usually made a lot of noise when they woke. Austin and A.J. shared a room with twin beds, and Jensen and Cole shared a room with two cribs. Debbie was enjoying the rare fact that they were "sleeping late", but after awhile she began to worry about them. She went upstairs, peeked into the room, and saw that Jensen's crib was empty. As she went further into the room, she saw that Jensen had climbed out of her crib, made her way across the room, and climbed up into Cole's crib. The two of them were there, playing together and having a great time! They were not hungry, but were happily playing, together in one crib.

David's daughter, Sarah, was five and her parents were signing her up for t-ball. She told her dad, "I want to be the catcher."

He said, "Sarah, that's the hardest job of all. Why do you want to be the catcher?"

"Because you get to wear all that neat stuff!" she said.

We were there during one of her games and she was wearing all that "neat stuff"—the face mask, the pads, etc. We sat right behind the fence and watched Sarah as she was "the catcher."

Our daughter Cindy's little one, Marissa, seemed to know the difference between her two grandmas. She would say she wanted to see the "black grandma" or the "white grandma." But her parents could not tell what she meant. She definitely had us separated in her mind, but why was she calling us "black" or "white"? It was a total mystery to all concerned.

Then one day, Marissa picked up two Barbies. In one hand she held a doll with dark hair, the doll in the other hand had blond hair. She said, "Two Barbies. Black Barbie and white Barbie!"

The light dawned! I had dark hair with just a little gray, and Jack's mother's hair was totally white! That's why we are the "black Grandma" and the "white Grandma".

After that explanation, I began trying to teach Marissa to call me "Grandma Nita" and Cindy began teaching her to call the other Grandma "Grandma Billie." She seemed to be getting it right. She knew when she would see Grandma Nita and Grandpa Charlie she had to drive a long way to get to our house. Grandma Billie and Grandpa Jack lived closer and when they would go to the Lake Condo they went with them.

But we knew she had it figured out when one day she said to her mother, "Grandma Nita makes quilts and Grandma Billie makes jello!"

Our youngest grandchild, Charlie, ran up to his mother (Cindy) one day after school soon after he started kindergarten. He said, "Mom, I was talking to my friend Gabrielle and I was telling her about Jesus, and she said, 'I don't know that person."

Then he continued, "I really need to tell her about Jesus, mom, because He loves her and she doesn't even know it!"

We went to see David graduate from seminary and as we got set up in our room at the hotel, I needed to get my laptop computer working.

I called the desk and asked if someone could come to my room to help me and be sure the computer was set up right.

The young man knocked on the door and came in. He looked all around, and seeing only an older couple, he said, "Who needs some computer help in here?"

"It's me," I said. "Come on in."

He looked around, puzzled, and said, "You?"

I said, "You didn't expect a grandma to need help with a computer?"

And he said, "No ma'am." (He could have been a little nicer—not making me feel so old.)

People are always confused when they see a grandma doing all this stuff with a computer—talking about wireless and HTML, internet and google. They don't expect a gray-haired woman to be busy on the computer. But this one is!

After we retired, Charlie did quite a bit of supply preaching in and around Jefferson County. He heard a joke and began telling it everywhere we went because the people enjoyed it so much. He would begin in all seriousness, and the people thought he was telling them something that actually happened, until they got the "zinger" and knew they had been taken!

He would say, "Juanita and I were on the way to church this morning, just driving along enjoying the ride, when we met one of Missouri's finest! We were just talking, and I was not paying attention to how fast I was driving, when suddenly I noticed this blue light in my rearview window.

"I pulled over and started to get out my license for the officer when I realized I had forgotten to buckle my seatbelt!"

Usually, at this point, the people would begin to look at me incredulously, as if to say, "He's telling us about getting stopped by the police!" You could hear an audible intake of breath as the congregation realized that this preacher was confessing to such an act!

Then Charlie continued, "So I grabbed that thing and buckled it, then got out my license and had it ready when the officer came up to my window."

The people would laugh, sort of embarrassed, and nervously wait for the next revelation.

"He took the license," Charlie would say, "looked at it, and said, 'Well, Mr. Nobles, any reason you are exceeding the speed limit this morning?'

"And I said, 'No, sir, I was just not paying attention. We were enjoying the scenery and talking and I didn't realize I was driving too fast.'

"By this time, he was up close to the window and he looked inside and said, 'Well, I see that you observe the seat belt law.'

"I said, 'Oh, yes, sir, I always remember to buckle up!'"

This always produced a lot of laughter throughout the congregation, because Charlie would show an honest face, professing his belief in the seatbelt law.

He went on, "Then I noticed that he had his head almost inside my window. He said, 'Well, tell me, then, do you always run your seat belt *through* the steering wheel like that when you buckle up?'"

At this point, the audience would always roar with laughter. They usually knew that this was just a story. Notice, I said <u>usually</u>. Sometimes people would ask later whether the story was true.

Once, we were at a fast-food restaurant in the town where we live when Charlie saw a preacher from another denomination who had been around town a long time looking at him strangely, as if he couldn't figure out who he was. Charlie was growing a beard at that time, preparing to be in our Christmas pageant at church, and the man kept on looking at him quizzically.

Finally, he said, "Are you Marvin Nobles?"

"Yes, I am," Charlie replied.

"Well, tell me then," the man said, as he stood up to shake his hand, "Is that seat belt story true?"

His reputation had preceded him! That preacher had not been in any of the Baptist churches where Charlie had preached, but the story had been told and retold until he wanted to know if it was really true or not!

Later, as we worked with the BUDD Builders, Charlie usually was asked to preach at some point during our stay with the group. One of the members, Jake Jones, would say, "Are you going to tell the seatbelt story? Because it's not worth going if we don't hear that one!"

Several years later, there was a sequel to the seatbelt story. Charlie had told that story in almost every church in Jefferson County and in many others as well, so he was famous for it.

I was driving back from Hillsboro after attending a Weight Watchers meeting. I had lost 5 pounds that week, so I was thrilled, and went to get a low-fat latte and head home.

A little way down the road, I saw a circling light like a police car behind me. I thought, "I didn't see anybody speeding, but evidently he's after someone, so I'll move over and let him go on."

But when I moved over, he pulled in behind me. Uh-oh, I was the one he was after!

I put the window down and got out my drivers' license, but as I looked in the rear-view mirror, I recognized the policeman. He was a man who had been a pastor at one of the Jefferson County churches while Charlie was Director of Missions. He came up to the car and I handed him the license. He looked at it, then looked at me, and said, "Juanita Nobles?"

I said, "Terry Michael?"

He said, "Any reason you were speeding today?"

I said, "I didn't think I was speeding."

He said, "You were doing seventy in a fifty-five zone!"

"Oh, my goodness," I said, "I have been at Weight Watchers and I had lost five pounds, so I was just drinking my low-fat latte and singing. I really didn't know I was speeding. I'm sorry."

He looked at me, looked at my license, and started tapping the license on his hand. Then he said, "Between Marvin and his seatbelt and you and your speeding, what's going to happen to Jefferson County?"

Then he said he would not give me a ticket if I would promise to put my speed control on and *WATCH IT*! I agreed, and we both went on our way. But my speed control was carefully set after that.

My dad served as bivocational pastor for churches in and around Dallas and North Texas for several years. At one time, they went to a little church in view of a call and mother went in and sat down while dad was talking to some men and getting ready for the service.

A lady came in, stopped at the pew where mother sat, and said, "Mrs. Preacher, you are in my pew."

Mother was startled and as she got up to move, the lady continued. "You just might as well know before we get started that this is where I always sit. Right here on the corner of the pew. The preacher knows that's where I sit and when I am not here, he is to come and see me that afternoon to find out what's wrong with me, because I'm *always* here unless I'm sick in bed."

Any time they went to a different church after that experience, she always asked, "May I sit here or is this someone's seat?" before she sat down.

After his death, my mother had an interesting, although terrifying experience. She lived in an area of Dallas where it was pretty dangerous. She was living alone, and all us children were encouraging her to move to a retirement home to be in a safer environment. She was active in her church and every week she drove some of the "older" ladies to their doctor's appointments. She stayed busy and was sought after by many.

One day, when she was about 85 years old, she heard a knock on the door. As she opened the door, a strange man came in, grabbed her in a hug and said, "Oh, Mrs. Wier, I'm so glad to see you again!" Another man came in behind him, so she had two strange men in her house.

She didn't know who these men were, and immediately thought, "Where is my purse?"

He told her his name was Cory and said that he had done some work on her roof a few years back when my dad was alive, and that his co-worker was out looking it over to see if anything needed to be done to update it. They asked if they could do anything—a leaking faucet, a squeaky door, anything they could do. Mother managed to excuse herself to go to the bathroom, and she went into the bedroom and hid her purse.

In a few minutes a third man came in and said, "OK, I've fixed the roof and the cost is $1800.00." They told her she had to pay them that amount of money.

Mother said she did not have that much money in the house, and Cory said, "My uncle owns the company, so if you will come with us and give him a check for $1800, we'll give you a kick-back on part of the money."

The neighborhood where the uncle lived was one Mother knew about, and it was even more dangerous that the one where she lived. She said, "I won't go to that part of town, but I have some money in the bank. I will drive to the bank and get the money."

They didn't want her out of their sight, so Cory said, "My partner and I will follow you in our car, and my boy will ride with you in yours. He'll go in with you while you get the money."

As she drove to the bank, a strange man sitting beside her, and two strange men following in another car, she was thinking, "What am I going to do?" She went up to the teller, asked for a piece of paper, and wrote on it, "*I NEED HELP.*" The teller took the note to the back, and came back with a manager, while another clerk called 911.

When the police car came up outside the bank, the two men who had started the job drove away, and so the police did not get them, but they did get the man inside. He said, "I don't know anything about this. They just hired me for today."

The Dallas paper wrote this up, praising an "elderly resident" for her quick thinking, and advising other senior citizens about the scam.

We are so thankful for her quick thinking. It probably saved her life.

Charlie came to me one day and said, "I just can't stand the thought of dying some day and leaving you because you get lost, you can't remember where you parked the car, you need me to help you—so I just prayed that the Lord would let you die first!"

I just stared at him for a minute. Then I said, "Boy, you are all heart, aren't you?"

Some time after that we were driving home from a trip to Branson, and I was in the driver's seat when I began to have severe chest pains. I had experienced this a few months before and had been in the hospital, but the pains were worse this time. It started in my chest and was moving up to my jaw and I was beginning to get a headache when I said, "I can't drive anymore. I feel funny."

Charlie looked at me and noticed that my face was very pale. I stopped the car and he got out and helped me move to the passenger seat, but the pain continued. He gave me two of his nitro pills and began searching for a hospital. We were driving on Highway 44, but had just come to a town, so he knew where to go pretty quickly. As he drove, he had his hand on my leg and I heard him whispering, "Lord, take care of her. Be with her."

We got to the Emergency Room and they got me in pretty quickly and began doing tests. They said the nitro was probably the best thing I could have taken. We stayed for several hours, doing tests and procedures to try to determine the cause of my problem. When I was released, they told me I had not had a heart attack, but I was to call my doctor and follow up when we got home.

As we got in the car and started home, Charlie was expressing how glad he was that I was doing better. I laughed and said, "Well, you did ask the Lord to take me first!"

He said, "Oh, but I repented of that! I didn't mean right now!"

Be careful what you pray for. You may get it!

David was ordained to the gospel ministry

22
CAMPING EXPERIENCES

We started camping because of Charlie's work with R.A.s.

He taught them camp craft, and we found that it was a cheap way to do family vacations.

During the early '60's while we were at Bogard we would often go to the "Going Out of Business" store in the nearby town of Chillicothe, Missouri, where we bought some inexpensive camping equipment. (There was a big sign on the front of that store which said, in big letters, **GOING OUT OF BUSINESS**. Then, in tiny letters at the bottom, it said, "**in 1969**".) Charlie could spend hours pilfering through the junk in that store, looking for some great treasure! He made a large box that would fit in the back of our station wagon and it held all our kitchen things—dishes, pans, and food—everything we needed to cook with while we were camping.

We used to love to go to the Crowder State Park at Trenton, Missouri, and we always tried to get the same spot; a large corner area where there was a lot of room for the kids to play. They would carry water to our campsite in a large plastic container and we had lots of fun "roughing it". We had a tent and an extra tarp to make a shelter over the table, cots and air mattresses, a lantern, and cooking equipment.

Charlie made all kinds of neat things for our campsite. He used a crooked stick to make a holder for the lantern that we hung in a tree and he carved poles to hold the tarp up, making a covering over our table. I learned to put liquid soap on the bottom of the cooking utensils,

217

making them easier to wash after being used to cook over an open fire. We made camper's stew and s'mores and had a lot of fun.

It seemed like it rained a lot when we went camping. More than once everything we had was soaking wet and there was no way to get it dry. We cooked on the back of the station wagon in the rain, sometimes. Many times we had to cut our trip short, go home, and spread everything out and let it dry.

One of our little trips became a casualty of the ever-present "schedule." We lived in Bogard and had planned to go camping on a weekend when there was a Brotherhood meeting in a town near Trenton, Missouri. So Charlie said he would take us to the park during the afternoon, get us all set up, we would have supper, then he would go to the meeting and come back and we would spend the next day there.

As we were driving to Trenton, I said, "Oh, no, we forgot Cindy's bottle!" Charlie looked at me and said, "Well, do you think we can wean her?" He meant, *"Do you think YOU can wean her?"* because he was not going to be there at bedtime, anyway. I thought, "She is a year old, I guess it's about time to wean her."

We never had any extra money, so it did not occur to me to go and buy her another bottle. So she got weaned in the tent. She rolled around on the tent floor and cried while Charlie was away at his Brotherhood meeting, but she never cried for her bottle again after that night. **We** weaned her!

We enjoyed going to one of the Missouri State Parks where Charlie would trout fish. While he was fishing one day at Bennett Springs State Park, Steve, Debbie, and David wanted to go exploring. "O.K.," I told them, "but don't get into the water."

They came back later, dripping wet, carrying their shoes in their hands. "What happened to you?" we asked them.

Steve said, "We fell in, but first I took off my watch, and we all took off our shoes, so they didn't get wet!"

We had lots of fun experiences camping. We liked to go trout fishing at Roaring River State Park. We loved to eat those fried trout! And Charlie loved to catch them.

Debbie was about five or six then. She caught a fish and she must not have understood that fish could only live in water. She was really proud of that fish. She kept it on her line and drug it around through the dirt. She thought that every time she would put it back in the water, it would swim. When it wouldn't swim, she called it "Dummard." She drug that poor fish all over the place, calling it Dummard because it wouldn't swim any more.

She told us later, after she was older, that she really thought that fish would swim whenever she put it back into the water. After all, that's what fish are supposed to do-- swim.

We had quite an experience once, before we even had a tent. We were out in West Texas, on our way to Carlsbad, New Mexico. Steve was about four, Debbie was around two, and David was just a toddler. Mary Kuhlman, a teenager in our church at Bogard, was along with us to help us with the kids. As we drove through a large, flat area with no houses or towns, Charlie saw a nice, clear open space and pulled off to make camp in that spot. We were just going to put our sleeping bags on the ground and sleep out in the open.

We got our stuff out and began unrolling the sleeping bags and blowing up air mattresses. Earlier in the day, we had stopped and Charlie had picked up some sticks to use to build a fire. He saw some rocks piled up and decided to build a fire on them because it would be easy to cook our supper there. He got the coffeepot out and had it filled with water, and was about to start the fire.

Steve had a little flashlight and was playing with it, shining it around, since it was getting dark. We were all busy getting things set up so that we could spend the night when we heard Steve say, "Daddy, there's a snake over there!"

Charlie shined his flashlight toward the place where Steve pointed, and saw a whole nest of snakes! He looked around at other spots and saw other snakes, then realized that we had pulled off into a gravel pit and it was working alive with snakes! Charlie said later that he knew that snakes like to make their homes in rock piles, but he didn't think about that when he pulled off the road into that spot.

We began frantically trying to get the air out of the air mattresses and get them back into the trunk of the car. Mary grabbed David and Debbie and jumped into the car. We managed to get into the car and get out of there. I remember Charlie saying, as we were hurriedly working to get things picked up, "The snakes won't hurt you if you leave them alone," but he said later he was just trying to calm us down.

We went on, but we had to spend the night somewhere. We had no money for a motel, and we had planned to camp, so we found a roadside park and put our sleeping bags on top of the tables and slept there. But we didn't sleep much. We kept waking up, looking for snakes!

We thought that God was surely watching out for us that night. If Steve had not seen those snakes and called our attention to them, we would have laid down and gone to sleep right there in the middle of them--and we might not have waked up!

We bought a used pop-up camper and then we really used it. When the canvas top wore out, we draped another tarp over that and kept on using it. We went to lots of state parks in that old camper.

We went on a little trip to the Diamond Mine in Hope, Arkansas, when we lived in Texarkana. We were going to dig for diamonds!

In the shop near the entrance we saw pictures of all the diamonds that had been found out in the big field. You had to buy digging tools and pans to shake out the dirt to see if you had found anything of great value. You could buy all sorts of stuff in that little shop, before you went out to dig for diamonds. We bought all our equipment and went out into the field to dig. It was hot that day, and we were walking over fields of dirt, looking for anything shiny. If we saw anything, we would kneel down and start to dig. After a while, we were all hot, tired, and disappointed that we had not found anything.

Then Cindy said, "I know where the diamond mine really is. It's in that little shop where you have to spend all your money to buy the stuff to dig with. That's where they take in the gold!"

We didn't have a camper while we were in Miami. Charlie had traded our old, beat-up camper for a set of golf clubs before we left Hannibal. Several of the people in our church knew we enjoyed camping, but that we had left our camper in Misouri. When it was time for our vacation, we were going to set out in our car. Then one of the families in the church said, "Why don't you take our Winnebago Motor Home since you like camping?" What fun that was! Cindy played with her Barbies, and David, Debbie and Steve played board games while we drove down the road. We discovered that we really liked "roughing it gently" in that nice motor home.

We went to St. Augustine, the Space Center, and Disney World. We told the kids to be sure and take good care of that camper. Charlie said, "Be sure to lock the doors when we're gone because we don't want anything to happen to this motor home. So, the last one out, be sure to lock the door."

It was a hot day, so we decided to stop at a little orange juice stand and get a cool drink. Charlie drove the camper close to the orange juice stand and parked. He thought we would just step off, get the drinks, and get back in the camper, so he left the keys in the ignition. But he forgot to mention that to the rest of us. Steve was the last one out, and he carefully locked the door to the motor home!

While we were drinking our orange juice, a thunderstorm came up and before we knew it, we were getting drenched! We ran back to get in the motor home and the door was locked! We ran back to the orange juice stand, but they were closing, so there was nothing to do but to stand in the rain. We had to find a phone, call a locksmith, and wait in the rain until we could get back in. But we couldn't blame Steve because he was just doing what his dad had said to do. We took good care of that motor home!

Charlie never used to wear shorts while we were camping, or any other time, either. I didn't dress the girls in shorts very often in the early years, and I didn't wear shorts, either. As the years went by, we began wearing them, but Charlie wore black socks and dress shoes with his shorts.

One day, after all the kids were grown, David took Charlie aside and said, "Dad, I'm going to help you learn how to dress. When you wear shorts, you don't wear black socks. And you don't wear those shoes! You have to get some little short white socks to wear with your shorts, and get some tennis shoes." David even gave him a pair of short, white socks to get him started.

Well, Charlie really appreciated that little bit of advice. He always wanted to look his best! He bought some white socks and some tennis shoes and began wearing them whenever he wore shorts.

One day, he and I were sitting in Shoney's eating lunch, when a retired couple got out of their car and started in. The man was wearing black socks and dress shoes with his shorts. Charlie looked at me and with a shocked expression on his face, he said, "Would you look at that? That old codger doesn't even know that he should wear white socks and tennis shoes with those shorts!"

I broke out laughing at him! Suddenly he was an expert on men's fashions!!

After we moved to DeSoto, we bought a fifth wheel camper from a man in our church. The first time we met Jeff DeGroot, our daughter's future husband, he and Debbie came to meet us at Bennett Springs, and we all stayed in that trailer. He had to sleep on the hall floor because he was 6'4" tall and that was the only place long enough for him to lie down. Of course, the hall floor was in front of the bathroom, so everybody had to walk over Jeff or around him when they wanted to go to the bathroom.

Then we got a larger camper. Our goal during retirement was to do volunteer building and Campers on Mission work, so that is what we did for ten years-- working with a crew to build churches wherever we went.

Many of the ladies were avid quilters and seamstresses. We made clothes for orphanages, quilts and things for old folks' homes, and sometimes we worked on things we wanted to make for our families or ourselves. I also took my piano keyboard in the RV so I could play whenever I wanted, or I could use it when we had meetings and church services. And with my computer I wrote stories and letters. We had come a long way from those early "roughing it" days!

We joined Missouri Campers on Mission and twice a year we met with the group to spruce up one of the Missouri Baptist camps for the boys' and girls' summer activities. We also volunteered at Windermere, which used to be the state Baptist Conference Center at Lake of the Ozarks. During one of those times at Windermere, the idea for BUDD Builders was born. A group of people who knew how to do basically everything in building a church joined together to go to a warm climate during the winter and build a church. Charlie was the one who found the places for us to go, and Bud McBroom was the work supervisor during our trips.

We spent time in Arizona and Florida, working on churches for several years. We estimate that we saved churches about two million dollars in expenses as these churches were built from the ground up. Sometimes we were privileged to be in the first service the church had in its new building before we pulled our campers out and headed for home again.

During that time, Charlie began to struggle with extreme dizziness. We were in emergency rooms several times when a dizzy spell would hit and he would be incapacitated, unable to even hold his head up. The episodes got closer and closer together until he was having them about once a month. They became more severe in intensity, too. During the time of the hurricane in New Orleans when people were being evacuated to other states to live, we were supposed to get some of the people in our area. Charlie was asked to head up a task force to house some of these people, so he drove to a town about thirty miles away to work out the details. While he was there, one of those spells hit while he was driving.

Fortunately he was close to Bates Creek, our associational Baptist camp, and he went there, and telephoned me to send someone to get him. I called a couple of guys in our church and when they drove up with him in their car, I told them to go straight to the doctor in Festus. I had called and made an appointment. Because he was in the midst of one of the spells, they were able to determine the origin, and it was severe Meniere's Disease, a disease of the inner ear.

It was too dangerous for him to be driving a truck and pulling the camper, so we had to sell our rig and stop going with our friends to build churches.

The dizzy spells kept on coming more and more often until in 2007 he had five spells in about seven or eight weeks. He was literally unable to hold up his head and very nauseous. We heard of a doctor in St. Louis who might be able to help him, so we went to see Dr. Robert Kletzker. We were sitting in his examination room, reading all the certificates on the wall, and noticed one for a Christian organization of doctors who help in some of the more needy countries.

After the initial examination, the doctor had his hand on the door, ready to go out, when Charlie commented on that certificate. Dr. Kletzker turned around, sat back down, and talked for several minutes about the work he does for primitive countries, helping people who have no means to get the treatments they need, and how much he loves the Lord.

Dr. Kletzer recommended a cochlear implant, and it was arranged for Charlie to undergo the surgery at Missouri Baptist Hospital. After the surgery the dizzy spells did not recur. He is a little unsteady on his feet, but at least he can be on his feet and not flat on his back in one of those spells.

The four Nobles kids in 2009

23
WEDDINGS, ORDINANCES, AND BAPTISMS

While we were at Elm Grove Church in Fort Worth, Charlie performed a wedding for Carolyn Walters. She had grown up in that church, and her family and Charlie's family knew each other well. She married a man who was a police officer and he later became a Texas Ranger. A few years ago, he was killed in the line of duty.

At their wedding ceremony, some of his fellow officers decided to play a trick on them. They decided to get the groom and put him in jail for the night.

Carolyn's father found out about the plan, so he got some handcuffs, and as soon as the wedding ceremony was over, he handcuffed Carolyn and her new husband together—in their wedding clothes—so that they could not be separated. They stood in the reception line and did the wedding cake and everything with their hands cuffed together. Bert Walters, Carolyn's dad, thought that would stop the other officers from playing their trick on them.

But the other officers just took both of them and put them in jail for the night—wedding dress, tuxedo, and all. They spent their wedding night in a jail cell. The next morning they released them and sent them on their way.

That's one joke that didn't leave them laughing. It was a long time before they could laugh about it.

In Bogard, the oldest of the nine Thye children was getting married. Earline was seventeen and just out of high school. She had been sick and was very pale. Some of us thought she might not even be able to get through the wedding ceremony.

Everybody was worried about Earline, and we were thinking about that instead of what we should have been doing. I was playing the piano for the wedding, and I guess I was really more worried about her than about the music, because I went right from the prelude to the Bridal March and forgot about the soloist.

After everybody was up on the platform and the vows began, I remembered that there was supposed to be a singer. I couldn't very well say, "Hey, I forgot, but you can sing now," so the ceremony went on without the usual song.

Earline and her husband are still married. But I learned a lesson. I learned to write down everything and keep it right in front of me on the piano. I never did forget a soloist again.

We were having the Lord's Supper in Sedalia at New Hope Church. It was after the sermon, as usual. The people were sitting quietly, the organ was playing, and the deacons were standing at the front waiting to pass out the crackers (or bread). As Charlie took the plate and said the Bible verse that he always said, he looked down at the plate and saw something move! He held the plate closer to his eyes and to his amazement everything on the plate was moving!

He looked up at the chairman of the deacons, Everett Pruitt, stepped up to him, and put the plate right under his nose. He whispered, "We can't serve this!"

Everett had his bifocals on and he couldn't see anything without getting it away from his face. So he pushed the plate back and stepped away to try to get a better look. Charlie immediately stepped forward and kept cramming the plate under Everett's nose and Everett kept stepping away, trying to see it! Finally Everett got hold of the plate and looked at it. There were little weevils crawling around all over and through the crackers!

The people could tell something was wrong, because the preacher and the deacon were stepping closer and closer to the people in the pews, and they wondered what kind of dance they were doing! Finally, Charlie said, "Folks, we can't serve this bread today."

Mrs. Glasscock, the lady who had prepared the bread, had very poor eyesight. At that point she stood up and said, "Why? What's wrong with it?"

Charlie said, "It's not edible."

Mrs. G. said, "Well, I'll go fix some more while you wait." She took the plate and started to leave. People were looking around, whispering, trying to figure out what was going on, and the organ was still playing softly.

By that time, Charlie decided that the mood of the service was broken, and it would be best to do the Lord's Supper another time, so he said, "We'll just reschedule and do this later."

That was one ordinance we never forgot!

Charlie had been preaching a revival and he was on the way home, late at night. He was really tired and ready to be home, when he heard a loud "POP."

He thought, "Oh, no, Lord, don't let that be a flat tire! I just can't change a tire now." He continued praying, "Lord, just let me get home without having to change a tire."

He kept on driving for about sixty more miles. He parked the car in the drive, came in the house very late at night, and went to bed. The next morning, he went outside and looked at the tire. It was flat and there was a hole in the tire big enough to put his fist through!

The Lord had answered his prayer! He had let him get home without changing a flat tire. So he changed it then. I know this sounds unbelievable, but it really happened!

In Hannibal, during a wedding ceremony, a groomsman was so scared and so stiff that he passed out. He was as stiff as a poker! He actually bounced three times on his forehead before somebody got to him. Charlie says he has seen men do that when they are standing at attention in the Army, but this was the first time he'd seen it in a wedding.

Then there was the baptism in Miami. Charlie was Minister of Evangelism there and he did almost all the baptizing. We usually had baptism at every service. One night, Charlie was preaching at another church and the pastor was supposed to do the baptizing. Our kids were singing, and I stayed there to hear them, so I was there when this happened.

When it was almost time for the baptism service to begin, the pastor, Luther Dyer, was sitting on the platform. One of the deacons realized that the pastor had forgotten that he had to do the baptizing that night because Charlie was gone, so he sent a note to the pastor. It said, "We have baptism tonight." The pastor received the note, looked at it, put it in his pocket, and continued to sit on the platform.

The deacon, knowing that the pastor had not understood, sent another note. This one said, "Marvin is not here!"

When the pastor, saw this, the light dawned! He got up and hurriedly left the platform to get ready to baptize the people who were waiting. Most preachers baptize in waders and they just put the waders on over their pants, but Luther always took his pants off and then got into the waders.

He also forgot that he had to go through the women's dressing room to get to the men's dressing room. As the pastor entered the women's dressing room, he had unbuttoned his pants and they were falling down around his knees. The woman who was helping a little girl didn't seem too concerned about this, but Luther was embarrassed and tried to grab his pants and hold them up while he got to the men's dressing where a man was waiting with the waders. Luther hurriedly stepped into the waders, but he stepped into them backward and his feet were facing the wrong way!

Rather than take the time to change, he just reached down and twisted the feet of the waders so that they pointed in the right direction, and went on into the baptistery. He went on with the baptism, but while he was in the water, the waders turned back around the other way, and his feet were turned backward!

As Luther tried to go up the stairs from the baptistery with his feet going backward, it sounded like a seal at the zoo! Water was splashing up and over into the choir! Loud splats were heard as Luther tried to get up the steps and out of the baptistery. It was a very memorable baptism service, especially after we found out about all the things that had happened.

Charlie and I went to Texas so that he could perform the wedding ceremony for his nephew, Eddie, and his bride, Donna. After the ceremony, they stepped off the platform to do the candle ceremony. As Donna stepped down, she stepped on her dress and the waistband of the slip broke. She could feel it falling off.

While they stood at the unity candle, Donna began to wiggle now and then. Charlie thought, "What is she doing?" As he talked about the candle, and the singer sang, Donna continued to wiggle a little. Then Charlie prayed, and she really wiggled because nobody was looking!

After the prayer, Donna stepped up and out of her slip and left it lying on the floor. She had finally wiggled out of it and she didn't have to worry about it falling off any more!

In Texarkana, a couple that did not belong to our church called and asked Charlie to marry them. He met with them, talked about the vows of marriage, and told them some of the rules that we had at our church, one of which was that there would be no pictures during the ceremony.

The time for the wedding came and bride's mother was late, so they had to wait. When she got there, she was drunk—or just a little bit tipsy. She sat on the front seat, and during the ceremony she took a Polaroid camera out of her purse and took a picture. You know what a Polaroid camera does when it zips out the picture. It went "Prrrrrt" and the woman began to giggle and dropped the camera on the floor. Meanwhile, Charlie was doing the serious ceremony of the marriage.

After the ceremony, as they were leaving, the woman shook hands with Charlie and put something into his hand. It was clear that she wanted him to look at it, but he didn't. He just put it in his pocket. Later he looked at it, and saw that it was a one hundred dollar bill! He told me later, "I don't think she intended to give me that. She probably thought it was a $20." But we put that money to good use, as we always did.

Once Charlie baptized a man who was a floater. He kept on trying to get him under the water and the man kept bobbing back up. Finally Charlie had to put his hand on the man's chest and push him down to get him baptized!

Charlie always had a lot of trouble with his throat when he was preaching all the time, so he always carried Vicks cough drops wherever he went. He kept them in his pocket, in the glove box of the car, and in the medicine cabinet in the house.

One night he was on the way home from a meeting where he had preached, and his throat was hurting. It was late and dark, but he reached into the glove box, found a little packet like the cough drops come in, opened it and popped it into his mouth. *WOW*! He had grabbed an Alka-Seltzer by mistake! It began to fizz and he had to get the car off the road fast and get that thing out of his mouth!

I'll bet that the next time, he was sure to look at the label before putting a pill into his mouth!

While we were in Miami, Charlie was asked to go out to a black church and preach. It is a real experience to preach in a black church, or to even attend services at one. The ladies all come in wearing white dresses and parade around the pews, singing, and then go to the choir. The preacher and the deacons file out of the little room where they have been praying when the service begins. The singing is like something you've never heard! The music is beautiful!

After the preacher preaches, another man usually goes to the pulpit and re-hashes what the preacher has said. They take a collection and pay everybody. After the offering is collected, some people count it while everybody sings. They take a little to the preacher, some to the singer, and go on paying everybody who had a part in the service while the singers are still singing. If they don't have enough money to pay everybody, they take another offering. This goes on until they have enough to pay everybody that had a part in the service.

At this particular service, Charlie went to the little room to pray with the preacher and deacons. After the singing, they introduced him and he got up to preach. He preached his sermon and sat down. Then one of the men went up to the pulpit.

He said, "Folks, I like this white preacher. Most of the white preachers comes out here and they tries to impress us with their big words. But THIS preacher, he puts those big words into little bitty bites, then he chews them up and spits them out in little words so's we can understand them. He don't try to IMPRESS us, he just PREACHES!"

We thought that was a great compliment and received it as such.

In 1998, Charlie received a call from a preaching school in St. Louis, the Pillsbury Institute of Applied Christianity. They asked him to speak at their Commencement exercises in May. They also said they wanted to confer the Doctor of Divinity degree on him.

The school was a part of the Christian Civic Foundation. Charlie was one of the first men who worked for the CCF in the 1960's, going into the public schools with a program of education about drugs and alcohol. He would receive an assignment to go to a school in our area of Missouri and would stay there all day, presenting a film and discussing what drugs and alcohol can do, urging the students to stay away from these things. Because of his early involvement in this capacity, they wanted to confer the D.D. degree on him. Of course, he accepted and spoke at the commencement.

It is only right that he should have received this honor. Some men work a few years, study hard, and receive an earned Doctor's Degree. Charlie worked all his life, gave his all and was given an honorary Doctor's Degree. We feel privileged that it was given to him.

After the degree was conferred, he said, "When people used to ask if I was a doctor, I'd say 'I'm not even a registered nurse.' Now I guess I can't say that any more."

Charlie was selected as Midwestern Seminary Alumnus of the year. He was D.O.M. of the year and preached the annual sermon for the Directors of Missions in New Orleans at the Southern Baptist Convention one year. He has also served on two Southern Baptist Convention committees

Charlie received his Honorary Doctor's Degree in 1998.
Friends with us are Ted & Connie Francis, and Jim and Judy
Raspberry

24
YOU CAN BE A MISSIONARY WHEREVER YOU ARE!

While we lived in Bogard, we decided that for our family devotions, we would study the places where Southern Baptists had missionaries. So we wrote to the Foreign Mission Board and soon received a large box in the mail. In it was a world map that showed all the mission points and lots of pamphlets about the missionaries and the places they served. We put the map on the wall above our table. Every day at mealtime we would pray for the missionaries and put a ribbon or colored pin on the place we talked and prayed about. We read and learned about the places where missionaries serve. We began thinking a lot about missions.

Then one day after we moved to Sedalia, Charlie saw an article in our state Baptist paper stating that a man was needed to serve in Nigeria, Africa, to begin a program for boys and men to teach them about missions.

Since he had been active in working with Royal Ambassadors and Baptist Men, he was very interested in this. We prayed about it and decided that we would volunteer for the job. He called Baker James Cothen, who was head of the Foreign Mission Board at that time, to tell him about our interest in becoming missionaries. Dr. Cothen said he would be flying through Kansas City in a week or two and would have about a two-hour layover, so we made an appointment to see him at the airport on that day.

On the morning we were to be at the airport, there was an ice storm in Sedalia. All the electricity was out and people were being advised not to get out unless it was absolutely necessary. But we went on to Kansas City, about a two-hour drive. Cars were overturned and in the ditches all the way, and we felt very fortunate to get there safely. Dr. Cothen seemed to be very impressed with us. He was very positive and encouraging, and after talking with him, we thought we would be on the mission field in a very short time. So we began the process of becoming missionaries, which involved a variety of things.

I had to go back to college to prepare to be a teacher to my own children, so I enrolled in Central Missouri State University at Warrensburg, about thirty miles from our home, and took a course load of twelve hours. At that time our children were ages four, six, eight, and ten. I was a housewife and a pastor's wife and was teaching twelve piano lessons every week. I was one busy lady—I was a multitasker before that word was invented!

We had to be approved and appointed before Steve was twelve, because they would not send anyone to a foreign field if they had a child above that age. They said when the children were older they had to leave home to go to boarding school, and it would be too traumatic for a child to go to a foreign country and immediately leave home.

We wrote our life stories, took many physical, psychiatric, and medical tests, and did everything we were told to do. Our children were excited about the prospect of going to Africa, too. We would sit in the living room at night at talk about what it means to be a missionary and what missionaries do, how we would live, and how different life would be for all of us.

We were flown to the places we had to go to do the various tests. I went to get a new pair of shoes at a store where one of our church members worked. I told him this would be my first plane trip and that I was apprehensive. He said, "Well, you know, you need some very light shoes to wear on the plane, so it will go up without a problem." I was so gullible I believed him, and when I got on the plane I carefully raised my feet off the floor so the plane would be able to get up in the air better! The plane took off from the Kansas City airport which was pretty close to the downtown area, and as it banked, I almost jumped into Charlie's lap, I was so afraid it was going to hit some of those buildings!

When everything was all done, nine months had passed. The Mission Board got all the information together and decided that Charlie was one of the best candidates they had ever had, and that he would make an excellent missionary. But, because of all the emotional and nervous problems I had experienced, they thought I should not be appointed. We learned that some couples had recently been appointed with problems similar to mine, and they had been sent back home because the stress was more than they could manage. In addition, at that time, a civil war was going on in Nigeria, and they didn't think I could handle that. We were very disappointed that we would not be going to the mission field, but felt that God knew best.

During those months, we became acquainted with a missionary couple on furlough from Africa. We visited together a lot while they were in Sedalia, and a few months after we were not approved, they wrote the Foreign Mission Board and recommended that they reconsider. They said, "We think the Nobles' would be very good missionaries."

Dr. Reneer, the professor from Midwestern who had helped me through my emotional problems, visited us in Sedalia. He wrote the Mission Board and said, "I think Mrs. Nobles is completely cured and would be fine if they were to be appointed as missionaries."

So, because of these two recommendations, the Mission Board telephoned us with a very unusual message. They said, "We have never done this before, but because of the recommendation of two fine sources, we want you to re-apply for appointment as missionaries. Let us take a look at you again and let us reconsider your appointment."

So we complied with their request. We filled out more papers, took more tests, and did what we were asked to do.

Again the same reply came back. Mr. Nobles would be a very good candidate, but we feel Mrs. Nobles should not be appointed. So we were not accepted.

This time, our disappointment was greater. Our children had been very excited, thinking that we might go to Africa. Our church had been waiting anxiously to see whether we would stay as pastor or go as missionaries. We had done all the preparatory work and were confident we would have been approved.

Shortly after that experience, we were called to the Calvary Church at Hannibal, which was right in the middle of a black community.

Many of the children came to church on our buses, and we learned that not all black people live in Africa. We learned that you can make a difference in the black community in America, and you don't have to go to a foreign field to minister to them.

The next church we served was Wayside Baptist Church in Miami, Florida, during a time when many Cubans and Spanish-speaking people were relocating there. We learned that not all Spanish-speaking people live on another continent. Many of the people we worked with were saved. Before we left that church, an average of 400 people were riding our church buses every Sunday and getting a witness about Jesus and His love. While we were there and my husband was serving as Minister of Evangelism at Wayside Baptist Church, approximately 225 people per year were baptized. My husband said he could go out on any night of the week, make three visits, and win a family to the Lord.

We ministered for five years in Texarkana, Texas, where the church grew from 200 to an average of 400. We went to Joplin, and then to DeSoto, Missouri. After five years at DeSoto, Charlie was called as Executive Director of Missions in Jefferson County, just south of St. Louis. We learned that not all people who need Jesus live somewhere else. Many thousands of people lived in that area and more than half of them did not attend any church. Several churches and missions were started in Jefferson County during the eleven years he served as Director of Missions.

Then one night as we watched the news in DeSoto, Missouri, we saw a picture of a church in Miami, Florida, with a big hole in its side. "That's Wayside!" we suddenly recognized. It had been severely damaged by Hurricane Andrew. So Charlie called the pastor at Wayside and said, "What can we do to help you?"

The pastor said, "People here have lost their roofs and there is no more roofing felt anywhere in Florida to be bought. If you could get some roofing felt and bring it to us, we would greatly appreciate it." Charlie called several men and got a group of about thirty people to go there and put roofing felt on people's houses so that they could be dry. A company in a nearby town gathered several truckloads of donated roofing felt and the men drove to Miami to do this work. After working for a week and roofing many houses, they took all the roofing felt they had left to a Spanish-speaking church in Homestead, Florida, and gave it to the pastor, so that it could be used there by others who would finish the work.

Then in 1996 a flood came to our area in Jefferson County. Many people in our own area needed help. Charlie called Campers on Missions and several people came and brought their rigs, parked them at Jefferson Baptist Association, and worked on houses that had been flooded in Jefferson County. We joined Campers on Mission ourselves after we retired and began doing volunteer work.

My husband and some other men organized a group of retired couples in 1996 called B.U.D.D. Builders (Building Under Divine Direction). The men were able to do any type of building work and the women made quilts for children's homes. We were in Pearce, Arizona, building the Sunnyside Baptist Church when a man drove up to the construction site and said, "Who's in charge here?" The men told them they guessed it would be Bud McBroom.

He said, "Well, I've been watching you old guys work. You get along well and I've never seen a group of men have more fun while they're working. I want to hire you to build a building for me."

"Oh, we can't do that," Bud said, "we're just volunteers and we don't work for money."

But later, Charlie thought, "Why can't we work for money, and put that money in a fund to help a church that needs a building but has no money?" So he and Bud and some of the other men discussed it, and after we got back home to Missouri, they called a lawyer and set up a not-for-profit organization called B.U.D.D. Builders. The men do contract jobs, but do not keep the money they earn. Instead, they put the money into a fund to help a church when there is enough money to do it. Bud McBroom figures the jobs and decides whether the men can do it, then Charlie and Bud call men who can come to help. The people for whom they are working pay a reasonable rate, and the money is used mission projects.

In Pearce, Arizona, the men started with the concrete slab and built the whole church building. We conducted the first service the day before we left. It was a wonderful experience to see how excited those people were when they were able to occupy their new church!

As years went on, many of the people in this group spent the winter months in Florida or Arizona working on a church. At home during the rest of the year, they would work for money. They were able to lay carpeting in a church that had no money and pay for the entire job. Sometimes they bought materials to use when a church was unable to foot the entire bill for the project they needed. After thirteen years, the group is still in existence. New people have joined and older people have dropped out when they were unable to continue the work. We are happy to see the group going on and working to build churches and help people.

While working in Graceville, Florida, the men built homes for retired preachers who needed a place to live in retirement. Many preachers who served during the 1950's, 1960's, and beyond, had lived in parsonages, and then retired without an adequate retirement fund, so they were in need of a home to live in during retirement. Our group built four homes and finished three others for the retired preachers, and built a larger staff house for visiting professors for the college. The next year they moved an old train station in and our men renovated it, building offices and conference rooms. They built dormitories and remodeled other areas where students lived during the three winters that BUDD Builders served there.

Some of the women helped with a nursing home, ministering to them every week and making wheel-chair covers for the residents or baby quilts for a pregnancy center. Other ladies did office work and helped in various ways. We did whatever we could to help where we could, as we were needed.

When we are at home in DeSoto, we do whatever we can in our own church and community to let people know that Jesus loves them.

No, you don't have to go overseas to be a missionary. You can serve Him wherever you happen to be.

The Nobles family in 2009 with all the kids and grandkids, except Austin, Debbie's son, who serves in the United States Navy

25
A HERITAGE TO REMEMBER

During the early 1980's Charlie's dad, Bill Nobles, was diagnosed with Acute Leukemia. This is a disease that causes a person's white corpuscles to eat up the red corpuscles, so that the body does not continue to make blood. A person can live for a while with this condition, but after a while, frequent blood transfusions are needed in order to stay alive.

After about two years with this condition, Bill Nobles had to be in the hospital a lot so that he could get blood transfusions. He grew weaker and weaker, and lost a lot of weight. He needed someone to stay with him when he was very sick, so Ed, George, and Melvin, who all lived near their parents, would stay with him at night when Charlie's mom was too tired to stay up and do things for him. When she was just worn out, and the brothers who lived in Fort Worth were, too, she would call Charlie in Missouri, and say, "Can you come and be with Dad for a little while and let me rest?" So he would fly to Texas from DeSoto and stay a couple of weeks.

Once when he was there, his dad was very weak. He was at home in the house on Silver Creek Road. He was so weak he couldn't sit up, but suddenly one night, Charlie heard him calling loudly. "Man!" he said. "Man, come here!" (He still called Charlie "Man" for as long as he lived.)

Charlie went into the room and his dad was sitting straight up in bed, pointing his finger at something. His dad, so weak he could not get out of bed, had managed to sit up and he was frantically saying, "Man, look out there! Look out there at all those people!"

Charlie talked with him a little bit, thinking that he must have been dreaming. His dad was very upset and excited about something and it was hard to calm him down. He continued his plea as he said, "Look at all those people. They need Jesus! Man, go and tell them about Jesus!"

Charlie said, "I will, Pop. As long as I have breath in my body, I'll tell all the people about Jesus." And then Charlie put his arms around his dad and helped him ease back down into the bed.

He has told this story many times when he was preaching. He said, "I promised my dad I would tell the people about Jesus, and that's what I plan to do. As long as I'm able, I'm going to tell them about Jesus, and I'll tell them Pop told me to do it."

Another time, Charlie was there and his dad was getting much weaker. The brothers knew that he was about to die, and they decided to take him to the hospital. They did not want him to die at home, in the house where their mother would have to stay the rest of her life.

When the time came to take him to the hospital, Charlie picked his dad up in his arms like a little child, and carried him to the car. He had become so weak and had lost so much weight, that he was very light. Bill said, "Where are we going?"

"Pop, we're taking you back to the hospital." Charlie told him.

Bill did not want to go back to the hospital, but they took him and checked him in. The brothers continued to stay with him all the time, taking turns as they could, and still work their jobs. Bill had talked with each of them while was sick, and on one particular night, Charlie was in the hospital room, sitting and talking with him.

Bill said, "I'm ready to go to Heaven. I've talked with each of my boys and I know they are all right with God and that I'll see them again, so I'm ready to go."

Charlie said, "Pop, you're going to be there soon. You'll see Jesus soon."

His dad nodded. He knew he was about to die.

Charlie moved his chair back into the corner and sat there, thinking about his dad and how weak he had become. He thought, "Pop has been a good father and a good husband. He has taught the Bible for years and has lived for God. But now his body is so weak. He can never get better because of this terrible disease." He felt impressed to pray, "God, why don't you take him home to Heaven tonight and get him out of this suffering body?"

In just a few minutes, he noticed a difference in his breathing, so he called the nurse. The nurse said, "It won't be long now. You had better call the rest of the family, because he will be gone soon."

Charlie went to call his mother and his brothers, then returned to the room and he and the nurse stood on either side of Bill Nobles' hospital bed, just watching him. Suddenly, the biggest grin Charlie ever saw came on his dad's face; then he relaxed, and he was gone. Charlie said that during that time, he could feel the presence of God more than he had ever felt. God was everywhere in that room, coming to get Bill Nobles and take him to Heaven.

Charlie, feeling the closeness of God, said to the nurse, "Isn't that beautiful?" She stared at him as if he had just committed a crime. By the look in her eyes, she seemed to be saying, "That's your dad that just died! How can you say it is beautiful?"

But to him it *WAS* beautiful. He had just seen a man who loved God go to be with God. Charlie could feel His holy presence in that moment. And we can be sure that we will go to Heaven, just as sure as he was that his dad was in Heaven at that very moment.

Charlie always told this story when he preached about living a victorious Christian life. He said, "God does not promise to keep sorrow and suffering out of our lives, but He does promise that while we are going through the sorrow and suffering, He will be with us, if we just trust Him and live for Him. He doesn't deliver us *out* of the sorrow, but he brings us *through* it by His grace."

Not very many years later, Charlie's mother, Thula, went to be with Jesus, too. She went to church one Sunday, then went to a party at the church and saw all her friends. After the party was over, she was tired. Ed took her to his house.

She walked in, sighed a tired sigh, and sat down in a chair. She leaned her head back, closed her eyes, and died. She had had a heart attack. It was another beautiful way to go to Heaven. God took her to be with him quietly, in the same way she had lived her life, quietly going about her business.

Be faithful until death, and I will give you the crown of life.   Rev. 2:10(NAS)

Our children were young and all were at home when my grandpa Wier became very sick and died. When we got in the car and started to Texas for the funeral, it was the month of February and it was very cold.

As we drove at night, the cold intensified and it started to snow. The snow got thicker and the highway was dangerous. Cars were slipping and sliding, many of them stopping on the side of the road or pulling into motels or restaurant parking lots. Those that continued to move did so very slowly and carefully. We were not prepared for emergencies. We had not brought blankets, we only had our coats, but it began to be evident that we, too, might have to stop.

Everyone in the family was asleep and Charlie was very tired as we drove through Oklahoma. He pulled over under a big overpass and said, "It will be a little warmer here. I've just got to sleep a little while. I'll sleep for a few minutes and then we'll go on."

I vaguely heard him because I was asleep too, but suddenly something made me wide awake! "We've got to get out of here!" I nudged Charlie and said, "We've got to go!"

He was too sleepy to move. He said, "Just a few minutes, then I'll drive."

The feeling kept on pushing me, so I said, "Get over! I'm going to drive!"

Sleepily, he said, "You can't drive in the snow. Just a few more minutes—"

I was not a very experienced driver at that time and had done very little highway driving, but something inside me said, "Get over! The Lord told me to drive this car!"

Charlie said, "I don't argue with the Lord." And he moved over and went right back to sleep on the passenger side of the car.

I was not used to highway driving, or driving in the snow, but something impelled me to get us out of that place, right then! I drove slowly and steadily until we got off that highway and after a while Charlie was awake. We stopped for coffee, and then he drove again.

We went on to Texas for my grandpa's funeral. A few days later we came back, but we had to go back a different way. The highway we had driven down on was still snow-packed and parts of it had been closed. We learned that if we had stayed under that overpass we would have been stuck there, closed in by the snow, and it might have been many hours before we could have been rescued.

God told me to drive that car. I did what He said, and He protected my family.

From the time I was a little girl, I prayed for my Papa to be saved. He had no use for God and would not go to church. I talked to him, my daddy talked to him, everybody tried to get him to turn to God, but he would not.

I was married and had teen-aged children when he finally decided to go to church. He was saved when he was an old man.

We were living in Joplin when Papa died. At Papa's funeral, I heard the preacher, one of my mother's cousins, tell about when he accepted Jesus as his Savior. He told about seeing Papa pray to ask Jesus to come into his life. He said that Papa faithfully attended church and was a different man during the last few months and years of his life.

As I sat there during that service, I could not cry. I could only rejoice and be happy for Papa, because one day, when I get to Heaven, he will be there, too. That is God's promise. If we love Him and trust Him and believe in Him, one day we will see the loved ones who have gone on to Heaven before us.

Isn't God good?

I used to think that after we retired, it would be wonderful. We would be able to do whatever we wanted to do, whenever we wanted to do it, so I thought! We talked and planned, dreaming of several trips we would like to take, and some places we would like to go.

Charlie retired on his 65th birthday, July 1, 1994, and he said, "I'm not ever gonna get snowed on again!" But I decided to teach school one more year so that I could buy some furniture that we needed to replace before our income became smaller.

During the summer after Charlie retired, we were in North Carolina visiting Debbie and her family when we got a phone call from Dallas. My dad, who was 78 at the time, had to have a second heart by-pass surgery, his first one having been fifteen years earlier. The doctors convinced him that if he had this second surgery, he had a pretty good chance of several more years of life. So he decided to do it.

I flew from North Carolina to Dallas to be with my mother and siblings during the surgery. A few days after the surgery, I had to fly back to North Carolina to meet Charlie, who had stayed there with Debbie and her family. My sister, Julie, and I were standing on either side of Daddy's bed when I said, "I planned to get you some flowers, but I just didn't get it done, and now I have to leave."

Daddy smiled, looked at us, and said, "My two pretty flowers are standing here beside me. That's all the flowers I need." And that was the last thing I heard him say, except for talking with him on the telephone.

In August, Steve came to visit. We, along with Steve and Cindy, took the camper and went to Hannibal because Steve wanted to go back and look at some of the places where we had been during his junior high school days. While we were there, Charlie experienced some chest pain, which was worse than anything he had felt before. So after we returned home he went to the doctor and had a stress test. He failed the test and was admitted immediately to the hospital for angioplasty on two of the veins to his heart.

When school started in September, I returned to teaching. Charlie spent his time doing things at home or at the church, or helping with projects at our church, the First Baptist Church of DeSoto, where he once served as pastor. He played some golf. He decided to work at our church as Senior Adult Event Coordinator, so he planned some trips for the Senior Adults and was involved in implementing the trips during that last year that I worked. But later he complained, "I got snowed on fourteen times that year!"

When school was out and I retired, we planned to go to Texas to see Mother and Dad. It had been a year since Dad's surgery, and he was feeling pretty good. But those Senior trips every month kept interfering with our time. We knew we would no sooner get to Texas than we would have to go back to Missouri for one of those trips. So we said, "We will go to Texas in June, and spend a few weeks with Mother and Dad."

It had been a year since my dad's surgery, and he was doing pretty well, in spite of the fact that he was experiencing congestive heart failure. He was seventy-nine years old, and was able to do some of things that he wanted to do.

But then Charlie began having trouble with his heart again. I insisted that he go to the doctor before our trip to Texas. He tried to put me off, saying, "I'll see the doctor after our trip to Texas." But as I expressed my concern about him to Debbie, she got on the phone with him and made him promise to see the doctor before taking that trip to Texas. She always could convince him when nobody else seemed to be able to do it.

This time when he went to the doctor, he failed the test again, and it meant another hospitalization. In late June he had to have open heart surgery, four by-passes. He was in surgery a couple of days before his birthday. We thought, "As soon as he recuperates, we will spend some time with my parents."

August came. We couldn't go to Texas then because we had a Senior Adult trip to the Smokies in September. So we decided to go in October.

Charlie was planning a Senior trip to Washington, D.C. for 1996, so he said, "Let's go up to Debbie's in North Carolina to take her some things for home schooling (some of my school things that I no longer needed), then spend a few days at Raymond & JoAnn's house in Virginia planning the trip for the Seniors for next year, then we'll come back home, get the camper, and go to Texas and spend six weeks with your folks around Dallas."

We planned to leave on Monday, so we would have a few days at Debbie's house, but a special vote was coming up at church on Wednesday, and the preacher asked us to stay for that. So we didn't leave until Thursday morning for North Carolina. We could only stay one day at Debbie's house, then we drove on.

We arrived in Manassas, Virginia, at Raymond and JoAnn's house, on Saturday, October 7. The next day, Sunday, they were involved in church activities all day, so we stayed busy doing that. We heard two wonderful sermons from the book of Revelation on that Sunday. A teen-aged girl who said she had not been in church for ten years came to the evening service and was saved. The services were Spirit-filled, and I was full of joy that night when we went to bed. We planned to begin our sightseeing trip the next morning, on October 9.

During the night, at about 2:00 a.m., the telephone rang. Since we were not at home, I was not alarmed—until I heard Raymond calling Charlie to the phone. It was my mother, telling us that my dad had just died.

Dad had taught his Sunday School class that morning, had gone to a birthday party for one of the department members that afternoon, and then, when he went to bed, he just closed his eyes and stopped breathing.

Charlie and I immediately started to Dallas, by way of St. Louis. We began that long, sorrowful trip at 3:00 A.M. and drove until 8:30 Monday night—926 miles. As we drove, we talked and cried and remembered. One of the things that came to my memory was the wonderful sermons about Heaven that we had heard the day before in Manassas, Virginia. God knew that I was going to need those assurances as we faced the long hours of driving. A lady had sung a song, Jesus Will Still be There, on Sunday morning, and Jesus really was there as we drove and remembered the good things. God gave me the assurance that my dad was in Heaven with Him at that very moment.

Once Charlie looked at me and said, "We hadn't even had a chance to compare scars yet." My dad was always showing us his scars from the many surgeries he had experienced. Now Charlie had a scar just like his, but they did not get to compare them. Dad was such a good friend to Charlie.

Another time he said, "I can just imagine Coy up there in Heaven, looking around to see if the corners are square or if everything is built just right." My dad was a master builder and whenever we went into a new building, he looked at the corners to see if they were square or if the builders had taken short-cuts and had not done their best on the building.

Then Charlie said, "Precious in the sight of the Lord is the death of His saints." (Ps. 116:15) And Dad truly was a saint. God honored him by allowing him to die in just the way he always said he wanted to go. He did not suffer or linger. He just lay down and closed his eyes, and

God took him. Now we can thank God for that, even though at the time, it was hard to accept.

The next morning, we drove to St. Louis. Cindy and Jack had made flight arrangements and flew with us to Dallas. When we got to Texas, Debbie came, and David and Margaret were there. Steve was unable to come from Germany, but we understood that.

I stayed with mother while Charlie drove back home to get our RV. When he came back we spent some time in Texas, but not as we had planned, with mother and dad.

We never know what is going to happen to our plans. But we can be sure of one thing-- Jesus will be there to comfort our hearts when we need Him most.

> *Now we know that if the earthly tent we live in is destroyed, we have a building from God, an eternal home in Heaven, not built by human hands.* *2 Corinthians 5:1(NAS)*

My mother, Allene Wier, is 90 now (in 2010) and lives in a retirement home in Denton, Texas, near my sister, Julie. She is a two-time survivor of breast cancer. She is a treasure to all who know her. She is supportive of her family and her church and her God. Recently she wept as she told me about an incident when daddy was a pastor and led some people to the Lord. She witnesses for the Lord, and when I think of her, I think of the verse, "I thank my God on every remembrance of you."

When mother was eighty years old, she bought a computer and learned to e-mail and she is even on Facebook so that she can keep up with family and friends. She makes greeting cards and address labels on her computer for her friends in the retirement home where she lives.

We recently celebrated her 90th birthday and Charlie Nobles' 80th in the same week—one in Missouri and one in Texas, with the whole family in attendance!

Looking back, I can see how thankful I am that God caused me to run across that street and be hurt in that awful wreck in Dallas. If it had not been for the wreck, my dad may not have been saved and we would not have been serving God all these years.

I am thankful that God led me to Decatur Baptist College. If it had not been for that place, I would not have met Charlie and we would not have spent these fifty-five years together in service of our Lord and Savior, Jesus Christ.

I thank God for the emotional problems I had in the early days of my marriage. If it had not been for those problems, I would not know the wonderful deliverance that comes when you say, "God, please do it for me because I can't do it for myself."

I thank God for our family—four children who are healthy and eight precious grandchildren, who have all accepted Jesus as their Savior.

And I thank God for leading me to write this book. It started out as some funny anecdotes for our grandchildren, but it has evolved into so much more—a tribute to a life filled with love and service and thankfulness!

Allene Wier, age 90, Juanita's mother, and Marvin Nobles, age 80

26
TRIBUTES TO A MAN OF GOD

These notes were gleaned from cards and letters we received through the years.

Bud and Betty McBroom, members of BUDD Builders, said: "To us, you are the most Christian man we know."

Ed and Sandy Backe, members of BUDD Builders, said, "Thanks for all the good times we shared on work projects."

Gary Taylor, a friend since Seminary days, and the current Evangelism director of the Missouri Baptist Convention, said, "Someone said, 'If I can see farther than others, it's because I am standing on someone else's shoulders.' You have definitely been great shoulders to stand on. You have had a great impact on my life."

Bonnie Collier, a member of First Baptist DeSoto, said, "Thank you for your calming spirit, your wise counsel, and your willingness to be a humble servant for our God wherever He leads."

Jerry Frazier, who has known Charlie since he was a little boy in R.A.s, then served in Jefferson County and is presently serving in a church in Virginia, says, "Thank you for being my 'Paul'. You kept me focusing on Jesus. You in a real sense were my father in the ministry."

Marvil and Melba Hawkins, former members of First Baptist DeSoto and currently serving in Crescent, Oklahoma, said, "You are a glowing example of a servant of the Lord, and we will always cherish the times we shared with you."

Cheryl Lake Stewart, who was a child when we were at Bogard, said, "I was saved under your ministry and Jesus became my Lord and Savior. It was also under your pastorate in Bogard that my dad learned to follow the Lord in a deeper relationship and was ordained Deacon."

Harold and Bess Myer, whom we have known since Seminary days, and for whom Charlie has preached a couple of revivals, said, "We are very thankful for all the ways you have touched our lives and led us through many experiences which have helped us be better servants of the Lord."

Carol Courtney, who was Charlie's secretary at Jefferson Baptist Association, said, "You have been a blessing to me through the years, not only as my boss, but as my friend. I thank God for you and for that friendship."

Darrel Girardier, Deacon at First Baptist DeSoto, said, "The Saturday Evening Post had stories titled 'The Most Unforgettable Character I Know.' God called Bro. Marvin to our church when we needed a pastor to heal our church, for we had been through a very trying experience, and God makes no mistakes. Bro. Marvin looks for the good in everyone. Under his leadership, when he was Associational Missionary, Bates Creek camp was brought to the level it is today. He belongs to a group of Christian men who travel to many states, building or remodeling churches. He is a kind man, ready to help when needed, whether it is to fill the pulpit or to visit someone in the hospital. I have known Bro. Marvin from the time he came to First Baptist, and I am happy that cowboy is my friend. Words cannot describe Bro. Marvin, so I will not try."

Rhonda Kamyk, secretary at Jefferson Baptist Assocation, said, "You are a special person in my life. Ever since the first week I met you I wished you were my father. You are a peacemaker, a calming in the storm. I hold dear so many precious memories."

Gianna Snyder Anderson, from New Hope church in Sedalia, said, "You two have been a pair in my mind and both have been so important in my early years that I have to thank you both. New Hope was critical in my view of how a person should live a worthwhile life. I can't imagine my life without music, and Juanita, on my 12th birthday, you helped me to pick a song to sing in church. Now I am busy in church with music and I can't imagine my life without it. Charlie, you knew our youth group needed direction, and you led the New Hope Church in Sedalia to call a red-headed kid from Southwest Baptist College. Roger Glidewell taught me that God wanted more than Sunday morning attendance And Charlie, I remember the time I came to see you all in Hannibal. I have never forgotten your witness that day in 1972 when you showed me how important it is to rely on God. Thanks for all you taught me both from the pulpit and through your lives."

Don and June Williams, members at First Baptist DeSoto, and . members of BUDD Builders, said, "Marvin, you and your family came to pastor First Baptist right after we moved here in 1979. You have been a great inspiration to our family, from being our pastor, working at Bates Creek when our son Steve was a camper and he had trouble breathing.

Bro. Nobles, you gave him injections of adrenaline medication for his asthma at camp. Then you both came home tired and weak, one from not breathing well and the other from no sleep. We enjoyed doing mission work with you and Juanita."

Kathi and Roger Glidewell, New Hope church in Sedalia, said, "Charlie, those years you were my pastor at New Hope are so precious to me. When things were not so stable at home, my church and pastor were always there for me. That's when Jesus became real to me. Thank you for being my pastor."

Andrea Maples, member at First Baptist DeSoto, said, "God always speaks through you and I love to hear your voice. Just the sound of your voice makes me feel comforted, calm and safe. I know when you speak that you will speak words of wisdom. I know when you pray that you ask God for guidance. Thank you for your years of service to God and for many more to come."

Edna Mae Abney, from New Hope in Sedalia, said, "You were my pastor and a great friend in the faith. You being my pastor showed me that the preacher was a human being, a good friend, and a regular person just like the rest of us. You were so kind and helpful in my spiritual growth. Thanks for being so patient."

Darlene and Bob Stone, from the Calvary Church in Hannibal, said, "I remember so many things and the good times we had. Among them was Juanita's beautiful voice, the revivals and the packed church on those nights, the Bus Ministry, its excitement and also the commotions that went along with it. Charlie performed our daughter's wedding. And I remember when you said you were leaving for Florida. You were a blessing to us as I know you have been to many others."

Jacque Charlton, from First Baptist, DeSoto, said, "It's April 20, and you have been on my mind. The reason is that April 20, 1980, I came to know the Lord and I haven't been the same since. You both played an important role in what was the most important event of my life, and this year I want to express to you again my deep appreciation for all you've meant to me. The best way I can think of to say "thank you" is to live a life worthy of the calling. Hearing your testimony, hearing the word of God taught faithfully, and being with other women my age was really the turning point for me. Then there was that good preachin'. Most important of all to me is the life I have seen you two live since you came here. You'll never know how much I respect you and will always keep you in my prayers. God bless you richly forever."

Jim and Judy Raspberry, from First Baptist DeSoto, said, "You are very special to us. It is evident that you love God and always show that love to others through your kindness and your humble spirit. You have been a faithful servant of God, and we pray He will give you many more years of service to Him. Thank you for your visits and wonderful prayers for me and my family."

Cindy Nobles Scanio, our daughter, said, "It isn't fair to expect Dad to have all the answers, but somehow he always does. Thank you for being such a wonderful example of Christian love."

Debbie Nobles DeGroot, our daughter, said,   "As children grow up they learn who God the Father is by watching their earthly father. Dad was a fine example for me. His example of love, not just for me, but for our church, our community, and for my mother, gave me a glimpse of the amazing love God has for each of us. I'm so glad he's my earthly father."

David Nobles, our son, said "My dad didn't have the money to give us all the latest gadgets but he did give us the gift of a college education.

We didn't have cool cars, but we had wheels to get us from A to B. We rarely went to restaurants, but we always had dinner. I never went snow skiing until I could pay for it myself—I took my wife and 4-year-old son with me. But I wouldn't trade any of that STUFF for what Dad did give me; the knowledge of how a man was to lead a family, even when he made mistakes and didn't know all the answers; a commitment to serve and worship God, and the drive to invite others into God's kingdom; and the knowledge that family ties are strongest when they're purchased with God's love. I thank God for the gift of being Marvin Nobles' son!

Kelly Crystal Sobaski, from New Hope, Sedalia, said, "Thank you, Juanita, for encouraging me to become a teacher. Thank you for all the influence you have had on my life. You are a very special person who continues to teach and make a difference in lives, but I wanted you to know how blessed I feel by you having touched my life."

John Lee, from Jefferson Baptist Association, currently music director at First Baptist Hillsboro, said, "Marvin Nobles is one of the greatest examples of a man of God that I have ever met. He always does what is right, he is always looking for the best in people, quick to forgive, slow to anger, loves everybody as much as they will let him love. Marvin was a great pastor, but he was an outstanding Director of Missions for JBA. I love Marvin Nobles. His greatest blessing to me is this: Marvin is my friend!"

Cliff and Donna Copeland, First Baptist DeSoto, said,
"When we think of you, we think of the word <u>love.</u> You have always had so much love for everyone and you still do. That is why we love you."

John and Ethel Pratt, from First Baptist, DeSoto, said, "When I hear someone talk about a man of God, you are the one that comes to my mind. When we talk about someone who has been an inspiration, your name is always mentioned. Thank you for helping to keep me on track for God."

James and Diane Leftridge, from First Baptist, DeSoto, said, "You are truly a 'man of God' and are highly esteemed by our family."

Vera and Arch McGougan, from First DeSoto, said, "You and your family brought harmony to FBC DeSoto a few years back. Our church had just gone through some turmoil and you brought peace and hope. You are a very kind and compassionate man."

Lucy Femmer, from First Baptist, DeSoto, said, "You are a very loving and kind man."

Jeanne Knight, from Oak Grove Baptist Church and later First, DeSoto, said, "Bro. Nobles, you came to Oak Grove in Fletcher when we needed you. You were always there with your patience."

Bob and Meg Stroder, from Calvary Baptist in DeSoto, said, "You have been a good friend over the years and a great DOM. We appreciate you and Juanita so much."

Lorraine Acre, from First Baptist, DeSoto, said, "Thank you for restoring so much love to our church."

Tom and Joan Jackson from First Baptist, DeSoto, said, "Thanks for all you do and have done through the many years of service for the Lord."

Jack Morris, from Jefferson Association, said, "Thanks for my many memories of our mission trips together."

Mary Jo Linhorst, from First Baptist DeSoto, said, "Thank you for your encouragement and the wisdom you have shared with me. Thank you for pushing me (gently) into more and more ministry and for helping me realize God's call."

Dave and Cathy Willis, Pastor, Friendship Baptist Church, said, "God was so good when He placed you in our lives. He knew we would need kind encouragement and loyalty. "

Steve Nobles, our son, says, "One night when my parents and I were reminiscing on the telephone about the past and our family life, Dad said, 'Well, we didn't have much, but we had enough love.' Daddy showed us love, he supported us—not only financially—and he taught us wisely—about God and about life. We don't have to agree about everything, but I appreciate his wisdom. I believe he is just about the wisest man I have had the privilege of knowing personally. I thank God for giving me my father.

Jack Gannon, First Baptist DeSoto, said, "I consider you a very special person and I am happy I have you as a friend."

Bob Brown, music minister at Wayside Baptist Church in Miami, wrote in a publication when we left that church, "The Highland Park Baptist Church in Texarkana, Texas, will be getting one of the finest pastors in the entire Southern Baptist Convention in Marvin Nobles. In his two plus years at Wayside, he has proved to be one of the most gracious men I have ever known. He has a pastor's heart of love and concern. The church will also be getting the most talented pastor's family in the whole world!"

Bill Curp, present Director of Missions for Jefferson Association, said, "One of the best times of my life has been following you in ministry. You have been a perfect gentleman and a great spiritual leader to follow. I have always enjoyed your council and advice and will continue to do so. Thanks for making my work a great place and a great enjoyment."

One of the things Charlie has always wanted is to be known as "a man of God." He is that, as is shown in all these tributes we received from people through the years.

Thank You, Lord, for the sunshine You have given and for the years in service to You.

May You say, *"Well done, good and faithful servant."*

LaVergne, TN USA
09 March 2010

175332LV00003B/2/P